Understanding Film

Also by Mike Wayne

Dissident Voices
The Politics of Television and Cultural Change

'*Consistently compulsive reading and a must for all students and specialists in the field of recent and contemporary television culture.*'
Professor Madeleine MacMurraugh-Kavanagh, University of Reading

'*A clearly written and uncluttered teaching text.*'
Media International

Political Film
The Dialectics of Third Cinema

'*Wayne injects a lively sense of political urgency into contemporary film studies and provides a valuable resource for teachers and students alike.*'
John Hill, Royal Holloway

'*One of those rare events in the publishing world which will enrich and possibly change our approach to film criticism.*'
Filmwaves Magazine

Marxism and Media Studies
Key Concepts and Contemporary Trends

'*Marxism could provide a powerful optic to understand the media and the contemporary world. This book shows how and why.*'
Filmwaves Magazine

Understanding Film

Marxist Perspectives

Edited by Mike Wayne

Pluto Press
LONDON • ANN ARBOR, MI

First published 2005 by Pluto Press
345 Archway Road, London N6 5AA
and 839 Greene Street, Ann Arbor, MI 48106

www.plutobooks.com

British Library Cataloguing in Publication Data
A catalogue record for this book is available from the British Library

ISBN   0 7453 1993 9 hardback
ISBN   0 7453 1992 0 paperback

Library of Congress Cataloging in Publication Data applied for

10   9   8   7   6   5   4   3   2   1

Designed and produced for Pluto Press by
Chase Publishing Services Ltd, Fortescue, Sidmouth, EX10 9QG, England
Typeset from disk by Stanford DTP Services, Northampton, England
Printed and bound in the European Union by
Antony Rowe Ltd, Chippenham and Eastbourne, England

Contents

Introduction:
Marxism, Film and Film Studies

Mike Wayne

Marxism and Film share at least one thing in common: they are both interested in the masses. Film it is true speaks to the masses rather more routinely, underpinned as it is by the institutional infrastructure of capital and state support (even where the state professes its belief in that phantom, the 'free' market), by a technology that multiplies and extends the reach of communication and through vernacular cinematic forms that knit together a variety of widely circulated storytelling and aesthetic strategies (from melodrama to music, narrative to special effects). The social reach of film explains the theoretical and practical interest that Marxists have shown towards the medium. Marxism itself speaks to and arouses the masses rather more sporadically (and some would say these days not at all), in those great ruptures in the continuity of things that we call revolutions, attempted revolutions or those less matured intensifications of social antagonisms that we call social crisis or cultural revolutions. Film has been remarkably attuned to these moments, these social convulsions whose aftershocks have rippled out across film theory and practice, inspiring, influencing and being reworked in new circumstances long after their original historical conditions of production have subsided.

ADORNO, BENJAMIN, BRECHT

Film as an established mass medium and developing cultural form had barely arrived on the stage of world history before the 1917 Russian Revolution opened up the prospect of an alternative modernity, very different from the capitalist one that had spawned the horrors of the First World War (1914–18). A number of key questions then arose for the Soviet filmmakers of the 1920s (Eisenstein, Vertov, Pudovkin, Shub) that were also taken up by a trio of German Marxists over the next two decades. In her essay Esther Leslie identifies some of the ways in which Theodor Adorno, Walter Benjamin and Bertolt Brecht tried to understand the relationship between film and society:

I

What effect did the integration of film into the capitalist culture industries have on it and its audiences? As a part of mass culture, what connection was there between film aesthetics and the reproduction of the capitalist social order? How did film technology and its industrial nature inscribe within it the contradictions of capitalist society? How does film and mass culture generally displace, suppress and marginalise class? What potential was there to disrupt, disturb and problematise film's relationship to capitalist socioeconomic relations? How does Marxist film aesthetics differ from those developed within the capitalist culture industry? What mode of consumption, what kind of spectatorship would alternative film practices seek to foster?

Of the three, Adorno came to the most pessimistic conclusions. With Max Horkheimer he produced the brooding *Dialectic of Enlightenment* in 1944. The chapter on the culture industry conjures up a devastating indictment on the integration of film into capitalist industrial production and consumption. This too is something that film and the masses share: the latter have their labour power industrialised for the pursuit of profit while film replays in their leisure time what is done to them in their labour time. Adorno and Horkheimer offer an unrelenting vision of an art form broken down into instrumentally calculated effects, subordinated in every particle to an efficient system of profit maximisation:

> the important individual points, by becoming detachable, interchangeable, and even technically alienated from any connected meaning, lend themselves to ends external to the work. The effect, the trick, the isolated repeatable device, have always been used to exhibit goods for advertising purposes[1]

One only has to think how long trailers of films today, which advertise the film as a series of 'effects', often leave you with the unsettling sense that you have virtually seen the film in abbreviated form. This suggests that the reduction of film to such a packaged commodity of 'tricks' with little internal integrity has hardly diminished. While some contemporary theorists are tempted to dismiss Adorno and Horkheimer as excessively pessimistic and prone to elitism, their critique should instead stand as a salutary reminder that concepts of diversity, subversion and resistance, which are today part of every 'radical' cultural theorist's lexicon, are also the stock-in-trade of capitalist mass culture and its endless self-promotion. Who exactly has been had in this surprising convergence?

On film aesthetics Adorno noted how the instrumental manipulation of filmic elements within a commodified process was concealed by the seamless way all the elements were melded into place. The 'unity' and harmony of the various elements was a false one just as social consensus within a class-divided society is premature and requires a repression of the conflictual and dysfunctional nature of capitalist society. Worse, film aesthetics aspires to represent a 'lifelike' picture of the world, a pursuit of verisimilitude that stunts the aesthetic possibilities of the medium and the imaginative capacity to think of alternative social possibilities. Even today, digital technologies seek no higher purpose than the faithful reproduction of the human body and environment as if there were still some indexical link, some original trace of light on photosensitive paper necessarily connecting the image to everyday perceptions of the real.

Adorno was one of the first theorists to consider at length the role of music and sound in films, a dimension of the medium that has only recently been rescued from neglect. As Leslie notes, for Adorno sound helped glue the film's elements together, breathing life into the human figure and affirming its apparent spontaneity, disguising its mechanical and mediated nature. One detects a tension around this difference between the finished film and the making of the film in those DVD extra features which 'go behind the scenes' of the finished text. The increasing cultural thirst to understand the processes that go into the making of commodities here comes into contradiction with the fetishised final product in which all trace of the labour process is erased. Hence the rapid editing and brevity of those scenes which show the shooting of the film, so as not to smash the 'magic' of the movies and reveal the gulf that exists between the prosaic production of scenes and the final shimmering product.

Today corporate synergies between the film industry and record companies mean the routine integration of film with the compilation CD score as the film is now routinely supplemented with a series of self-contained pop songs. One is aware of the tension between such economic imperatives and the classical narrative structure in those moments where the song has to be brought to a stop before its natural length threatens the classical narrative's absolute commitment to eliminate superfluous material. In *The Full Monty* (Peter Cattaneo 1997), when Gary tries to illustrate what he has in mind to his unemployed friends, he begins stripping to a diegetic soundtrack of Hot Chocolate's 'You Sexy Thing', but comes to a premature stop when he burns himself with his cigarette. At the same time the record needle (inexplicably) makes the sound of it scratching off the vinyl. The performance has come to a stop on the image track because the plot 'point' has been made, thus preserving the 'full monty' for the film's climax and more importantly staving off embarrassing homoerotic questions for his watching friends. The insistence on ending the soundtrack at the same time (without logical diegetic motivation even, thus flouting the narrative's own principles) betrays the nervousness of having any filmic elements becoming uncoupled or unhinged from one another: behind this lies an entire economic system devoted to authoritarian order, containment and the smooth uninterrupted through-put of product.

Benjamin and Brecht on the other hand represent somewhat differing responses to thinking about the place of film in relation to capitalist modernity. While Adorno emphasised its integration into structures of domination, the more 'activist' sensibilities of Benjamin and Brecht, while hardly disagreeing that the mass media were subordinate to capital, explored the potential of film (and other media forms) to undercut and outflank those relations of domination. For Adorno, film was *too close* to mass culture and its spectators were in turn too close to it, too integrated into its effects and manipulations. For Benjamin, by contrast, the technology of mechanical reproduction meant the increased participation of the masses in cultural life, at least a little bit, on their terms. The reverential awe (or aura) encoded into the reception of traditional art, was replaced by art forms that were close enough to live and breathe in the everyday spaces and rhythms of the city, of urban life, with its movement and its technologies. Inspired by new media technologies, both Benjamin and Brecht developed theories that sought to disrupt perceptual habits (Benjamin's 'optical unconscious', Brecht's defamiliarisation strategy or 'alienation effect') and reveal the social and cultural structures that are invisible to everyday perception.

A sequence from Darren Aronofsky's *Requiem for a Dream* (2000) reveals an Adornoesque view of television and a Benjaminian/ Brechtian view of film as a vehicle of critique. Sara, strung out on prescription appetite-suppressant drugs, settles down to watch her favourite quiz show, which she hopes one day to be on. She imagines herself in the show as a contestant, her electronic image (and ego ideal) a slimmer, more beautiful version of her real self. But then both her electronic self and the typically smarmy quiz-show host rematerialise in her own working-class apartment, and what seems intimate and comfortable suddenly becomes intrusive. Sara's ego ideal and the compere begin laughing at the decor while she struggles to explain and justify herself. The quiz-show audience in turn begin to laugh at her while suddenly her home is turned into a television studio set, with people removing her furniture, while cameras, lights and microphones are brought in. As chorus girls dance threateningly around her chair, Sara's electronic self smooches with the compere. It is a brilliant fantasy sequence, a Benjamin-like optical beam illuminating the contempt in which mass culture holds its consumers, a very Brechtian-like revelation, through defamiliarisation, of the threat and social violence lurking beneath television's technology and seductive razzmatazz aesthetics, and a painful glimpse into the vortex of hidden self-loathing and aching lack of fulfilment which underpins the fantasies promoted by the culture industry. This is a good example of those more transcendent and critical dimensions of art that Marcuse wrote about:

> The truth of art lies in its power to break the monopoly of established reality (i.e., of those who have established it) to define what is real ... The aesthetic transformation becomes a vehicle of recognition and indictment.[2]

GRAMSCI AND SEMBÈNE

The process by which consciousness comes to a point of critical recognition is something that is of particular concern to the work of Gramsci and Sembène. In her essay Marcia Landy brings the Italian revolutionary Antonio Gramsci (1891–1937) and Senegalese filmmaker Ousmane Sembène into a productive mutual illumination of each other's concerns through the prism of a single film, Sembène's *Camp de Thiaroye* (1987). Gramsci was a leader of the Factory Councils movement that saw the working class occupy and (briefly) seize control of Turin's large industrial sector in 1919. However, the crisis of Italian capitalism in the wake of the First World War created an opening not for the political forces of the left but of the far right. The 1920s saw the rise to power of Benito Mussolini's fascist party and Gramsci was to spend the last eleven years of his life in Mussolini's jails. This failure of the left to secure a fundamental social and economic transformation and the success of the fascist right in temporarily offering a solution to the problems of capitalism within the capitalist order, underlined for Gramsci what he already knew: that culture, as a weave of habits, values, customs, institutions (the Church, the school system), popular knowledge, folklore and specific artefacts (including print media, radio and film) played a crucial role in inhibiting the political imagination and in bonding people to the capitalist system.

The struggle for moral and intellectual leadership in the sphere of culture is the struggle for hegemony. But it *is* a struggle and Gramsci's originality lies in his recognition that cultural domination is never simply a top-down process of imposition. Gramsci understood hegemony as a force field of contestation between different groups; a dialogue even, but crucially not a dialogue between equals because capital and the capitalist state have awesomely more resources at their disposal to shape the agenda and implement policies and practical changes. As an unevenly conducted dialogue, no hegemony is ever static, but is rather always a battle on the move. The forging of hegemony is the process by which the dominated or subaltern groups are brought into the social, economic and cultural order and that order is in turn brought *into them*. This process of inclusion and internalisation requires the dominant groups to adapt where necessary, concede ground where necessary, channel resistance and dissent where necessary into less disruptive forms, co-opt the leaders and leading ideas of the subaltern where necessary as well as project their own agendas and values. So in this unequal dialogue and struggle, all sides are changed (but not equally) by the other, and all sides (but not equally) internalise aspects of the other's values and perspectives. The social democratic welfare state represents the outer limit of what capital and its agents have, historically, been able to internalise and concede in the face of working-class demands. Today, however, as the competitive struggle to accumulate profits intensifies, capital must delegitimise that particular institutional class compromise and establish a new neo-liberal order in which capital compromises rather less and labour concedes rather more. The struggle for moral and intellectual leadership is today fought out in such topics as war, the environment, sexuality, public services, poverty, wealth and trade: these are the multiple fronts, the multiple sites of struggle, accommodation, co-optation, compromise and resistance. Cultural representations in a variety of forms are part of this struggle.

Sembène's work, like Gramsci's, is incredibly attuned to the role of culture in the struggle for power. This is indeed one of the key characteristics of Third Cinema. Sembène's films are themselves counter-hegemonic texts, challenging the dominant cultural order. Take the Second World War, for example. Its popular conception, reiterated endlessly by war films, is that this was a battle for freedom and democracy against fascism. As Landy notes, Sembène's *Camp de Thiaroye* suggests a more complex picture by reminding us that the so-called European democracies were also colonial powers determined to hang on to their territories and that European fascism generally and the Holocaust specifically, where millions of Jews, communists, homosexuals and gypsies died in fascist Germany's concentration camps, was essentially the return to European soil of the horrors and barbarism which Western 'civilisation' has visited on the colonised for centuries.

The emphasis on struggle means that the formation of 'common sense' (on for example the 'meaning' of the Second World War) is never the formation of a homogeneous, uniform affirmation of the capitalist society. Any radical intervention into common-sense must ask itself what knowledges can be built upon (and just as importantly, what memory traces of the past can be reactivated) and what habits of thought need to be challenged. It is the double-sided nature of common sense that any critical intellectual practice needs to appreciate. Gramsci is concerned with the role that intellectuals play in shaping and inflecting cultures. There is neither an identity nor an absence of communication between intellectuals and common sense (the 'philosophy' of the subaltern classes), but a complex exchange (as hacks on the tabloid press know only too well) which has historically been framed within national contexts and narratives of national history, past, present and envisaged future. At the same time, Gramsci deconstructs the category of the intellectual, noting that everyone is at some level an intellectual with particular knowledges of the world, conceptions and skills. It is only within a class- and labour-divided society that the intellectual becomes a specialised activity, a 'career' and mode of (wage) labour. Thus intellectuals too are in turn shaped not only by the dominant culture but also by the culture and the people whose work does not designate them as intellectuals. And so in a transformed society, and in the struggle for a transformed society, one of the things that has to be on the agenda is precisely the role of the intellectual and their relations with others, and how that relation can be opened up and democratised; how intellectuals can call into question the very basis of their social power in a context in which the democratisation of power is being fought for.

There is, however, no reason to suppose that intellectuals are any less likely to be bonded to the capitalist social order by the sticky innumerable threads built up over time, than anyone else.

Academics are becoming noticeably more cautious and quietist in the field of film studies: specialisation, cultural populism, scholarly 'objectivity' contradictorily combined with relativism dressed up as 'critical scepticism', vocationalism, research funds increasingly orientated to industry concerns, publishing companies churning out endless 'introductions' to this or that aspect of the field (here knowledge becomes a mere 'tool' for getting good grades, not the same thing necessarily as doing challenging work) – all this amounts to a shrinking space for counter-hegemonic practices. Meanwhile the UK undergraduate in an increasingly Americanised Higher Education system has become a debt-laden consumer; knowledge is instrumentalised (the fantasy ticket to a 'good job', even as the degree qualification suffers from that phenomenon typical of a society built on artificial scarcity: inflation); competition is rife; working much of the time to support themselves, most students cannot enjoy education for its own sake and the time and space for self development that that implies is being, has been, stripped away. How deeply the internalisation of these logics goes, how far it presses into and constrains the political imagination, how ingrained our conformity goes behind merely external gestures of dissidence or individuality – this is what Gramsci's concept of hegemony asks us to consider. Gramsci and Sembène's film enquire into our attachments to certain forms of life, the channelling of hopes, the satisfaction in certain consolations, the temptations to carve out our own little bits of 'territory' at work or in our cultural satisfactions, the limits to our imaginations which condemn us to the cycle of capitalism with its hermetic circuits of capital (endless accumulation).

ALTHUSSER AND IDEOLOGY

The origin of modern film studies as a subject on university curricula more or less coincides with one of those punctual moments of radicalisation, the late 1960s and early 1970s, that breaks through the surface of capitalism from time to time. At this moment, a time of optimism and disappointments, the work of the French Marxist Louis Althusser had a major impact and made the study of ideology and 'the subject' (the socialised individual) de rigueur. I wrote earlier of 'internalisation', and the debates around ideology associated with Althusserian-influenced cultural criticism offered one way of thinking about how this process might work through language and visual systems of representation. The concept of ideology brought the study of culture, texts and art back kicking and screaming to questions of social power and conflict, from which it had been insulated by liberal and conservative approaches. It is this 'moment' of Althusserian-inspired theory (and the fierce debates that went with it) that Deborah Philips charts in her essay.

Althusser stressed that ideology is grounded in institutional practices and concrete social relationships – it does not float about in the ether, nor does ideology simply exist in people's heads (a notion that suggests we could reject/eject those ideas quite easily). It should be noted that, by and large, the main thrust of Marx's conception of ideology (idea systems) did indeed stress its material roots, without offering any detailed institutional analysis. Marx and his co-writer Engels in *The German Ideology* (written in 1845–46), for example, defined ideology as precisely ideas that *imagined* themselves to be independent of their material conditions of existence (their main target was German idealist philosophy generated by the universities). Thus ideology critique must return ideological ideas to what they repress, their rootedness in class-divided material practices. In imagining themselves to be independent of actual social and economic relations, ideologies project themselves as spontaneous and naturalised givens, their 'obvious' or apparently universal nature concealing very specific class interests and the historical (and geographical) limits of their claims.

It was less the insistence of the inevitable interface between ideology and social practices which distinguished Althusser's conception of ideology from Marx's, as the different kind of 'imagining' ideology offered in his thesis. Ideology was not so much ideas that imagined *themselves* independent of material circumstances (a conception that suggests that individuals could fairly easily move 'out' of those ideas) but ideas that *necessarily* offered the subject an imaginary relationship to *their* real conditions of existence. We will come to the nature of this imagining shortly. What needs to be stressed is how this conception inscribed the subject into ideology in a way that Marx and Engels, with their nineteenth-century rationalist confidence in distinguishing between ideology and science did not. Writing prior to the Freudian revolution, Marx's critical analysis was directed outwards, towards society and he had little in the way of a vocabulary that could investigate how the society he identified might inscribe itself into the very agent/subject which seeks to change that society. This has become the paradox of our time as the reach of capital in terms of production and culture, and the reach of the state, has exponentially increased.

For Althusser, the imaginary characteristic of all ideologies was the way they construct subjects as autonomous, free agents, internally unified and operating in a more or less unified world (except for the presence of various 'others' who must be kept at bay or in check). It was for this reason that ideology critique came to develop sophisticated decoding strategies that undermined the appearance of unity and seamless integration. For Althusser, the very activity of 'making sense' was constitutive of both subjectivity and ideology. This is true even if one responds negatively to a dominant discourse. For example, even a negative response to an appeal to 'the national interest' (e.g. don't strike, it's against the national interest!), constitutes subject-formation and an imaginary relation (of unity) with some group(s) that the subject perceives as resistant to the smoothing-over of difference and antagonism which any appeal to the national interest requires. In other words, for Althusser, there is no getting 'outside' ideology in general, although one might reject specific ideologies.

To believe that there is no getting 'outside' ideology introduces an indiscriminate level of generalisation into the debate about ideology that is problematic. If we maintain the definition that ideologies are idea systems generated by class differences and other unequal social relations that then require some sort of rationalisation, then to say that there is no 'getting outside ideology' is to say that there is no getting beyond such relations of domination. Such a proposition is hardly a rallying cry for change. Althusser slid towards this position on ideology because of his rather uncritical appropriation of the work of the psychoanalyst Jacques Lacan. The production of ideology moved from something that designated unequal social relations (which could in theory be changed), to a property *inherent* in language and communication (which we were stuck with). Althusser's concept of ideology as an imagined relationship that facilitates effective operation within society and social groups without acknowledging the contradictions of self and society, borrows strongly from Lacan's notion of the imaginary.

The Lacanian notion of the imaginary refers to the *misrecognition* of unity and cohesion that the infant has about its own body and its relationship to its parent(s). The pre-language infant identifies visually with the parent, seeing in this powerful actor an image of its own (imagined) self. The infant's entry into the world of language and representation generally (what Lacan calls the symbolic order) forever displaces the closed narcissistic space of the imaginary. But that basic ontological or primordial 'ideological effect', in which the subject seeks to shore up the unity, integrity and power of itself and its preferred objects of identification, lives on in and through language. This is despite the fact that language and representation generally is a slippery business, articulating meanings that constantly shift into new terrain, carrying with them a freight of meanings that exceed individual intentions, clash with and are relativised by other utterances, and so forth. All of which undermines the subject's fantasies of itself as the unified *source* of meaning. Indeed, for Lacan, the 'unconscious' is less some repressed desire 'within' the subject, than these inevitable gaps in the structures of meaning-making (the space between signifiers and signifieds) which undermine the subject's own sense of unity. Radical critique then seeks to unstitch the subject from its misrecognition of seamless unity in the self and its sociocultural environment; it seeks to productively identify how any symbolic act is an unstable assemblage of disparate signs and meanings (the influence here of modernist aesthetics as much as Marxist political theory is worth underlining).

As Philips notes, in some ways Althusser was developing Gramsci's work on the role of consent, consensus and common sense in helping the stability and endurance of capitalist society. If at a macro level Althusserianism marked a step back from Gramsci's more subtle and historically grounded analysis of hegemony, at a micro level, Althusser's work led to certain advances in how the subject was constructed and crucial advances in hermeneutics (textual readings). Althusserian criticism explored the role of cultural texts in 'positioning' the subject to make sense of itself in ways that conceal contradictions within the social order, the text and by implication, the spectator. Thus for example, whereas Sembène's film *Camp de Thiaroye* insists that reading the social order is a complex decoding of social contradictions and that the meaning of individuals' actions is not always immediately present to them or the spectator, mainstream films usually offer a certain immediacy in the readings and identifications on offer.

By contrast, we know that Ned Kelly is the hero of *Ned Kelly* (Jordan 2003 Aus/UK/Fr) because the spectator sees him right at the start of the film saving his brother from drowning. We later see him wrongly accused of horse theft and so forth (the film thus quickly associates Ned with nature, against the corruption of society). We are placed in a position of intelligibility by the narrative construction of the action and our perspective on it. The problem with this presentation of narrative knowledge as easily and immediately obtainable is that it disguises the more problematic questions around the links between poverty and crime and the police and big landowners (who only appear via Ned's romantic interests). Instead we have Ned the hero vs. the police as the villains – which they may well be, but abstracted from any context their villainy is seen as the result of individual stupidity and jealousy on the part of the police. On the other hand, this subject position does not quite work for the film because the popularity of Ned as an outlaw and the social isolationism of the police from the rest of the community (see the bar scenes) suggests that the law is rather more *systematically* problematic. So here we have a flat contradiction in the film's representational strategies. But in terms of the systematic nature of police oppression, the film can do no more than suggest police brutality as being the result of wearing the uniform (making little men 'big') rather than the result of social factors. Thus the formal strategies which the film deploys to tell its story lead it towards romanticism (Ned is a hero, pure and simple) and sentimentalism (even the top police chief chasing Ned respects him) and this undermines the critical elements embedded in the folkloric story of the bandit and outlaw (the knowledge of class injustice) that is part of popular consciousness (see Gramsci again). Finally the arbitrariness of the police strikes the modern spectator as archaic, prior to all the rights that the citizen now (apparently) has secured from the state (we see no judicial process for example, the film ends with Ned's capture). And this too constructs a reassuring position for the *modern* subject: things are not like that today! Radical filmmakers have sought to disrupt these consoling fictions of linear progress in historical dramas by the use of anachronisms. Peter Watkins' *Culloden* (1964 UK) and *La Commune* (1999 Fr) for example, Derek Jarman's *Caravaggio* (1986 UK) and *Edward II* (1991 UK) or Alex Cox's *Walker* (1987 US) come to mind.

The attention to the way representations *constructed* subject positions for readers or spectators meant attending in great detail to the language of a medium and the way it stitched its various materials together into a semblance of unity (shades here of Adorno's critique), offering the subject a similar semblance of a unified position of intelligibility in reading the text. If I can be autobiographical for a moment, I still well recall the liberating and revelatory engagement with Althusserian-inspired critiques of literary and film texts. Having been educated to appreciate the *unity* of the text and assume that its apparent coherence (itself judged to be the result of the artist's own unified control over their material) was the highest aesthetic ideal, my own political horizons expanded considerably once I discovered the legitimacy of investigating the text for the kind of contradictions, tensions, silences and sheer incoherence I have schematically indicated in relation to *Ned Kelly*. As Pierre Macherey and Etienne Balibar argued (both of whom collaborated with Louis Althusser) in relation to literature:

> literary productions must not be studied from the standpoint of their unity which is illusory and false, but from their material disparity. One must not look for unifying effects but for signs of contradictions (historically determined) ... which appear as unevenly resolved in the text ... the materialist analysis of literature rejects on principle the notion of 'the work' – i.e., the illusory presentation of the unity of a text, its totality, self-sufficiency and perfection (in both senses of the word: success and completion).[3]

Within film studies, the journal *Cahiers du Cinema* realigned itself in the wake of the events of May 1968 and developed a criticism explicitly orientated to ideology critique. Famously, *Cahiers* offered a typology of the different relations that could occur between film texts and ideology. They suggested for example that a film might have radical political content, but be contained within ideology by its narrative form. Such a film as Oliver Stone's *JFK* (1991) comes to mind. Although radically questioning of American democratic institutions and society in some respects, the film suffers from a massive and uncritical investment in the 'lost' father figure of the assassinated President, itself underpinned by the heroic protagonist's quest for the truth of a single event (rather than, say, a social and historical analysis of the role of political violence in the US of the kind that Cuban filmmaker Santiago Alvarez produced in his 1968 short film *LBJ*). Conversely, a film which on the surface appears to be fully within the dominant ideology might on closer analysis be revealed to be 'riddled with cracks; it is splitting under an internal tension'.[4] *Cahiers'* own analysis of such a film, John Ford's *Young Mr Lincoln* (1939) was, however, rather unsatisfactory. Their historical and institutional contextualisation of the film (which was overly monolithic and devoid of contradictions) remained largely disarticulated with the textual analysis that followed, which was more Freudian/Lacanian than Marxist, despite early promising observations on how the film dissociates Lincoln from party politics and social interests.[5] This illustrated just how problematic Althusser's borrowing of Lacan was for a Marxist analysis that wants to link texts to class struggle, modes of production, cultural and political traditions and specific historical conjunctures, rather than some amorphous 'desire'.

JAMESON AND LUKÁCS

One of the paradoxes of Althusser's thinking was that, having suggested that ideology is rather more pervasive and entrenched than was previously thought, Althusser, like Marx, held on to a conception of scientific (that is non-ideological) practice. This contradiction was to be carried over into post-Althusserian currents as well, particularly in postmodernist theories, where the pervasiveness of ideology and the undermining of knowledge which that implied, was now reinterpreted and reconfigured as a general cultural relativism. This actually meant the death of ideology-critique. The concept of ideology, even when blown up to a general necessity for all social agents and made equivalent to the business of 'making sense' or symbolic production generally, still holds out the (albeit) faint possibility of a non-ideological position. A full-blown cultural relativism, however, has no need to entertain the notion that some representations and discourses might just have the edge over others in terms of their adequacy to the real. If for Althusser there was no outside ideology, for later theorists influenced by postmodernism, there is no outside culture. As with Althusser, however, there remained the fundamental paradox by which epistemology (questions of knowledge) kept returning: how did the postmodernists know that knowledge was merely relative to this or that cultural construct when such relativism precludes making any such general knowledge-claim?

The American Marxist cultural theorist Fredric Jameson made an early and important intervention into debates around the postmodern and is the subject of my own contribution to this anthology. As the cultural logic of capital, postmodernism was for Jameson a fact of life which the radical critic had to work within and against. He worked within it by taking seriously a number of features of cultural life within contemporary society that made it extremely difficult to articulate a collective politics of social transformation. But he worked against the postmodern by insisting that it was itself a product of the socioeconomic mode of capitalist production and that the task of a Marxist criticism was to track such a cultural phenomenon back to its repressed material roots (Marx again) by sifting through it and (following on from Althusser) examining its contradictions and silences.

It is useful to compare Fredric Jameson's critique of postmodernism with his intellectual 'predecessor', the influential Hungarian Marxist cultural theorist, Georg Lukács' critique of what he saw as modernism's penchant for relativism. For it is indeed striking that Jameson in many ways adapts Lukács' critique of the modernist avant-garde (with its generally minority publics) and applies it to the new conditions of the mass media and culture and the transnational capital which produces and promotes it. Lukács' intellectual formation was forged in the first three decades of the twentieth century. His essay 'The Ideology of Modernism', written in 1957, brands modernism as anti-realist, which was not (or so Lukács argued) a judgement on its forms and techniques, but on its epistemological principles which suggest that the 'objective world is inherently inexplicable'.[6] It should be noted that, whereas in Adorno, Benjamin, Brecht and Althusser there is positive value to be found in aesthetic strategies which disrupt and disaggregate cultural forms in order to break apart their oppressive containment of contradictions, for Lukács, the shattering of narrative worlds and perspectival certainties is a sign of an unleashed subjectivism, which attends only to the surface features of life under capitalism, missing the fact that beneath the appearance of flux, fragmentation and unpredictability lies an ever more integrated and concentrated socioeconomic system.

Jameson will argue that such a shattering of perspectives has become generalised well beyond a few specific avant-garde texts, and finds this problematic, for the same reasons as Lukács: namely that our capacity to represent the systemic nature of transnational capitalism is undermined. However, he is less dismissive of postmodernism than Lukács is of modernism, partly because while for Lukács, modernism was a specific cultural current, for Jameson, postmodernism constitutes the visible horizon of contemporary life, backed as it is by the transnational culture industries. And with his post-Althusserian hermeneutic tools of textual analysis, Jameson sees more value in probing texts for their symptomatic *unconscious* relations to the capitalist mode of production than Lukács did with modernism.

For Lukács it is not the forms and techniques of modernism in and of themselves that are the problem (he contrasts Thomas Mann's realist use of the interior monologue with Joyce's modernist (anti-realist) use of the same technique); rather it is the excess of form or style over the referent that is problematic. Jameson slightly tweaks this by arguing that it is the *imitation* of style or a plurality of styles that is foregrounded in postmodernism, to the detriment of the referent (the world the signs refer to). This emphasis on style is symptomatic in both cases of a profound cultural relativism. Within modernism, the hero 'is strictly confined within the limits of his own experience' with no 'pre-existent reality beyond his own self, acting upon him'.[7] This surrender to subjectivity is also evident in the postmodern resistance to engaging with the way the real impacts on and conditions perception, representation and meaning. There is a greater emphasis within the postmodern on 'experience' being shaped by media messages and forms (rather than the modernist subject's own inner psychological dynamics), but this is to say that within postmodernism the media is the real.

Lukács notes that once the dialectic between subjective and objective reality is broken, the 'human personality must necessarily disintegrate',[8] hence the typical condition of the modernist subject is psychopathological. This in turn echoes Jameson who draws on Lacan's linguistically inflected account of schizophrenia as a way of conjuring up what life is like for the subject under postmodernism. For Lacan, schizophrenia is essentially the breakdown of the subject's ability to operate within the symbolic order. Here language suffers a breakdown of the signifying chain, with signifiers rupturing from any settled connections to signifieds (as they do in dreams). Jameson is not saying that everyone is schizophrenic under late capitalism, but rather that on a smaller although pervasive scale, the subject's capacity to use signs to map the world around them is problematised. The Lukácsian-Jamesonian contours of a critique of culturalised relativism are evident in Amrohini Sahay's review of the film *Memento* (Christopher Nolan 2000 US), which, it is suggested, offers a new postmodern model of subjectivity congruent with the labour flexibility required under capitalism's new information-rich modes of production:

> The world of 'signs' out of which Leonard [Shelby] forges his 'identity' thus remains fundamentally ambiguous and open-ended; yet in order to 'act' he is forced to construct the momentary semblance of a 'stable' self which can 'orient' him in the present. Shelby thus stages the new corporate dogma of identity under globalization: that is, as a form of self-invention in which the subject 'lives' not by reliance on any definite, clear, and coherent understanding of the world, the logic of its operations, or his/her place in

them, but on a 'moment-to-moment', contingent and pragmatic basis which needs to be constantly 'revised' and 're-done' based on new information.[9]

Similarly, Jameson offered a celebrated reading of the postmodern Bonaventure Hotel in Los Angeles, which he argued has a deliberately unmappable interior space that represents (and encourages) the individual subject's difficulty in grasping 'the great global multinational and decentred communicational network' of the postmodern epoch.[10]

With the collapse of any sense of a structured objective world, the subject also collapses, reduced to 'experiential fragments' in modernism[11] and fragmentation in postmodernism.[12] Lukács writes of 'the dissolution of personality',[13] Jameson, 'the death of the subject'.[14] With the objective world dwindling, the subject has no basis on which to make any judgements or assessments as to the validity of its subjective understandings of the world; the dynamic reciprocal relationship between subject and object has been shattered. Thus for Lukács, modernist art suffers from a loss of *perspective*.[15] Perspective implies evaluation and selection, tested against the world independent of the senses. But as the relative becomes absolutised, so judgement and the adequacy of judgement from a particular vantage point, become meaningless, because impossible to assess. So too with postmodernism which Jameson associates with a loss of critical distance, a loss of the capacity *for* criticism in the face of wall-to-wall commodities. Criticism is thus replaced with blank pastiche. Warhol's soup cans '*ought* to be powerful and critical political statements' but are not.[16]

It is hardly surprising then that when the world becomes so unknowable, so lacking in objective features independent of our senses and cultural constructions, it very soon turns into a nightmare, a terrifyingly opaque 'utterly strange and *hostile* reality'[17] cut off from any sense of knowable past or different future or contemporary causal determinants. The best-known modernist exponent of this nightmare reality was of course Kafka, and today popular film culture is replete with similar kinds of paranoid visions. Just as Lukács acknowledged that modernism was a protest against capitalism (but an epistemologically impoverished one) so Jameson argues that the paranoia film is a distorted representation of advanced capitalism. Yet the surprisingly strong continuities between Jameson's arguments vis-à-vis postmodernism and Lukács' arguments vis-à-vis modernism, ought to caution us against the notion of a linear history and clean breaks with the past implied by the prefix 'post'.

While Lukács may be criticised for underestimating the critical and cultural possibilities of modernism, and indeed the possibility of turning modernism in critical theory (Benjamin, Adorno) or cultural practices (Brecht) to Marxist ends, Jameson (as has often been pointed out) overestimates the dominance of the negative aspects of postmodernism and indeed (more importantly) overestimates the dominance of the postmodern, full stop. I explore this in relation to the media conspiracy films that have become popular in recent years, while delineating Jameson's method for reading texts in relation to their repression of the capitalist mode of production. Nevertheless, as with Lukács, so with Jameson, these theorists have provided formidable paradigms with which to think within and against.

ALLEGORISING CAPITALISM

If postmodernism has an economic underpinning, it is in the increasing role played by information technologies in production and the attraction to capital of investing in the hardware and software of cultural consumption. In a sense, 'the postmodern' might be a rather hyperbolical way of saying that our era sees economics as increasingly inscribed by cultural questions and frameworks while culture is itself increasingly penetrated by the logics of commodity capitalism. Despite, then, the rising tide of relativism and cultural diversity (both real and apparent) it is hardly surprising if cultural texts are also a hotline to and offer allegories of entire economic structures and modes of production. Indeed, perhaps no other cinema in the world can represent (albeit ideologically) the sheer *power* and pervasiveness of capital like Hollywood, not least because in Hollywood, as in America generally, corporate capital and culture are so interconnected. It is precisely just such an allegory of capital that Anna Kornbluh detects in a cluster of Hollywood films that return nostalgically to the 1970s. These films mull (in disguised form) over the decay of the post-Second World War economic/political/cultural and psychological order (sometimes called Fordism) that shaped the subject and the transition in the 1980s to the neo-liberal world that found its first *electorally* successful politicians in Ronald Reagan and Margaret Thatcher. (The Chilean dictator Augusto Pinochet test-ran the New Right's economic policies after his *coup d'état* in 1973, which overthrew the Marxist president Salvador Allende.) The neo-liberal world order saw the role of the state radically refashioned: no longer offering protection against the worst abuses of the market, the state becomes an enthusiastic promoter of the cash nexus and market 'choice'; the labour market is restructured both in terms of the 'content' of occupations and their structure and practices (e.g. a casualised and flexible workforce) while the old gender divisions that made men the 'breadwinners' and women, largely, housewives, are swept away as women are sucked into wage labour in large numbers. Meanwhile what is happening in the real economy has an increasingly problematic relationship with finance capitalism, with its speculative search for future markets and profits (witness the dot.com boom/bust), its rule by investor 'confidence' and its endless oiling of consumer debt which keeps the economy turning for capitalists and proletarians alike, only deferring the inevitable 'correction' for another day.

For Kornbluh, *Boogie Nights* (Paul Thomas Anderson 1997) and *Blow* (Ted Demme 2001) are symbolic representations of this excess, this out-of-kilter economy where surplus and lack sit side by side. Frustrated desire and permissiveness are the transmuted stand-ins for structural economic change driven by levels of consumer demand that are frenetic, destructive and unsustainable. At one level this representational strategy is an ideological one, because structural economics becomes a question of individual morality and choices, something that it is evidently easier to offer some resolution of and judgement about without radically questioning the socioeconomic order. At this level, representational strategies converge with ideological strategies that seek imaginary resolutions to real social contradictions (a formulation typical of Althusserian-influenced criticism). At the same time, even structural changes must work through individual desires and fantasies; subjects do have to internalise the (new) logics of the system for the system to work. In showing that and in suggesting the damage done to subjects in the process, these films reveal the human costs of the system, opening it up to criticism and revealing the contradictions and internal tensions within the ideology of individualism, an ideology that always betrays the promises it offers.

It is worth noting how the allegorisation of capital is distinctly (and ideologically) gendered in the films Kornbluh discusses. In *Boogie Nights* the mother figure stands in for economic constraints and the angry, harsh dissatisfactions that generates within the family context. Kornbluh notes how the film dramatises the subject's own internal making (and unmaking) within this context as Eddie leaves the alternative family of the porn industry and maternal mother figure of Amber Waves (the positive representation of the regime of surplus) to compulsively replay his earlier experiences where emotional reciprocity (or exchange) is lacking. This attention to the way the individual subject carries the psychic scars that bear witness to their own biographical mediations of a brutal social order, is central to Kornbluh's contention that libido (gratification) is central to any political economy. A socialist political economy would fulfil the promises which capitalism must constantly make and just as constantly betray.

This is a point that Marcuse insisted upon and which has been subsequently developed by the feminist theorist Jessica Benjamin. Although Marcuse is often misunderstood as a theorist who promulgated a polymorphous sexuality to subvert bourgeois sexual morality, his argument was actually rather different. Indeed the reduction of sexuality to sex is already a reification (the isolation and atomisation) of a broader set of psychic dynamics. Eros for Marcuse is closer to an everyday and generalised, not specialised, sense of sensuality which includes a caring and loving environment, an emotional reciprocity which recognises as legitimate the intertwining material (bodily) and emotional needs and demands of the subject. As he argues:

> every process that preserves life, from the first union of the germ cells to the formation of ... communities ... stands under the aegis of the pleasure principle: it is precisely the polymorphous character of sexuality that drives beyond the special function to which it is limited, toward gaining more intensive and extensive pleasure, toward the generation of libidinous ties with one's fellow men, the production of a libidinous, that is, happy environment. Civilization arises from pleasure: we must hold fast to this thesis in all its provocativeness.[18]

MARXISM AND AUTHORSHIP

The question of how individual biographies mediate the social and economic relations of their environment is also the key issue for any Marxist engagement with the thorny question of authorship. Within film studies, the question of authorship remains on the scene like an embarrassing close relative, its presence is unwanted but a complete break with it seems more trouble than it is worth. The rise of Althusserian Marxism in the 1960s naturally led to a major attack on the notion of authorship, since it was an excellent example of the ideology of the subject. The 1950s saw film critics appropriate the notion of authorship and assign it to select film directors as a means of legitimating the study of a medium that many within the intelligentsia saw as irredeemably impoverished by its commercialism and the 'low' tastes of its mass audiences. The concept of authorship bathed (some) films in its own high culture/quality status. But by the late 1960s authorship was widely seen by many within academic film studies as the ideology of the subject writ large. And they had a point. Conventional notions of authorship saw the meaning of the text as originating almost solely from the author, which effectively erased the role of culture and collective systems of representation and society from the process. At most, some biographical elements from the author's past might be gestured to and then seen as 'reflected' in certain themes, while the author's 'mastery' of the medium would be discerned in their ability to write (or film) with a distinctive signature. The other major problem was that not only was culture and society erased, the author, as an example of the ideological subject, was conceived as a unified and unifying producer of meaning(s). Conceiving the subject or the texts that issue forth from their intentions as a site of contradiction, could not be admitted.

Authorship was initially then supplemented by structuralism, which attempted to shift attention to the language system that authors inevitably depended upon. But authorship (which locates meaning as deriving from the conscious or unconscious intentions of the author) and structuralism (which locates meaning in the system of language itself) were fundamentally incompatible. As Althusserian Marxism went into decline, post-structuralist approaches announced the 'death of the author' (Barthes) or, more productively, suggested that authorship was an institutional 'discursive' construct, a fiction, but with real effects (Foucault). Yet while the *dominant* version of authorship had rightly been taken to task, we cannot do without some sense of agency, collective and individual. As Marx once famously formulated, men and women make their own history, but not under conditions of their own choosing. There is no reason to suppose that authors of cultural texts are any less able to consciously shape meanings than academics. However, clearly, conscious intentions do not exhaust the meanings of texts, while intentions and consciousness itself are shaped by multiple, overlapping but conflictual as well as internally contradictory contexts: cultural, institutional, social, political, economic and historical. No seamlessly unified subject or text can emerge from this situation, but equally, and contrary to the post-structuralists, agents are not so fragmentary, contingent upon or dispersed by language systems that agency (and authorial style) itself becomes impossible, or is a mere 'effect' of institutions that want to market authors. The inability to overcome this antinomy between a conceptualisation of authorship in which the author is the primary source of meaning and a concept where they are virtually the source of nothing, merely an effect of language or institutionalised discourses, means that film studies has yet to settle its accounts with the role of the director (to whom authorship is usually, although not always, ascribed).

It is within this context then that Colin McArthur engages with the way class has been evacuated from critical discourses across film studies generally via a case study of Alfred Hitchcock. One of the dominant critical discourses which have displaced class is that of psychoanalytic feminism. Its focus on the 'look' or the gaze of the spectator and its construction within the network of shots and *mise en scène* of the text has given it a powerful hermeneutic presence within a subject dominated by textual approaches. McArthur thus chooses to explore precisely the question of the look within Hitchcock's films, but yoking it to the question of class and Hitchcock's biographical formation within the class profile of the petty bourgeoisie. This is a class fraction whose capacity to generate 'a libidinous, that is, happy environment' (Marcuse) is restricted in ways that are specific to their in-between position between the working class and the bourgeoisie proper. McArthur's approach, then, redeems the more untheoretical approaches to authorship which take the film as the reflection of the life of the author without paying attention to the formal process of construction involved in the cinematic text (and its contradictions) while at the same time he re-grounds authorship study historically in a way that auteur-structuralism, for example, was signally uninterested in. Specifically McArthur draws parallels between Hitchcock and his contemporary (from a similar class background), the cartoonist H.M. Bateman. Bateman's drawings thus provide evidence of a visual rhetoric organised around anxieties and insecurities which, McArthur argues, were typical of the lower, self-employed middle class of the period. McArthur then traces this visual rhetoric (particularly around the *stare*) and its attendant anxieties, into Hitchcock's films. The methodology is exemplary in its attentiveness to historical and social contextualisation and questions of formal construction.

HOLLYWOOD AS MONOPOLY CAPITALISM

McArthur's essay is not concerned with the industrial context of film which inevitably shapes and influences the work of film workers. The two essays by Douglas Gomery and Toby Miller do focus our attention on the question of the film industry, its economic and legal institutional context and policy determinants. There is an obvious need for specific and detailed analysis of the history of film's modes of production, provided by Gomery in relation to Hollywood. For the structures and strategies of production powerfully shape and influence textual outcomes. There is for example a relationship between the aforementioned *Ned Kelly* and the fact that it was produced by an Australian subsidiary of Working Title. Working Title of course is the hugely successful UK-based production company responsible for such films as *Four Weddings and a Funeral* (Mike Newell 1994) which grossed more than $250 million worldwide, *Notting Hill* (Roger Michael 1999) which grossed $116 million in the US market and *Bridget Jones's Diary* (Sharon Maguire 2001), which took more than $72 million in the US. Working Title, however, is not some plucky independent outfit somehow swimming against the tide of monopoly capitalism. Rather, as the wholly owned subsidiary of the US major Universal-Seagram, it is very much part of the new face of monopoly (subsidiary) capitalism. Critical studies of globalisation, post-Fordism and postmodernism provide us with the appropriate framework with which to understand how Working Title functions within a Cultural Transnational Corporation such as Universal-Seagram. The role of Working Title in the UK, and by extension, the subsidiary's subsidiary in Australia, is to plug into national/regional cultures, talent and narratives and articulate them as suitably deracinated products for an international market via the American market. *Ned Kelly*'s co-optation of the Australian rebel/outlaw (making the film a slightly exotic western) and the muting of the class dynamics which produce this figure is hardly unconnected with these international conditions of film production.

Douglas Gomery's essay charts something of the history of the film corporation – the central unit for economic analysis and institutional analysis. As with Toby Miller, Gomery points to the ways that the American state has supported and provided the legal framework for the development of monopoly power within the film industry. Monopoly capitalism does not abolish competition but intensifies it between, and latterly within, fewer and larger corporations. Thus risk management is still imperative in that filmmaking is ultimately a high-risk speculation: trying to anticipate what kind of film will catch large-scale public interest and maximise profits. Gomery notes the internal structures and corporate strategies that have been developed to minimise risk and maximise profits, and, latterly, the integration of the film commodity with a host of other outlets, merchandise and inter-corporate alliances and sponsors. As he argues, contemporary Hollywood represents an awesome concentration of economic power into the Big Six, who make the decisions, within the accumulation imperative, that profoundly shape and limit the range and nature of worldwide film culture. Gomery's work draws our attention to something important. Film is a commodity, as we know, but this in itself tells us very little about what specific forces are shaping particular films. It is crucial to understand that films emerge out of the *market strategies* which companies develop and which they develop in turn as a response to their position within the market at any one time as well as broader cultural and political trends. Companies may deploy different strategies at different times or simultaneously and a film might be the product of some new strategy innovation, some emulation of another corporate strategy or the continuation of its own well-established one, or some combination of these. The notion of corporate stratagems allows us to understand how the process of commodification works as an evolving and differentiated process.

HOLLYWOOD AND CULTURAL POLICY

As Toby Miller argues, the global dominance of Hollywood is often said by its supporters to derive from Hollywood's freedom from state support, a liberation which means that risk-taking buccaneering free-market entrepreneurs rise to executive decision-making levels, crafting products that meet audience demand. The model of cultural policy that is said to underpin Hollywood's success is seen not to have much in the way of a *cultural* policy at all and only a minimum of film industry-related policy. All this is then set in contrast to European film policy that often has explicitly cultural goals (cultural diversity, cinematic representation of national life, culture as a means of increasing mutual understanding across social, cultural, geographical and other differences). This is underpinned by state subsidy of training and production, fiscal measures (tax breaks) and sometimes restrictions on imports and obligations on national exhibitors or broadcast television to show a percentage of indigenous product. Historically, cultural policy is attractive to those states whose national film industries are on the receiving end of the Hollywood hegemony (which is pretty much every nation state) because it is a way of countering the influence of 'foreign' cultural values, promoting a version and vision of the nation that state elites can be proud of, tying nation and state more closely together in this vision and securing for the state popular support and/or support from sections of the populace, particularly the 'opinion-forming' middle class. Cultural policy is, in short, as Miller argues, a component of the hegemonic process and a good example of the contradictions of that process, when the state ends up directly or indirectly supporting films that question the state and/or the nation. Nevertheless, there is a contradiction for radicals, because while state mechanisms are the only means of sustaining indigenous production in the face of Hollywood domination, there are all sorts of questionable assumptions – which Miller identifies – often underpinning that state support and which feed through into a more or less 'promotional' national film culture or one which is orientated towards fairly exclusive (middle) class-taste groups.

However, the same 'unregulated' economics of the market that have seen Hollywood triumph are also now pressing in on state policies across the board. As coordinated through the World Trade Organisation and the International Monetary Fund, the international trend is towards competitiveness (meaning wiping out smaller competitors), growth (of profit margins), employment (suitably casualised and insecure) and trade liberalisation (dismantling the few mechanisms left by which to call transnational companies to account); in short, cultural considerations are dropping down the state agenda (although it is difficult and perhaps even dangerous for the state to entirely eliminate them) while economic considerations are coming to the fore. Yet the state itself is profoundly implicated in promoting and sustaining the fiction and the practice of the 'free' market model. As Miller demonstrates, Hollywood benefits from state subsidies, state laws and regulations and state promotion nationally and, crucially, internationally. Nor is this support merely a concern for Hollywood as an industry. There has long been a tacit recognition of the role Hollywood has in selling America both at home and abroad (see for example the way Hollywood elites were invited to Washington to discuss George Bush's 'war on terror' in the wake of 9/11). That recognition *is* a cultural policy, but because Hollywood is on top (of the rest of the world), it is one that does not have to declare itself as such. It seems less a policy than a universal fact of economic life.

SOCIALISM AND THE STATE

The association of Marxism with oppressive and totalitarian regimes in the twentieth century has done more than anything to discredit and undermine it. Thus it seems that while Marxism may work well enough as a theoretical critique of capitalism, as a practical alternative, it has been disastrous. This is not an irrational conclusion and only the deeply complacent would not be worried by the record so far. However, it is worth noting that the 'practice' which is assigned the *name* of Marxism, actually bears some striking resemblances to the socioeconomic order of capitalism. The rhetoric of the regimes that made Marxism their official ideology in fact amounted to no more than an ideological legitimisation of class rule. This class rule is sufficiently *different* from Western capitalism, because of its abolition of the *private* ownership of the means of production and market mechanisms of exchange, to make that rhetoric appear formally credible, but strongly *continuous* with class rule nonetheless, insofar as the mixed mode of domination (state and private capital) gives way to a mono-mode relying on the state alone. For Mészáros such societies were/are *post capitalist* but not *post capital*, for they still maintained the basis of class rule, *'command over labour'*[19] via state-owned productive property.

Marx and Lenin had seen the state as a *problem*, as a sign of class power and the means by which broader social contradictions were both preserved and managed (and not in any way genuinely reconciled). Yet twentieth-century proponents of Marxism, socialists and social democrats, increasingly saw the state as a means to desired ends, if only it could be captured electorally or through the armed seizure of power. Outside the West, there were two main streams feeding into the establishment of regimes that declared themselves to have an affinity with Marxism. There were first the movements for national liberation against colonial occupation (the Chinese revolution for example, against Japanese occupation), but these were precisely *national* movements and whatever progressive advances they represented over colonial or neocolonial influence, they were not about the kinds of social transformations which involved control resting with the 'free association of the producers' (as Marx put it). The second stream of historical forces which produced so-called 'Marxist' regimes did not even have the merit of popular revolutions to underpin them, but were rather the direct result of military occupation by the Soviet Union after its role in combating fascism during the Second World War. This was the case, for example, with much of Eastern Europe after 1945. North Korea was the product of both these historical forces. Korea had had a fairly weak national liberation movement against Japanese rule, but the decisive determination of the nature of North Korean 'socialism' was the fact that Korea was carved into two in 1945 by the Americans who occupied the South (and who established a capitalist Korea) and the Soviets who occupied the North and who replicated their model of state control through the leadership of Kim Il Sung.

As Hyangjin Lee makes clear, in the absence of a popular movement for social change, North Korea represents state-imposed change from above, the antithesis of Marx's argument that the emancipation of the working class has to be the *act* of the working class. The rise of Stalin in the Soviet Union in the late 1920s brought with it two characteristics familiar from bourgeois politics: the fetishistic elevation of the Great Leader (faithfully emulated in North Korean films) and a nationalistic politics complete with absurd cultural boasting (again farcically emulated by North Korea). Nationalism always works to downplay internal class differences within the nation by appealing to common values and interests that are said to override social antagonisms.

The state, now merged with the Party, as a centralised body of coercive force and political and cultural power, incarnates the wisdom of the Party/Great Leader, thus rendering the masses in the same position of passivity and non-participation as in orthodox capitalist countries. In relation to North Korea, Lee uses Gramsci's concept of 'passive revolution' (used in relation to the historical formation of capital) to understand the North Korean film industry's representation of social change. This is a representation that reproduces state power, state paternalism and state authority; a form of cultural communication utterly shorn of any ambition to develop the audience's independent critical faculties. Aesthetically it is close to the conservative and conformist model of 'Socialist Realism' that was developed within the Soviet Union in the early 1930s. As in politics so in culture, the Socialist Realism of Stalinist rule imitated the forms and morality of popular bourgeois culture. As Michael Chanan notes, Socialist Realism was characterised by stereotypes, formulaic narratives, revolutionary optimism (happy endings), continuity editing, lack of ambiguity or controversy and sexual prudence. In terms of filmmaking it was basically Hollywood with a more collective gloss and socialist (instead of individualistic) rhetoric. In the context of North Korea, Lee shows how a language of revolution and progressive social transformation is gutted of its radical meanings and adapted to the celebration and legitimisation of class power and inequality, a grotesque inversion and parody of its authentic aims.

The question of the state appears in Xudong Zhang's essay in a somewhat different guise, via a reading of Zhang Yimou's film *The Story of Qiu Ju*. The Chinese state, although the product of a peasant-based popular revolt against colonial domination, quickly adopted the model of state control over productive labour that characterised the Soviet Union and its satellites. However, recently the Chinese authorities have also been reintroducing private property relations and market mechanisms of the most brutal kind, thus making for a highly complex and contradictory socioeconomic situation into which *Qiu Ju* makes a remarkable intervention.

If in Korea, filmmaking is entirely subordinated to the state, a small elite of filmmakers (called the Fifth Generation) has won some cultural autonomy from the Chinese authorities. Much of their international recognition has derived from the sort of muted modernism typical of art cinema, complete with strongly authorial codes. Xudong Zhang finds in *The Story of Qiu Ju* a decisive shift away from an earlier aestheticisation of rural life. Instead, there is an engagement with rural life on its own terms, in its concrete everyday materiality. If Zhang Yimou's *Red Sorghum* (1987) opens with a spectacular aesthetic construction of the particularity of individual desire, Xudong Zhang finds in *Qiu Ju*'s opening an equally radical engagement with the particularity of the social and collective world of rural life. Both cases function like Benjamin's optical unconscious, to reveal material realities denied by the *formal* laws and ideology of the Chinese state. If individual desire once had no formal recognition within the Chinese state, then the 1990s rush to embrace the market and private property means that any such declaration of desire today risks collapsing into capitalist apologetics. The delineation of the concrete specificity of a social collective life in *Qiu Ju* reveals what both market economics and state 'socialism' have in common: precisely their *abstraction* from just such daily social realities and the radical disjuncture between material reality and formal law and ideology which that causes.

Abstraction is the process by which the absence of democratic control over social production returns as a series of impositions and laws that are inevitably indifferent to how people *actually live*. This is easy to observe in the gulf between the plans for production scripted by the bureaucrats at the centre of the state and the realities of production that workers and peasants actually undertake with the actual resources and will power available. But it is also (less easily) observable in the gulf between the market system's economic imperative to find equivalence between all exchanges (the wage exchanged for work, the disposable income exchanged for consumer goods, supply equivalent to demand, etc.) and social relations based on a fundamental *non-equivalence*, where an elite has amassed fantastic quantities of social wealth. It is not only the market system's blindness to its own social inequalities which is at work, but a more general indifference to the particularity of *all* relations and qualities generated by human beings in their interaction with each other and nature. Ideally, capital works to assimilate everything to the homogeneous laws of the cash nexus so that it can continue, like some monstrous parasite, to grow (accumulation for the sake of accumulation). From economic equivalence there arises within most capitalist societies a legal formal declaration that we are all equal in the eyes of the law. The fact that this is daily contradicted in all sorts of ways indicates that this is true only in the *abstract*, not in the grist, the materiality of life.

A good example of how the impetus of equivalence fails to do justice to the particularity of social (and cultural) relations is inscribed within the subtitling of *Qiu Ju* itself. Irrespective of the genuine difficulties which translation poses when it comes to subtitling, there is a widespread culture of sloppy translation within the subtitling business. As Xudong Zhang argues, the English translation of what it is that Qiu Ju seeks is either 'justice' or 'apology', both used interchangeably as if they were the same thing (equivalent). But in fact, the heroine of the film demands 'shuofa', which Zhang tells us means neither justice nor apology but something like 'explanation'. What Qiu Ju seeks is a way of integrating what has happened to her husband back into the social relations of rural village life in a way that is meaningful to her and everyone else within the community. What this indicates is the central importance of the politics of knowledge tacitly embedded into everyday life. The political right have always criticised the state precisely on the grounds that it cannot substitute itself for the knowledge that is deployed in the production process.

And this is the basis of the right's demands that the state should be rolled back, limited to providing minimal legal conditions for economic activities. However, the right's understanding of the importance of tacit knowledge is necessarily individualistic and largely restricted to the entrepreneurs who 'make things happen'. The idea that knowledge is collective and shared is clearly incompatible with a system based on the private ownership of the means of production.[20] Capital's accumulation imperative is also indifferent to the specificity of social and cultural relations, processes and outcomes. Xudong Zhang concludes his essay by locating the repetition and specificity or singularity which marks Qiu Ju's quest in relation to the Marxist dialectic as articulated by Walter Benjamin. While capital returns in all its grinding homogeneity concealed by new technological and social features, the struggles of labour have a genuine multiplicity but are themselves forced to return since there can be no satisfactory resolution to social antagonism between capital and labour. We can see in the tacit webs of knowledge and custom that constitute the rural universe of the peasant, the dialectical prefiguring of an advanced system of production, which, based on the free association of the producers, would also depend on tacit knowledge and revolve around the consent, sharing and cooperation that capital must repress.

Our final essay, by Michael Chanan, orientates us to the questions posed in the relationship between revolution and film. After the seizure of power, the real, incomparably more difficult task begins: the tasks of further revolutionising people's thinking, their habits, values and sentiments. If people are going to participate in social life, then that requires a transformation in outlook. For example, the bourgeois cultural revolution in the West took at least two centuries to drive through. This required breaking down the old habits and ties of feudalism and building up the new values and perceptions around private property, profit, territory, nation, family life and urban living, all of which radically reshaped traditional conceptions of space and time. The socialist revolution also needs an ongoing cultural revolution: how, for example, can men participate productively in social life if they retain strong elements of sexism in their outlook? How can middle-class people contribute productively to social life if they retain strong elements of elitism and superiority over working-class people? How can people develop cooperative modes of working and living if they retain subtle attachments to racism? Any authentic revolution is a process of education and re-education for all concerned: but it is emphatically not the top-down process which has attached the term 're-education' with faintly sinister connotations, but rather a collective and participatory process of learning and changing. After any seizure of power then, the question of culture, which is one of the key means through which people intuitively comprehend their world and make sense of it, becomes crucial.

Debates on the left continue about the nature of the 1959 Cuban revolution and its trajectory across more than four decades. I would situate it within the progressive wing of the national liberation movements of the era, freeing itself from neocolonial subordination to North America. It was a genuinely popular revolution and if it did not have the classic base in working-class insurrection as the Bolshevik Revolution did in the factories and army in 1917, neither did it degenerate into Stalinist tyranny as the world's first socialist state did. What Russia 1917 and Cuba 1959 share is that they opened the gates for an incredible unleashing of cinematic creativity and innovation in the first ten years which made major contributions to world film culture. In both cases cinema was conceived as more than merely a tool of propaganda, but also as a crucial means for raising consciousness and developing the critical and cultural capacities of the audience. There was no hint of patronising audiences in cinemas where political radicalism and aesthetic experimentation converged. If there was sometimes a gulf between the cinematic avant-garde and the audience in Russia, Cuban filmmakers several decades later, working within a higher level of cultural development generally, indisputably made films for the Cuban masses. Chanan's juxtaposition brings out the lines of continuity and difference between the two historical moments and the cinematic movements that flourished within the two revolutions as well as the respective attitudes of the Russian and Cuban states to those movements.

CONCLUSION

What is it that Marxism offers film studies? It offers I think a remarkably rich tradition of analysis and debates central to understanding an industrial cultural form such as film. Marxism raises questions about relationships at every level of the social order; without necessarily collapsing into reductionism, it reminds us how important socioeconomic relations are and any authentic Marxism understands the complexities of the cultural arena within those relations. Marxism provides, potentially, a substantive antagonist to those socioeconomic relations in their dominant form (capitalism) at a time of much conformism and resignation. It draws attention away from the exclusively textualist concerns which have fashioned film studies and highlights economic institutional power complexes, particularly corporate and state actions. Marxism demands that we historicise everything rather than taking it to be a natural immutable fact. It provides the tools with which scholars can self-reflexively critique their own position within the class structure and wonder how that position inevitably leads to unthinking internalisation of dominant practices. Marxism's historicisation refers not only to the past and present, but to the future as well. Marxism allows us to think beyond the now. Its sensitivity to utopian currents within cultural practices (and technologies) as well as resistance and contradiction helps us glimpse the prefigurings of alternative ways of living and loving which are today so urgently needed.

NOTES

1. Theodor Adorno and Max Horkheimer, *Dialectic of Enlightenment* (London: Verso, 1973), p. 163.
2. Herbert Marcuse, *The Aesthetic Dimension: Towards a Critique of Marxist Aesthetics* (Basingstoke: Macmillan, 1990), p. 9.
3. Etienne Balibar and Pierre Macherey, 'On Literature as an Ideological Form', in Terry Eagleton and Drew Milner (eds), *Marxist Literary Theory* (Oxford: Blackwell, 1996), p. 283.
4. *Cahiers* Editorial, 'John Ford's *Young Mr Lincoln*', in Bill Nichols (ed.), *Movies and Methods Vol.1* (Los Angeles: University of California Press, 1976), p. 27.
5. A good summary of *Cahiers'* difficult analysis of the film can be found in Robert Lapsley and Michael Westlake's *Film Theory: An Introduction* (Manchester: Manchester University Press, 1988), pp. 120–3.
6. Georg Lukács, 'The Ideology of Modernism', in *The Meaning of Contemporary Realism* trans. John and Necke Maunder (London: Merlin Press, 1963), p. 25.
7. Lukács, 'The Ideology of Modernism', p. 21.
8. Lukács, 'The Ideology of Modernism', p. 25.
9. Amrohini Sahay, '*Memento* and the Cultural Production of the New Corporate Worker', *Red Critique* <www.geocities.com/redtheory/redcritique/MarchApril02/memento.htm> (accessed March 2003).
10. Fredric Jameson, 'The Cultural Logic of Late Capitalism', in *Postmodernism: Or, The Cultural Logic of Late Capitalism* (London: Verso, 1991), p. 44.
11. Lukács, 'The Ideology of Modernism', p. 26.
12. Jameson, 'The Cultural Logic of Late Capitalism', p. 14.
13. Lukács, 'The Ideology of Modernism', p. 28.
14. Jameson, 'The Cultural Logic of Late Capitalism', p. 25.
15. Lukács, 'The Ideology of Modernism', p. 33.
16. Jameson, 'The Cultural Logic of Late Capitalism', p. 9.

17. Lukács, 'The Ideology of Modernism', p. 36.
18. Herbert Marcuse, *Five Lectures: Psychoanalysis, Politics, and Utopia* (London: Penguin Press, 1970), p. 19.
19. István Mészáros, *Beyond Capital* (London: Merlin Press, 1995), p. 610.
20. Hilary Wainwright, *Reclaim the State* (London: Verso, 2003), pp. 1–29.

I

Adorno, Benjamin, Brecht and Film

Esther Leslie

T.W. ADORNO AGAINST FILM

The eleventh of September 2003 was the hundredth anniversary of the birth of Theodor Wiesengrund Adorno. As one of the many public acknowledgements of this event, Alexander Kluge was interviewed about his former teacher who in 1962 became his friend. Given Kluge's own work as a filmmaker and television producer, he was asked to comment further on Adorno's relationship to film. Kluge recalls that 'Adorno dismissed film and cinema totally'.[1] This blunt statement comes as no surprise. In various writings, Adorno dismissed film as a commercial industrial product of no value for art, or indeed for the living of genuine lives. The complement to this was that film was of considerable instrumental and economic value to the ruling class. For Adorno, film was a commodity, made for profit. While it sucked up their money, film enslaved viewers mentally. Film made itself easily available for purposes of domination for, unless it was abstract, adventurous or technically incompetent, film delivered a 'semblance of immediacy', that is, it conjured up a convincing look of reality.[2] Film's immediacy increased its capacity to lie about the world, whilst appearing as if it were telling the truth. Film was infantilist and infantilising, in the sense that it turned its audience into passive children and it drew on their bad, sadistic and negative impulses. Film accustomed the audience to the repetitive brutalities of life under capitalism, in a sort of training for what Adorno called the 'life in the false', that is, a life lived in an over-technologised, brutal, mechanical, alienating environment. It was for this reason that film was enthusiastically received by audiences, who are complicit in their own subjugation and exploitation:

People give their approval to mass culture because they know or suspect that this is where they are taught the mores they will surely need as their passport in a monopolised life. This passport is only valid if paid for in blood, with the surrender of life as a whole and the impassioned obedience to a hated compulsion.[3]

Adorno dismisses the oft-bandied about reason for films' success: the supposed 'stultification' of the masses generates a demand for film because these masses need easily assimilable culture of a simplistic variety. This is a line, he argues, 'promoted by their [the masses'] enemies and lamented by their philanthropic friends'.[4] Instead Adorno insisted that the masses' eager take-up of film denoted something quite rational. Film's service as a training mechanism was important for those who watched films, as they felt they might understand thereby something of what those in power desired of them.

If Adorno was critical of film's visual capacities, on the issue of sound his judgement was equally sceptical. The palate of sounds in a film was one of its most predictable elements. In the book *Composing for the Films* (1944), written together with Brecht's collaborator Hanns Eisler, Adorno bemoaned the way in which film music relies on clichés or 'highly specific and thousandfold tested effects in specific situations'.[5] Film music attempts to pre-interpret the action, so if a scene takes place in Holland or Venice some recognisably Dutch or Italian music is used. If a wedding is on screen, the Bridal March wells up. Life is represented as a set of predictable situations, from which one cannot escape, and reality is banalised through sound's library of effects. Music in film served reactionary ends, but it also impacted upon the existential experience of film. Film music sanded over what Adorno perceived as the terrifying cracks of the filmic experience, providing a 'soul', a kind of auratic effect that made the figures on screen appear less as shadowy ghosts and more as real human beings with emotions. Film music glues everything together in the experience of cinema, anaesthetising its pains and putting a veil over the reality of the experience – a human encounter with the machine. Film music

> brings the picture close to the public, just as the picture brings itself close to it by means of the close-up. It attempts to interpose a human coating between the reeled-off pictures and the spectators. Its social function is that of a cement, which holds together elements that otherwise would oppose each other unrelated – the mechanical product and the spectators, and also the spectators themselves. The old stage theater, too, was confronted with a similar need, as soon as the curtain went down. Music between the acts met that need. Cinema music is universalised between-the-acts music,

but used also and precisely when there is something to be seen. It is the systematic fabrication of the atmosphere for the events of which it is itself part and parcel. It seeks to breathe into the pictures some of the life that photography has taken away from them.[6]

Sound as music and as speech populated film with characters who seemed human. Sound made film seem a fully human articulation, rather than a technical concoction, which, for Adorno, existed to make profits in a deeply anti-human age. Audiences were beholden to spectres, which were animated by a semblance of life, but this life was given it by the machinery of cinema. Real life is 'indistinguishable from the movies', Adorno and co-writer Max Horkheimer asserted in their chapter 'The Culture Industry: Enlightenment as Mass Deception', from *Dialectic of Enlightenment* (1944).[7] Sound film stunts the imagination, with speech nailing the meanings of the movies before the eyes of spectators who can but hastily and desperately follow the 'relentless rush of facts'.[8] With film a technologically enhanced sense-experience is born, which replaces our vision with its own, asserting its consciousness in place of ours, and mollifying by its soundtrack the horrors attendant on our recognition of its mechanical deadliness, and, by association, the world's own technical lethality.

For Adorno, cinema is the consequence of the application of industry to the arts. Film is made purely with an eye to its exchange value.

Cultural entities typical of the culture industry are no longer *also* commodities, they are commodities through and through.[9]

Involved in market machinations, film, like other products of the 'culture industry', loses its artistic integrity and quality, tending towards standardisation, stereotypes and simplicity. In the process film creates appropriate audiences, who are equally standardised and homogenised. Denial or resigned acceptance of the unhappiness in the world was what the culture industry was organised to promote. Adorno abhorred the manipulative effect on people's minds of cultural forms that conveyed easily interpretable messages. This was a residue of his experience of Nazi propaganda and his knowledge of propagandistic mass culture in the Soviet Union. It also stemmed from his experience in California, the apex of US commercial culture. Adorno distrusted work that gave instant gratification. Its effect, he thought, was to lead to a technologically dependent, uncritical populace susceptible to any totalistic ideology, be it fascist, Stalinist or consumerist. In 'Transparencies on Film' (1966) Adorno notes how film consists of 'mimetic impulses which, prior to all content and meaning, incite the viewers and listeners to fall into step as if in a parade'.[10] The metaphor evokes the recent German history of Nazi pageants and rallies. In the 1940s essay 'The Schema of Mass Culture' Adorno notes how reality becomes its own ideology through the spell cast by its faithful duplication. Through a mimetic technology, a myth of the positive is drawn. A positive aesthetics represents the world positively. Pictures of happy people experiencing the world or images of objects in that world are shown in recognisable form, naturalistically. Through this very act of seemingly photocopying the world, the world as it exists now is affirmed and re-affirmed. No change can be imagined and art acts as a consolation, suggesting that this is really our happy world, attainable for us now. Through realism, art becomes a vehicle for showing the world as it is, though this 'world as it is' may be highly ideologically coloured. Such a realist aesthetic might also show misery in the world, with recognisable pictures of suffering. Again, though, this would act as an affirmation of what is, even as it denounces it, and it is unlikely to change anything, offering only catharsis and not opening on to reality but remaining self-contained. Art is deployed instrumentally as a vehicle to show a world 'out there'. Adorno's negative aesthetics aims to make art the focus of something different. Art should not be instrumentalised or deployed utilitarianly. Art marks a space for a relationship to the world that is not directed by the constraint to imitate the surface of reality. It holds on to autonomy: both for artists who create without constriction, including the obligation to imitate the surfaces of the real world, and for recipients whose imaginations are stimulated and who are born as active viewers in the encounter. This does not, however, mean that the world as it exists is absent from the artwork. In 'Commitment' (1962), Adorno insisted that work such as Kafka's disturbing novels or Samuel Beckett's absurdist drama, in their rejection of empirical reality, in their refusal of naturalistic representation and figuration, in their emphasis on distorting the real, arouse a fear, a shudder, an indignation in their audiences that is more in accord with the truth of our existence.[11] In addition, their asceticism, internal complexity and intellectual snarls are a counterweight to the quick-fix popularisations of Hollywood and pop music. Their relentlessly negative visions provide maps of current unhappiness. As Adorno phrases it in 'Commitment':

He over whom Kafka's wheels have passed, has lost for ever both any peace with the world and any chance of consoling himself with the judgement that the way of the world is bad; the element of ratification which lurks in the resigned admission of the dominance of evil is burnt away.[12]

T.W. ADORNO FOR FILM

Film's persuasive rhetorical power lies in its ability to mimic the external features of reality. 'Transparencies on Film' (1966) was written once Adorno had had time to reflect on the outcomes of this idea first voiced in the 1940s. Though generally consistent in his analysis, he mentioned that conformist and repressed behaviour everywhere had not been the only consequence. Adorno conceded one small point to film. The realistic portrayals of 'the *dolce vita*', wild parties, playboy lifestyles and the like, while often intended by the screenwriters to be understood as immoral, 'reflect an element of collective approval' in their very presence on the screen, such that sexual mores in conservative countries transform in a progressive, liberatory direction.

In its attempts to manipulate the masses the ideology of the culture industry itself becomes as internally antagonistic as the very society which it aims to control. The ideology of the culture industry contains the antidote to its own lie. No other plea could be made for its defence.[13]

Film offers a chink of hope, through the very mechanism that makes it also so hopeless for resistance to the status quo. But this was too little for Adorno. There was, however, another aspect that presented some element of hope. Adorno was aware of the existence of a new German cinema, which had forcefully denounced the 'Daddy's cinema' of its predecessors. 'Transparencies on Film' opened with a defence of the 'incompetence' of this new wave of German filmmakers, one of whose number was Alexander Kluge:

Works which have not completely mastered their technique, conveying as a result something consolingly uncontrolled and accidental, have a liberating quality.[14]

In error and incompetence there was a chance of escaping both the domination by the machinery and subjection to the filmmaker's limited worldview or the culture industry's ideology. In this essay

Adorno insists on the 'refusal to interpret, to add subjective ingredients', arguing that thereby subjectivity is not relinquished as such, because it can never be – he makes an analogy with the fact that silence retains significance despite its non-articulation – but at least psychological intention is denied.[15]

In the interview in 2003 Kluge reminisces about Adorno's attitude to film in the last years of his life. He suggests that Adorno was able to conceive of a film aesthetic that counters aspects of film's commodity-form in the culture industry: Kluge notes that Adorno 'respected the auteur-film, especially the French ones':

> It surprised him that such a thing is possible at all within the film business. He found Godard's *Breathless* foolish, but interesting. It was too Protestant for his taste, but very decisive and radical aesthetically, in its montage. He was interested in the extent to which Eisenstein's montage is of a rhetorical nature, and how, in contrast, Godard's montage comes from the material itself, from the incompatibility of two viewpoints. It is the third image, the image between two images that are montaged together, which one does not see, but which keeps the film moving. That is typical Adorno, this thought that there are no images and only the invisible images count.[16]

Adorno's film aesthetic refuses the image, for the image is liable to reproduce an illusion of reality, thereby confirming reality's coordinates. But, Adorno's aesthetic insists, film is not just composed of its ostensible images. Film is as much an art of what falls between each frame, each image. Film is as much composed of its absences, moments of decision for editor or director. In these gaps perhaps something interesting was hidden, precisely because it was obscured. Brought out into consciousness, this negative image might be telling. Through such a perspective Adorno might be able to bring film into the orbit of his negative aesthetics. A negative aesthetics is concerned with absence, the lack of a positive vision of life mediated through art. As a kind of intensification of this negative aesthetics of film, Kluge recounts the details of a discussion that he had with Adorno about a film in 1968:

> We made a nine-hour film about the student movement in Frankfurt at the Institut für Filmgestaltung. Adorno said to us that we should film blind. If one records something without intention, then something will always be tracked down. What it is will only be seen subsequently. The film that is

recorded without intention is cleverer than that which you intend. That was Adorno's point of view.[17]

For Adorno, the film should be blind – or the filmmaker blind, for if there were blindness in this very art of vision at least then something objective and true might be caught. Adorno's 'blind film' offered the possibility of capturing filmic truth. Here – under fairly extreme filmic circumstances – was the possibility of making something that did not serve capital, corral the audience into ideological submission and banalise human existence. Adorno's 'blind film' would evade the clichés of planned filmmaking. It would allow film to record something objective in the world, without the conscious interventions of filmmakers or participants, who all conspire to produce something staged for the film. Perhaps something more akin to an unmediated reality would emerge, from this mediated form. Or perhaps what came out would be more authentically filmic, given that the filmic apparatus is, in some sense, solely responsible for the images recorded. The 'subjective' aspects of film – represented by a set of roles, director, camera operator, editor, screenplay writers, researcher etc. – give way to an 'objective' film, where the productive capacity lies with the machinery, the camera, its lenses, the recording material. It is as if film itself is endowed with a consciousness. This is a relatively positive reading of film, based essentially on a negation of what mainstream film had come to be by the 1960s – scripted, plotted, acted, dramatic cinema.

WALTER BENJAMIN AND FILM

Adorno's idea of 'blind film', a film that sees on our behalf, is a kind of recuperation of the technical basis of cinema. As such it reworks Walter Benjamin's idea of a filmic 'consciousness', first mentioned in 1927. Benjamin's evaluation of film is more hopeful than Adorno's, but it shares with it a sense of film as a technological product that is viewed collectively. Both conceive film, if properly understood, as it seldom seemed to be, as distinct from previous modes of representation such as theatre, painting or the novel, even if these might appear, at first glance, to be similar. In 1927 Benjamin composed a defence of S.M. Eisenstein's *Battleship Potemkin*. He defends the film against the criticisms of Oscar Schmitz who 'marshals some heavy artillery from the arsenal of bourgeois aesthetics', which is to say Schmitz judges the film using criteria derived from judging a novel.[18] Schmitz attacks

Battleship Potemkin for its introduction of politics into art. Benjamin retorts that all works of art imply 'political tendencies', 'since, after all, they are historical configurations of consciousness'.[19] A work of art is produced out of the possibilities of consciousness, reflecting a social state of knowledge, a set of expectations about human life, behaviour and morals and a stance towards these that reinforces or challenges the social conventions. But all this embedded background is not necessarily visible in the moment of an artwork's appearance, because it appears as part of the texture of the time. The composition of this consciousness, what Benjamin terms 'the political tendency', remains unconscious, until a fissure or fracture point occurs and brings it to the surface. Such a fracture emerges, notes Benjamin, in technical revolutions, significant technological changes in which ways of doing things, or even the things done, are altered because new technological possibilities become available. Film is just such a technical revolution. Benjamin argues that in film 'a new realm of consciousness comes into being', through which people get to grips with the nasty disconsolate world. It is unclear whether film (the camerawork, the montage) or the people watching the film possess this consciousness. The distinction is irrelevant though – both film and audience participate in this 'new realm of consciousness':

> To put it in a nutshell, film is the prism in which the spaces of the immediate environment – the spaces in which people live, pursue their avocations, and enjoy their leisure – are laid open before their eyes in a comprehensible, meaningful, and passionate way. In themselves these offices, furnished rooms, saloons, big-city streets, stations and factories are ugly, incomprehensible, and hopelessly sad. Or rather they were and seemed to be, until the advent of film.[20]

Cinema blasts apart this 'prison-world', so that we, from the comfort of the cinema seat, may take extraordinary adventures in the widely scattered ruins. Film's experience of the world extends our own. Film extracts a beauty from everyday environments. All is streamed past our eyes and made a site of looking, a point of fascination. This, Benjamin argues, is liberating. It allows us to penetrate the secrets contained even in very ordinary reality, through its mediation and through the opportunity given us for reflection. Problems emerge, though, he notes, with plots. Plots fall back on clichés or templates from theatre, not allowing the tendencies immanent to film technology to dictate development. Benjamin's point here could be expressed as:

film is technological and so it should be about technology, in terms of both its form and its content. In terms of form, film has an array of technological devices at its command: slow motion, speed-up, close-up, montage, image/sound montage and so on. In terms of content, technology can form the basis of film in many ways. The world we inhabit is technological. Film technology is simply a subset of the technologies that structure our lives more widely – in homes, offices, factories, streets. To this extent film allows a grappling with the forces that structure our experience in the world. Technology is not one homogeneous entity for Benjamin. He illustrates this idea by pointing to two examples, slapstick films, such as Charlie Chaplin's or Buster Keaton's, and Soviet montage cinema. American slapstick movies play with technology, technology gone wild, technology as over-lively. It is humorous and indicates something of the potential a 'liberated technology' might open up.

> The obverse of a ludicrously liberated technology is the lethal power of naval squadrons on maneuver, as we see it openly displayed in *Potemkin*.[21]

Because film is a technological form, the heroes of film, notes Benjamin, have to be those who have direct experience of technology in their daily lives – the proletariat, the workers who daily engage the machinery that produces commodities and reproduces daily life. The proletariat is a collective. It works and experiences collectively, just as the spaces of its leisure are the collective spaces of industrial and urban modernity.

Benjamin's notion of a filmic consciousness is developed further a few years later in his 1931 essay 'Little History of Photography'. According to a Freudian model, if consciousness exists, then there must also be an unconscious. Film and photography are understood in terms of this unconscious.

> For it is another nature which speaks to the camera rather than to the eye: 'other' above all in the sense that a space informed by human consciousness gives way to a space informed by the unconscious. Whereas it is a commonplace that, for example, we have some idea what is involved in the act of walking (if only in general terms), we have no idea at all what happens during the fraction of a second when a person actually takes a step. Photography, with its devices of slow motion and enlargement, reveals this secret. It is through photography that we first discover the existence of this optical unconscious, just as we discover the instinctual unconscious through

psychoanalysis. Details of structure, cellular tissue, with which technology and medicine are normally concerned – all this is, in its origins, more native to the camera than the atmospheric landscape or the soulful portrait.[22]

For Benjamin, filmic material captures that which has been socio-historically repressed, screened out by the regulative workings of social consciousness, or ideology. To this extent, Benjamin dissents from Adorno's negative assessment of film as an immediate duplication of reality. There is always something more to see in a reality mediated technologically, and, through this mediation, reality becomes its own critic. The filmic 'optical unconscious' suggests that film itself, the cinematic strip, the processes of montage, could exceed the intentions of the filmmaker, even if it is not filmed 'blind'. Film presents its own unconscious to the audience. This unconscious might consist of chance details, instances where the material captured behaves in ways previously unintended or is seen in ways invisible to the naked eye, and, thereby, film makes something socially significant and legible. Caught in the viewfinder and projected in the cinema is an unconsciously perceived space. Externalised in film it becomes available for analysis and so increases the sum knowledge of reality.

The movie-camera is a mechanical eye, more powerful and more capable of seeing than the natural eye. Human capacities are replaced by machinic ones. Such a concept draws on the ideas of the Soviet film avant-garde. Vertov, for example, had conceived of an unconscious filmic space in which reality is 'caught unawares'. Vertov's documentary-based cine-movement, *Kino-Pravda*, claimed that its filmwork 'observes and records life *as it is*', and they pursued 'life caught unawares' through the form of documentary, the newsreel, 'that factory of film footage in which life, passing through the camera lens, does not vanish for ever, leaving no trace, but does, on the contrary, leave a trace, precise and inimitable'.[23] Here was a duplication of reality, such as was condemned by Adorno, but Vertov and Co. were confident that reality itself was a counter to the fake reality of fiction film. Benjamin wrote about these ideas in 1927 in an essay on the state of Soviet filmmaking, when he described 'attempts to make films straight from life, without any decorative or acting apparatus'.

They are produced with a 'masked' apparatus. That is to say, amateurs adopt various poses in front of a dummy set, but immediately afterward, when they think that everything is finished, they are filmed without being aware of it. The good, new motto 'Away with all masks!' is nowhere more valid than in Russian film. It follows from this that nowhere are film stars more superfluous. Directors are not on the lookout for an actor who can play many roles, but opt instead for the characters needed in each particular instance. Indeed, they go even further. Eisenstein, the director of *Potemkin*, is making a film about peasant life in which he intends to dispense with actors altogether.[24]

Not only might the camera's technological relationship to reality allow an unconscious space to be captured, the actors too could be unconscious of the fact that their lives are being recorded and retransmitted. Promised herewith is an end to dissimulation and lies. The veils thrown over reality by Hollywood studios and after filmmaking – in its very structured and controlled use of plotting, sets and styles of acting – are stripped back, and film promises an honest technique of engaging with reality and a new way of seeing.

Adorno spoke of 'blind film', a filmmaking in which the technology does the seeing, detached from human vision. Benjamin wrote similarly of new ways of seeing, which have been mediated technologically. Human vision is supplemented by camera vision and, in this way, a new region of consciousness opens up, one that was previously invisible to the eye. In both cases, fundamental human capacities are given over to substitute technologies. Human existence is understood historically and perception is mediated through machinery. Perhaps, though, Benjamin's optical unconscious, like Adorno's blind film, pushes further than that, replacing human intention with a machinic consciousness, an automation of perception. There are two motifs at work in Benjamin's and Adorno's attitude to film. One motif is the importance of the machine, or the way in which the machine mediates the world to humans. To this extent, filmic technologies mirror the increasing importance of the machine in industrial capitalism and the corresponding demotion of the human, or specifically the worker who operates the machine. The other motif is the valuing of the unconscious, of the non-intentional, that which escapes the domination of the rational and the diktat of the concept. Benjamin worried that in sound film this aspect might be lost. In 1938 he acknowledged Adorno's suspicions of film as a manifestation of the pacifying and banal 'culture industry'. Sound film had to be seen as a regressive step. Silent film, he argued, 'tended to evoke reactions that were difficult to control and therefore politically dangerous'.[25]

Therein lay the revolutionary potential of film. Benjamin stresses the way in which this reproduction of reality was effective, in the sense that it had effects. It produced reactions that could not be predicted in advance. Sound in film, like film music, may close down the space for unpredictable responses and enlivening reactions. It prevented an active appropriation of film's objective and analytical rendition of the world.

AURA, DISTANCE AND APPROPRIATION

Film's ability to provoke reactions and be appropriated is crucial for Benjamin. Benjamin argued that in an age of technical reproducibility, the security of art's status as special or sacred was undermined, or threatened, precisely by mechanised modes of reproduction.[26] The mass reproduction of art, specifically in the making available of postcard representations of canonised artworks and in the production of limitless copies of photographs and films which exist in various places at any one time, brought about the decline of what Benjamin termed art's 'aura'. 'Aura' is a quality that appends itself to unique . works of art, paintings or sculptures that, in order to be seen, demand viewers trek to their place of existence, and having made such a journey, the viewer has to be overwhelmed by the actual vision of the singular item. Aura involves the notion that unique, authored works of art exude a special presence and effect, akin to magical or mystical experience. Auratic artworks disempower the spectator, privileged and lucky enough to have unique communion with the art object. They force the spectator into the position of a passive beholder who laps up the vision of untouchable, valuable genius. Benjamin was fascinated by mass reproducible art because it promised a change in these rules, signifying one of those 'technical revolutions'. Technical reproduction could make copies of artworks that already existed, increasing the familiarity of audiences with these works. In a sense, the journey no longer needed to be made, because some sort of knowledge of the artwork could be gained through its reproduced version. Benjamin renders this change in spatial terms. The artwork meets the viewer halfway. As photograph or postcard it finds its way into the hand of the viewer. This is notwithstanding the fact that 'aura' may be bolstered, in a strange and paradoxical way, in the epoch of mass reproduction. Certain works of art are frequently reproduced and they become known to many people who are stunned once they have made the journey and are exposed to the presence of the unique original item. This aspect of reproduction of original works is, however, of less importance than the fact that now certain artworks are made only for a celluloid existence. Photography and film possess no original. Each print from the negative is as 'original' as each other print. Each film in the can is as valid as all other copies of the same film. This change in production – crucially a development into re-production – generates a change in modes of looking and understanding art. The possibility of a demystified appropriation of culture by audiences, Benjamin thought, could be most strikingly perceived in the cinema. In the cinema audiences engaged energetically with what was on show. They were no longer in awe before it. They discussed it and criticised it, in ways that they might not discuss a novel or an artwork.[27] At the same time, the very culture industry that Adorno excoriated was producing an apparatus for discussion and reflection on film, in magazines and fan clubs. This led to a familiarity with film, its actors, its processes, its financial dealings. Demystification could occur, with films, techniques, actors opened up to criticism and mockery. (But, warned Benjamin, an institution such as the Hollywood star system attempted to reinstate that awe before the product, by glorifying certain individuals, creating hierarchies, making them superhuman, reinforcing what Benjamin saw as the rotten shimmer of commodified star personality by creating cults around them, in much the same way as dictators cultivated a superhuman image of themselves through painting, photography and film.) The more cultural forms lost their 'aura', their mystical character, their existence as object of beauty for a select few, the more these artworks would become dispersed amongst the population, available to everyone. In tandem with this shift in balance comes a reworking of the status of the artists – or producer. Benjamin's remarks on technologically reproduced culture are concerned with conditions of reception; the implications for audiences. Necessarily Benjamin is also interrogating the position of the producer of culture, who produces under different historical conditions; for example, he picks up on the large degree of anonymity of producers in the culture industry.

People reacted to cinema, insisted Benjamin, with all their critical faculties alert. He saw film watching as an active mode, or perhaps reactive, but certainly attentive (unlike Adorno's terror of the loss of time for reflection in film's relentless flow of images). Film was perceived more casually than paintings. It not only meets the viewer halfway in terms of coming into the orbit of the viewer, it also allows its meaning to be appropriated more quickly. It allows this because it speaks a language that is familiar already to its viewers. Film is a product of technological industrial modernity. Benjamin compares the flow of the filmstrip through the projector to the flow of goods on a conveyor belt. He imagines the factory worker who has become accustomed to this rhythm reliving it quite easily in the cinema. Film's multifaceted representation of life, with its shifting angles and deluge of data, is also akin to experience in the city, the very place where cinemas might be located. But film is not a positive and pacifying representation of daily factory and urban life, simply because daily life itself is not positive and pacifying. At the root of film's aesthetic is the shock. As Benjamin puts it in a footnote to his 'The Work of Art in the Age of its Technological Reproducibility':

> Film is the art form corresponding to the increased threat to life that faces people today. Humanity's need to expose itself to shock effects represents an adaptation to the dangers threatening it. Film corresponds to profound changes in the apparatus of apperception – changes that are experienced on the scale of private existence by each passer-by in big-city traffic, and on a historic scale by every present-day citizen.[28]

Film, for Benjamin, was modern and the very equal of the society in which it was viewed. Film was able to represent the very speed and complexity and fluctuating impermanence of city life. City life is about speed, fracture and incessant movement. The *only* apt means of representing the era was the apprehension of things in constant flux: a cinematic recording. Benjamin claims that even photography now seems unfit for recording the sum and substance of the city. Photography's fixed one-dimensionality contributes only one static perspective. The snapshot is superannuated in comparison with agile and multifaceted cinematography. Film is the only form capable of analysing new temporal and spatial urban relations and capable of representing them in meaningful ways to inhabitants of those spaces.

BRECHT'S EPIC THEATRE AND BENJAMIN'S THEORY OF FILM

Benjamin's film theory was strongly influenced by the Marxist playwright Bertolt Brecht. This is curious, because Brecht chose to work in the medium of theatre and not cinema. Brecht undertook cinematic projects for money in Hollywood but it was not his favoured medium. Brecht preferred the flexibility of theatre, which allowed for spontaneous changes, the reaction to a moment. Film, in contrast, is fixed and unchangeable. However, Brecht's formal analysis of 'epic theatre' suggested to Benjamin a way of conceptualising film, and, vice versa, film offered a language through which Benjamin could describe Brecht's epic theatre.

From the 1920s onwards, Brecht writes plays and develops his theory of epic theatre in close conjunction. For example, with the play *The Threepenny Opera*, Brecht includes a set of notes, directed at people who might be wishing to perform the play and at people generally interested in theatre. In these 'Notes to the Threepenny Opera',[29] Brecht asserts that he has changed the function of theatre, in terms of subject matter and also, or especially, in terms of form. Theatre has become a place of critique. Critique is directed at theatre itself – and its malpractices are countered by a 'literarization of the theatre'. Critique is directed at traditional ways of acting – and countered through the 'alienation-effect'. Criticism is directed at the traditional role of the spectator – now reformulated by Brecht as part of a 'new art of spectating'. Brecht insists that the theatre stage must no longer be the site of performance of an illusory slice of reality. If it is to play a political role – and that is indeed the role Brecht wants it to play – it must be a different sort of arena, a platform, a site of an experiment, a political space, wherein audiences can learn something about the world in which they live. As a Marxist, Brecht insists that people's actions are less a product of their autonomous needs and desires, and human nature and psychology, and more the product of an objective network of social relations, in whose all-encompassing web people's lives have become entangled. These social relations need to be shown – as just that – social, and also historical, not naturally or divinely given. Epic theatre is supposed to make social and political processes available for analysis. Epic theatre, then, is a theatre in which typical situations from life are presented for the purposes of analysis. Each of these typical events, almost like tableaux, is a 'social gestus'. The 'social gestus' is to produce a shock of recognition of the familiar made unfamiliar.

In 'What is Epic Theatre? II', from 1939, Benjamin set out a number of headings that encapsulated Brecht's practice: 'The Relaxed Audience'; 'The Plot'; 'The Untragic Hero'; 'The Interruption'; 'The Quotable Gesture'; 'The Didactic Play'; 'The Actor'; 'Theatre on a Dais'.[30] Aspects of what Benjamin described under these headings related to his particular characterisation of film (which means, what he thought film could do, if it broke from emulated conventional theatre). The audience – a collective – is at ease and 'follows the action without strain', for it is 'of a sort that the audience can validate at crucial points on the basis of its own experience'. The plot might well be a recycled old story. Its suspense is not connected to its denouement but to the movement between particular scenes, the way it unfolds. The hero is best characterised by Galy Gay, the protagonist of the play *Man is Man* (1925), who 'is nothing but a bodying forth of the contradictions which make up our society'. Galy Gay is a man who flows with the tide, a man subject to social circumstance, an extremely adaptable character. No moral standpoint is taken by Brecht in his play. In *Man is Man* humans are seen to be victims of circumstance, there is no essential human nature and no essential human goodness. A component of this educative function, which teaches the importance of social relations on lives, necessitated the display of social lives. This, recognised Benjamin, is why much of Brecht's work, and also that of other epic-style writers, is set in very social spaces, pubs, factories, and so on. This objective factor, the influence of environment, manifests itself, according to Benjamin, in Alexander Döblin's city-novel *Berlin Alexanderplatz*, which concentrates its action on public arenas: transportation system, pubs, streets. Another way of introducing life into art was through subject matter, i.e. examples of the incursion of the state or law into individual lives. The reappropriation of life into art, the disclosure of the public image-space inside the private individual, was a political act. The historical forms of individuality that formed such a central plank of assertive bourgeois ideology are now superseded. To assert them now is to evade the project of realism. For Brecht realism takes its cue from the technological and social exigencies of the moment: new technologies and the mass nature of man. To work with those new exigencies demanded experimentation and the invention of new aesthetic techniques. Brecht insisted that proletarian audiences were open to audacious aesthetic experimentation and were more likely to switch off in the course of reading a long nineteenth-century French novel, or an imitation of one.

Interruption is the rhythm of epic theatre, that is to say interruptions of the flow of life in order to provoke astonishment and to 'defamiliarise' the action. Benjamin illustrates this by outlining a pregnant scene in which a family is interrupted by the entrance of a stranger. Each actor is caught suddenly 'in the act', and in being so caught, all the relationships between the characters and the types of things that they do are laid bare. Epic theatre undertakes an untangling of the surface appearance of reality to lay bare the actual determinants and underlying structures. It is rather like Benjamin's idea in 'The Work of Art in the Age of its Technological Reproducibility' of a camera probing, isolating, magnifying and illuminating processes. This implied a different type of acting, and it was one that Benjamin saw well suited to film acting. For the film actor, who performs in front of a camera and who might shoot scenes in any order, no empathy is required but, rather, a distanced and even critical relationship to the role is inevitable.

As Benjamin notes: 'Like the images in a film, the epic theatre moves in spurts.'[31] Epic theatre is 'didactic', because it is designed to be appropriated, discussed, criticised by its audience who compare their situation to that of characters in the play and learn from it, or teach others in their discussions. This is underlined by the interrupted narrative and moments of direct address from the stage to the auditorium. One device used by Brecht to break up the flow of the play involves the decoration of the theatrical space. Brecht uses titles and boards, in what he calls 'a primitive attempt at literarizing the theatre'. 'Literarisation' Brecht defines as a way of putting across ideas, interspersing the performed with the formulated, introducing the footnote to theatre. These slogans and placards act as the chorus also does: they reveal what is about to happen, they comment on what has happened. Sometimes the captions are posed obtrusively against the visual. Brecht also sees the boards and placards having an effect on the audience. In reading the projections on the boards the spectator becomes aware of their own existence in a theatre. They become self-conscious. Brecht compares it to someone smoking. Smoking was an activity Brecht liked to promote in his theatre. As long as the spectator is smoking, they are concerned with themselves. It is pointless to try to spellbind such a viewer, because they cannot be lost in the action as long as they are aware of themselves. Brecht argues that by divesting theatre of illusory pretence, by knocking down the invisible 'fourth wall', the customary empathetic relation of the observer to the artwork is prevented. Brecht wants to change the relationship between the audience and the stage and its actors. He wants to cut away the emotional, identificatory basis of theatre. An emotional, dramatic theatre is not a realm in which the critical, political theatre he desires can be carried out.

The forms of epic theatre correspond to the forms of the new technologies: radio and film. Benjamin is convinced that film is inherently epic. It enables spectators to come in at any point. It is like radio, another technological form into which the public can switch on or off at any moment. Audiences and artworks, actor and producers have all come down to one level. Benjamin provides a spatial metaphor in relation to epic theatre:

> Epic theater takes account of a circumstance that has generally been overlooked. It might be called the filling in of the orchestra pit. This abyss, which separates the players from the audience as though separating the dead from the living, this abyss, whose silence in a play heightens the sublimity, whose resonance in an opera heightens the intoxication; this abyss, which of all the theater's elements is the one that bears the most indelible traces of its origin in ritual, has steadily decreased in significance. The stage is still raised, but it no longer rises from unfathomable depths.[32]

With the coming of sound film, the orchestra pit was fully eradicated from the cinema space and the audience moved even nearer to the screen.

Brecht preferred theatre, but he did have some involvement with film, including some bad experiences in Hollywood, where he lived from 1941–47 – his negative view of the US film industry is recorded in a number of poems, including his 'Hollywood Elegies', a set of biting poems written for Eisler's 'Hollywood Songbook'. But there was one film in which he had a hand, from the closing days of the Weimar Republic, which exemplified the potential of film as theorised by Benjamin, on the basis of Brecht's 'dialectical theatre'. The film *Kuhle Wampe oder Wem gehört die Welt?* (To Whom Does the World Belong) was a collective presentation, made in 1931/32, with the screenplay written by Brecht and Ernst Ottwald, direction by Slatan Dudow, camerawork by Günter Krampf and music by Hanns Eisler. It was produced by Prometheus Film-Verleih und Vertriebs-GmbH, Berlin, a communist film production and distribution organisation founded in 1925.[33] The film was made by a collective. It was a low-budget production. The actors came from left-wing theatre groups or were non-actors playing themselves. In the film there is no hero and there is no resolution. The film concludes with the suggestion that through solidarity the world can be reclaimed. Much of the film takes place in ordinary Berlin, rather than in film sets. It is consciously constructed in opposition to the narrative style of Hollywood. The film is episodic, in an echo of Brecht's dramatic theory. It consists of four loosely linked parts, divided by self-contained pieces of music accompanied by images of apartment blocks, factories and landscapes. The first part deals with the fruitless search for work and subsequent suicide of an unemployed youth. The second part deals with the eviction of his family and the pregnancy of the family's young girl, who is then compelled by her family to get engaged to her boyfriend to avoid moral opprobrium. She breaks off the engagement. The third part shows a Communist Party organised proletarian athletic meeting (using 4,000 members of the Communist-led Fichte sports club), the girl's abortion, and her finding her way back to her lover on the terms of a 'free union'. The fourth part takes place on a Berlin train, where various people discuss a newspaper article about the dumping of 'excess' coffee beans in order to maintain its price on the world market. In *Kuhle Wampe* the characters are social types whose lives unfurl on screen. This does not necessarily mean that there is no emotional identification with them, and there are certainly traumatic scenes – such as the suicide of a young worker – which are affecting. However, the circumstances of tragedy are always at the fore, so that the audience does not just lament the death of a man who is barely sketched out in the film, but rather reflects on the insanity of a world that brings about such a waste of life. The music by Eisler works to underline the intended critical reception of the film. Eisler described his opening scene when numerous young workers pedal furiously to reach factories where 'hands' are being taken on for the day. They ride against each other, providing a graphic image of how the members of the working class are set in competition with each other under capitalism:

> A slum district of drab, dilapidated suburban houses is shown in all its misery and filth. The atmosphere is passive, hopeless, depressing. The accompanying music is brisk, sharp, a polyphonic prelude of a marcato character, and its strict form and stern tone, contrasted with the loose structure of the scenes, acts as a shock deliberately aimed at arousing resistance rather than sentimental sympathy.[34]

Image and sound are set in opposition to each other and thereby open up a gap for critical reflection on the part of the audience, rather than the audience's sinking into the story. At the same time there is something of Eisenstein's *Kino-Fist* here, the idea that the violent montage of images stimulates aggressive and angry impulses in the audience, an anger that is to be directed against the ruling class. Various resources specific to film are deployed here, most notably editing – or more specifically montage, creating contradiction and connections between images and between image and soundtrack. The use of real-life situations alongside acted segments was also made possible by film. Close-up, distance shots and off-camera action underlined aspects of the action, directing audience attention and adding another layer of commentary. In addition the filmic unconscious laid bare Weimar society for its inhabitants and subsequent viewers to scrutinise. Through these filmic techniques, in conjunction with the array of dramatic techniques adopted from Brechtian and agitprop theatre, social awareness is sought, fulfilling Benjamin's demand at the end of 'The Work of Art in the Age of its Technological Reproducibility', that Communism politicise art.

THE UPSHOT

Adorno and Benjamin are differently disposed towards film, and show that Marxist approaches to film may lead to quite disparate conclusions. Adorno is usually disapproving, except when he can find a 'negative' aesthetic of film, which might provide some hope for film as a critical, exploratory tool in the world. Benjamin is more positive, confident that film allows a new technologically enhanced and accessible mode of encounter with the world. Despite their different evaluations, their analysis is footed on a common assessment of film's and cinema's significance. Both regard film and cinema as part of a collective experience in various senses. It is made and watched collectively. This means that film and cinema are inescapably social products with social significance. As Marxists, Adorno and Benjamin desire a total analysis, which can encompass aesthetic issues as well as economic questions, and which considers film in terms of its production as much as it considers cinema as a site of viewing or consumption. Both place film and cinema within the wider context of social relations in urban modernity. Adorno and Benjamin both focus on the technological aspects of film, an aspect that makes it qualitatively different from previous modes of art. This technological aspect means that film and cinema are essentially modern and the very equal of wider technical modernity. As such, film is peculiarly attuned to re-present that modernity, to good or ill effect. Both Adorno and Benjamin attribute to this technological art form a kind of agency or active pre-digesting of the world. This might be understood negatively in Adorno's sense, as film's manipulation of reality and its presentation of an ideological compote, which forces audiences into submission to its fabrications and inventions. Benjamin's more optimistic version of this presents film as a probing analytical dissection of reality by technology, which is then laid out before audiences for their critical appropriation and comment. Neither theorists' position on film is rigid, though. Benjamin and Adorno suggest counter-cases to their own analyses. For Marxists, there has to be an element of actual practice in the world revising the theory. This is seen most starkly in Benjamin's critique of the reactionary deployment of film by the Nazis for propaganda purposes, a case that appears to reverse all that he has said about film's critical and democratic disposition.[35] As a Marxist, Benjamin is aware that the character and possibilities of film are influenced by the state of the class struggle. His analysis is an analysis of potential, in the context of a recognition of the distorting effects of capitalist property relations and profit motives.

While Adorno's and Benjamin's positions are distinct in many respects, it is not simply the case that Benjamin favoured film, while Adorno despised it. They were debating the meaning of a young cultural form and its context, its actuality and its potential. The fault lines of capital and the eruptions of the class struggle pervaded both form and context, as they still do today. Film remains a mass form, though one amongst many now. Adorno and Horkheimer perceived a tendency that – despite recent sunny pronouncements about niche culture, cultural proliferation, audience empowerment and the world of choice – has continued unabated into our era. What Adorno and Horkheimer described as 'the system which is uniform as a whole and in every part' still persists and, despite well broadcast assertions of diversity and choice, in this world too 'all the living units crystallise into well-organised complexes'.[36] Indeed the monopolistic tendency is even more pronounced nowadays than when Adorno wrote this, when, for example, in the United States media concentration is far greater than ever before – a huge world market divided up between the 'big ten' media conglomerates, with their billion-dollar interests in publishing, television, film, video and radio, music, theme parks, the internet and sports. Concentrated ownership across these areas makes it so much easier to cross-promote products, i.e. to produce material in multiple formats, as in the Disney animation film that becomes video, theme park attraction, book, feature in magazines, pop hit, toy and accessories, and McDonald's or Burger King 'freebie'. US films do the rounds internationally, a process made simpler because the major film companies own distribution companies, multiplex cinemas, video chains and television stations. It all locks together tightly and forms an unavoidable bulk. Films are made solely in order to place products, turning them into lengthy advertisements. This is a world of exhausted internationalised formats, where repetition is compulsive, as *Big Brother 2, 3* and *4* and *Celebrity Big Brother*, or *Celebrity Survivor*, or another so-called Reality TV show or quiz show format, replicate around the world. Boredom inhabits this process as a permanent threat, and so hopes are high for short memories as the next re-recycling comes round, and celebrities rise and fall, to give the illusion that something is really happening, when really everything in essence stays the same: the business as usual of the expropriation of surplus value. Adorno's pessimistic analysis recognises this and it explains how and why this happens and what the psychological impact might be. But on the other hand, there is today a proliferation of media technologies, which make it possible for Benjamin's vision of audiences as producers to take shape, even if all the aspects of distribution, multiple reproduction and so on still remain intractable matters of finance and power. In a more modest sense, Benjamin's notion of a demystification of culture and an accessibility of culture mediated technologically would appear to have been realised in the widespread media literacy of a large part of the world. In a very real sense the aesthetics of film and other media forms have become politicised, with a very foregrounded discussion of the reality of images, the gap between image and illusion, questions of 'spin'. It is evident in a new wave of struggle in the realm of signs, through which much anti-capitalist and anti-globalisation activism has occurred – in parody adverts or subvertisements, in detourned corporate logos, in billboard and website subversion, using the latest technologies of culture to mock ideological fictions. 'Globalisation' produced its antithesis, a globalised resistance – or, more specifically, resistance to world capitalism on a world scale. Any decisive political consequences of such literacy are yet to be realised.

NOTES

1. The interview appeared in the newspaper *Der Tagespiegel* on 11 September 2003. A transcription of the interview by Peter Laudenbach is available online at <www.kluge-alexander.de/interv_tagesspiegel_adorno.shtml> (accessed 6 November 2004).
2. T.W. Adorno, 'Transparencies on Film' (1966), *The Culture Industry*, ed. J.M. Bernstein (London: Routledge, 1991), p. 155.

3. T.W. Adorno, 'The Schema of Mass Culture' (1942), *The Culture Industry*, p. 80.
4. Adorno, 'The Schema of Mass Culture', p. 80.
5. See T.W. Adorno and Hanns Eisler, *Composing for the Films* (1944) (London: Athlone, 1994), p. 57.
6. Adorno and Eisler, *Composing for the Films*, p. 59.
7. T.W. Adorno and Max Horkheimer, *Dialectic of Enlightenment* (1944) (London: Verso, 1995), p. 126.
8. Adorno and Horkheimer, *Dialectic of Enlightenment*, p. 127.
9. T.W. Adorno, 'Culture Industry Reconsidered' (1963), *The Culture Industry*, p. 86.
10. Adorno, 'Transparencies on Film', p. 158.
11. T.W. Adorno, 'Commitment' (1962), in Ronald Taylor (ed.), *Aesthetics and Politics: Debates Between Bloch, Lukács, Brecht, Benjamin, Adorno* (London: NLB, 1977), p. 190.
12. Adorno, 'Commitment', p. 191.
13. Adorno, 'Transparencies on Film', p. 157.
14. Adorno, 'Transparencies on Film', p. 154.
15. Adorno, 'Transparencies on Film', p. 159.
16. *Der Tagespiegel*, 11 September 2003.
17. *Der Tagespiegel*, 11 September 2003.
18. Benjamin, *Selected Writings*, volume 2: 1927–1934, ed. Michael W. Jennings, Howard Eiland and Gary Smith (Cambridge, MA: Harvard University Press, 1999), p. 16.
19. Benjamin, *Selected Writings*, vol. 2, p. 17.
20. Benjamin, *Selected Writings*, vol. 2, p. 17.
21. Benjamin, *Selected Writings*, vol. 2, p. 17.
22. Benjamin, *Selected Writings*, vol. 2, pp. 511–12.
23. Dziga Vertov, 'The Cine-Pravda: A Report to the Cine-Eyes', 9 June 1924, in Richard Taylor and Ian Christie (eds), *The Film Factory: Russian and Soviet Cinema in Documents 1896–1939* (Cambridge, MA: Harvard University Press, 1988), p. 113.
24. Benjamin, *Selected Writings*, vol. 2, pp. 13–14.
25. Walter Benjamin, Letter to T.W. Adorno, 9 December 1938, *Selected Writings*, volume 4: 1938–1940, ed. Howard Eiland and Michael W. Jennings (Cambridge, MA: Harvard University Press, 2003), p. 118.
26. This argument is most cogently expressed in his 'The Work of Art in the Age of its Mechanical Reproduction' 1935 (which is variously anthologised). The Harvard edition of Benjamin's *Selected Writings* has amended the English translation of the title to the more accurate 'The Work of Art in the Age of its Technological Reproducibility'.
27. Adorno stacks up similar motives in a completely different way. Music 'brings the picture close to the public', reanimating the aura that technological reproduction has indeed stripped away.
28. Benjamin, *Selected Writings*, vol. 4, p. 281.
29. Bertolt Brecht, 'The Literarization of the Theatre', in John Willet (ed.), *Brecht on Theatre* (London: Methuen, 1964), pp. 43–7.
30. See Benjamin, *Selected Writings*, vol. 4, pp. 302–9.
31. See Benjamin, *Selected Writings*, vol. 4, p. 306.

32. Benjamin, *Selected Writings*, vol. 4, 1938–1940, p. 307.
33. For further information on Prometheus and the involvement of the Communist Party in film, see Bruce Murray, *Film and the German Left in the Weimar Republic: From Caligari to Kuhle Wampe* (Austin: University of Texas Press, 1990).
34. Adorno and Eisler, *Composing for the Films*, pp. 26–7.
35. See, for example, the third version of the essay in Benjamin, *Selected Writings*, vol. 4, p. 270.
36. Adorno and Horkheimer, *Dialectic of Enlightenment*, p. 120.

2
Gramsci, Sembène and the Politics of Culture

Marcia Landy

In *Le Camp de Thiaroye*, the director Ousmane Sembène encyclopedically probes relations between Africa and the West. The film portrays the contradictory character of subaltern existence, the nature of history and storytelling as the means of bringing past and present into politically productive crisis, the possibility of cinema as a pedagogical instrument, and the role of common sense as both debilitating and enabling in the process of constructing collective notions of 'the people'. Most importantly, *Le Camp* dramatises the importance of rethinking the category of the intellectual, including in its mixture of narration the role of Africans, of the French, and of the filmmaker as he strives to produce a cinematic text that complicates questions of knowledge and of action toward the ends of political transformation. In this essay, I contend that Sembène's cultural and political concerns converge in significant ways with those of the Italian Marxist, Antonio Gramsci.

Sembène's Marxism, as Françoise Pfaff has said, is neither doctrinaire nor reductive.[1] I believe that his form of Marxism can be best understood through an analysis of Gramscian key concepts: the existing and possible relations between intellectuals and subaltern life, the presence of history and memory, the debilitating and enabling aspects of common sense as folklore for an understanding of the politics of culture, the nation and the pedagogy of sameness and difference, as retarding or enhancing culture. Sembène's knowledge of filmmaking on a global and historical scale, of US and European cinema, is evident in the ways he uses the cinema as a pedagogical medium and particularly as an essay on the politics of culture. His cinematic texts offer 'a close and critical scrutiny of the role of media as an increasingly important source for the production and dissemination of knowledge'.[2]

The ideas of Antonio Gramsci's represent a challenge to orthodox forms of Marxism that adhere to distinctions between a rigidly determining economic base and the social and cultural superstructure.

If culture assumes a commanding position in both Sembène and Gramsci, it is because they, in contrast to Marxists committed to a more orthodox position of the central and determining role of economics, saw that social, political and economic transformation is impossible without a corresponding transformation in knowledge, behaviour and belief.

In what follows, I concentrate on one film, Sembène's *Le Camp de Thiaroye* in order to examine the full range and complexity of both thinkers' engagement with Marxism. While this film can be considered as exemplary of other Sembène films, its address of fascism adds a cogent and timely analysis of contemporary cultural politics.

INTELLECTUALS AND SUBALTERNITY

An organic intellectual from Senegal, Ousmane Sembène was a dock worker, a political organiser, a political critic, a writer, and ultimately a filmmaker with such films to his credit as *La Noire de …* (1966), *Mandabi* (1968), *Emitai* (1971), *Xala* (1974), *Ceddo* (1976), *Le Camp de Thiaroye* (1987), *Gelwaar* (1992), *Faat-Kine* (2000) and, most recently, *Moolaadé* (2004). His films, from the 1963 documentary, *L'Empire Sonhrai*, offer a range of styles, themes and points of view, but the continuity informing them has most of all to do with his notion (akin to Gramsci's conception of culture) that 'Le cinéma est l'école du soir du peuple (Cinema is the night school of the people).'[3] Sembène remains committed to the pedagogical value of film as an instrument for social change despite the economic and political difficulties he experienced in bringing films to African audiences.[4]

Sembène's films are addressed primarily, though not exclusively, to African audiences, and their pedagogy lies in Sembène's ability 'to reach out effectively to both literate and non-literate Senegalese viewers'.[5] Aware that antagonism arises when subaltern groups in a position of retreat either are successfully wooed by the dominant group or regard their survival, for the moment, as lying in accommodation rather than revolt, Sembène probes the conditions of accommodation and revolt. The film is a parable, the filmmaker, a *griot*, that is to say, a historian/storyteller of his culture and its politics. His work is committed to a critique of prevailing conditions and to producing new forms of thought.

In his discussion of the character of the artist as 'native intellectual' and his relation to the past conditions of colonisation, and the present possibilities for knowledge and action, Frantz Fanon wrote,

The artist who has decided to illustrate the truth of the nation turns paradoxically toward the past and away from actual events. What he ultimately intends to embrace are in fact the cast offs of thought, its shells and corpses, a knowledge which has been stabilized once and for all. But the native intellectual who wishes to create an authentic work of art must realize that the truths of a nation are in the first place its realities. He must go on until he has found the seething pot out of which the learning of the future will emerge.[6]

Fanon's comments about the role of the artist as 'native intellectual' reinforce Gramsci's historically and economically inflected interest in the function of intellectuals and artists as representing a political force for a new cultural and political hegemony. His comments also illuminate Sembène's filmmaking.

In the *Prison Notebooks* (1926–1937), Gramsci made the following general observations that offer an unconventional conception of the role and nature of intellectuals. He wrote:

When one distinguishes between intellectuals and non-intellectuals, one is referring in reality only to the immediate function of the professional category of the intellectuals, that is, one has in mind the direction in which their specific professional activity is weighted ... This means that, although one can speak of intellectuals, one cannot speak of non-intellectuals, because non-intellectuals do not exist ... There is no human activity from which every form of intellectual participation can be excluded.[7]

Gramsci's notes on intellectuals are set in the context of creating 'a new stratum of intellectuals', one that 'becomes the foundation of a new and integral conception of the world'.[8] In short, he regarded intellectuals as serving a variety of roles, distinguishing between rural and urban intellectuals and between traditional and organic types. In the case of 'traditional' intellectuals, they, as heirs of previous historical and social formations, were associated with the Church, philosophy and academic life. The role of the 'organic' intellectual is tied to prevailing modes of economic production, and, given the constant changes mandated by capitalist production, this role is dependent on economic and political changes in society that affect subaltern life. 'In the modern world,' he wrote, 'the category of intellectuals has undergone an unprecedented expansion.'[9] Thus, Gramsci challenges idealist and ahistorical views of intellectuals. Similarly, Gayatri Chakravorty Spivak reminds us to look to the various ways in which the international division of intellectual and manual labour and their efforts on education, language, and social practices underpin and determine cultural and political conceptions of nation, race, gender and ethnicity.

Hussein Abdulahi' Bulkan also reinforces the Gramscian insistence on the importance of understanding the differing and conflicting roles of intellectuals. He writes:

> The phenomenon of neocolonialism would indeed find no realisation without the presence of two necessary conditions: (1) the formation of an intelligentsia born amidst the oppressed but bound in a symbiotic class relation with the oppressor, and (2) the gradual peripheralisation if not the total destruction of the indigenous culture as a world hegemony of Euro-American cultures is imposed.[10]

Bulkan's observations are at the centre of many contestations over the relations between 'indigenous' and 'Euro-American' cultures and are at the very heart of postcolonial theory.

Sembène's *Le Camp de Thiaroye* takes place during the return and anticipated repatriation of Africans after their service in Europe during the Second World War, which included the experience of a German POW camp. Their return home and their incarceration in a 'repatriation' camp dramatises how their treatment at the hands of the French colonisers reproduces the same exploitation that was characteristic of their life in Africa prior to the war and during their service in Europe. The filmic discourse reveals its investment in producing intellectuals who can learn from failure and conceive of different responses to oppression. *Le Camp* travels through the various levels of address of colonial violence from, in Frantz Fanon's terms, an 'assimilation of the culture of the occupying power' to a memory of 'bygone' days wherein old legends are 'reinterpreted in the light of a borrowed estheticism and of a conception of the world which was discovered under other skies' and finally to the 'fighting stage' where 'Instead of according the people's lethargy an honored place in his esteem, he turns himself into an awakener of the people.'[11]

The film charts these various stages of 'awakening'. The character of Sergeant Diatta dramatises the dilemma of the 'assimilated intellectual'. He is not the isolated hero of conventional cinematic narration. He is rather an instance of 'the principle that the pretensions and interests of any character as an individual must be shown up as false and insufficient'.[12] For example, Diatta has thrown his lot in with traditional intellectuals, with Captain Raymond, with his French wife, and the artistic culture of the Europeans, in part because he is alienated from the indigenous culture. He does not yet envision a new way of producing knowledge as an organic intellectual, although, through his character, the film reveals the destructive and fatal consequences of divorcing the culture of the coloniser from the politics of colonialism.

Sembène is not interested in the psychology of the French coloniser, in apologising for their actions or in excoriating him as an individual; he is more interested in how French nationalism is inseparable from colonialism, and the film pursues this connection. He seems closer in *Le Camp* than in any of his previous films to portraying the French multidimensionally, providing a spectrum of the various military figures that defend and maintain colonialism, from the 'leftist' Captain Raymond, ultimately mired in his own national culture, to the general who is totally committed to the nation (whether Vichy or not) and completely indifferent to the needs of the Africans.[13]

In the case of colonised countries, culture has historically served both as a means of consensus and coercion on the part of the coloniser and as an impetus on the part of subaltern groups toward new forms of action and liberation. *Le Camp* dramatises the ways in which coercion *and* consent on the part of the French functioned to maintain European state power not just in the past but also into the present. Specifically in relation to cinema and the state, Sembène has said:

> We have no illusions. The problems of Senegalese cinema are bound up with a cultural policy still to be defined by Senegal. We also know that film problems cannot be resolved in ignorance of the other aspects of the social life of a country.[14]

Le Camp embodies the struggles of the African subaltern to arrive at an understanding of inherited social, cultural and political conditions as a means to produce new forms of social life. In particular, the film is a parable of failure that extends beyond the characters to the audience in its attempts at providing an incentive to thinking about the past and the present.

THE PRESENCE OF HISTORY AND MEMORY

In contrast to official history, memory is fluid. What is required in order to re-examine and challenge the dominance and clichés of official history and its connections to reigning versions of colonialism, is the bringing to light and reconfiguring the sediments of memory that constitute buried layers of the past. The cliché freezes the past and makes it available for constant recycling and repetition. However, when the clichéd image or word is jammed, there is the possibility of an awareness of the uneasy relationship between past and present.

Memory is central to Sembène's work. In a discussion of memory in Sembène's *Ceddo* (1976), Mbye Cham reveals how the narrative is not inert historical reconstruction, but 'recasts the structures of power and power relations in the nineteenth century'.[15] The film

> counteracts the official Senegalese-Islamic version of the West as the sole source of Africa's cultural contamination and degradation with a new version which splits Islam's roots away from Islamic soil, casts Islam as heavily infused with Arab culture, and conflates it with Euro-Christianity.[16]

Sembène's irreverence towards official history unseats idealistic and universalistic notions of culture, social structures, and of progress.

Gayatri Chakravorty Spivak identifies the problems of a form of historicising blind to the history of imperialism. Historiography as represented by well-meaning Western intellectuals often reveals a lack of knowledge 'in the history of imperialism, in the epistemic violence that constituted/effaced a subject that was obliged to cathect (occupy in response to desire) the space of the Imperialist's self-consolidating Other'.[17] Recollection of the past, dependent as it is on the position of the historian/storyteller, falls prey to a number of lapses in memory that bear directly on the efficacy and credibility of the historian and on representations of subalternity.

Speaking of his conception of the role of cinema in relation to the functioning and importance of popular memory, specifically in his film *Le Camp de Thiaroye*, Sembène has said that the film is 'the memory of history which we keep alive'.[18] *Le Camp* uses a set of events, the return of the men from Europe, as a pretext to examine how to make good sense of what passes for cultural knowledge but is in fact the form of common sense emphasised in Gramsci's writings on language, history, and culture.

The film does not remain within the confines of African culture, though it takes place on African soil. The global dimension of the events reminds the spectator that Africa has never been insulated from the outside world and that the cultural residue of the colonialist past is scattered everywhere. In describing Third Cinema, Gilles Deleuze writes that in the case of Glauber Rocha and of Sembène:

> story-telling is itself memory, and memory is the invention of a people ... Not the myth of a past people, but the story-telling of a people to come. The speech-act must create itself as a foreign language in a dominant language precisely in order to express an impossibility of living under domination.[19]

For Europeans, the memory of fascism has remained 'alive'. In the histories of fascism, in European and Hollywood film, the story of fascism has been more often associated with Europe and has taken place on European soil. Sembène's film challenges this history through focusing on the African memory of fascism and makes a connection between fascism and colonialism, something that Eurocentric views have neglected.

Le Camp involves not merely a consideration of the repressive forms of French political power but how they are intimately connected to the economic dependency of Africans. The substitution of African elites for the former French colonisers and the use of violence on the part of these elites to maintain their hegemony are not only an indication of the various forms this power can assume but, more importantly, are revealing of how the exercise of political power is tied to the exploitation of labour. The interplay between the escalating efforts of the French to keep the African men confined and submissive and the various conferences of the men in their attempt to receive a just monetary exchange underscores this connection between the politics and the economics. The Africans attempt to maintain a sense of equilibrium, stay focused on the immediate problems – getting their pay and returning home – but are thwarted in their objectives.

A consideration of European colonialism and its linkage to fascism can profit from a Gramscian analysis of the role of the state and of its connection to conceptions of civil society. Civil society is often equated with the 'private sphere' and with personal 'freedom', religious institutions, the family, and other cultural affiliations, whereas the state is usually identified with governmental power. However, Gramsci did not pose a simple binary distinction between civil society and the state. In calling attention to the interpenetration of these seemingly distinctive arenas, he wrote:

> In the (anyway superficial) polemic over the functions of the State (which here means the State as a politico-juridical organisation in the narrow sense),

the expression, the 'State as veilleur de nuit' corresponds to the Italian expression 'the State as policeman' and means a State whose functions are limited to the safekeeping of order and of respect for the laws. The fact is glossed over that in this form of regime (which anyway has never existed except on paper, as a limiting hypothesis) hegemony over its historical development belongs to private forces, to civil society – which is 'State' too, indeed is the State itself.[20]

He explored the assimilation of civil society into the state

to help him comprehend several contemporary developments: the resilience of capitalist regimes despite profound economic and political upheavals; the success of fascism in Italy, a movement which arose in civil society, outside 'normal' politics; and the differences between Russia and the West.[21]

Both state and civil society utilise force and consensus to maintain power, and fascism was exemplary in its mobilisation of consent and coercion to establish hegemony.

In his notes on Italian history that pertain to the Risorgimento, Gramsci records political failure in Italy's attempts to become a unified nation and this failure becomes the basis for an understanding of later developments in Italian history; namely, the rise of fascism.[22] Gramsci's writings on culture and hegemony were deeply implicated in historical analysis, and his examination of the relation of civil society to the state[23] is characteristic of his commitment to historical analysis as are his discussions of folklore and common sense.

Gramsci does not merely document specific moments of Italian history but performs an analysis of the historical process itself. One of the oft-quoted aspects of his historical analysis of the Risorgimento is that it was a 'passive revolution', or what he also termed 'revolution/restoration'. In investigating the Risorgimento, the struggle for Italian unification, Gramsci is addressing not only a moment in time that has been superseded but one that bears the signs of repetition and can be with care extrapolated to the present. Of 'passive revolution' he wrote:

the course of events in the Risorgimento revealed the tremendous importance of the demagogic mass movement, with its leaders thrown up by chance, improvised, etc., nevertheless in actual fact taken over by the traditional organic forces – in other words, by the parties of long standing.[24]

Gramsci's particular use of the concept of revolution here is ironic, since what he is describing is a restoration of the old order under a new rubric and with a new rhetoric through state reformism. This restoration is characteristic of the triumph of the bourgeoisie and of the defeat of subaltern groups, very much in the spirit of Marx's description and analysis of working-class defeat in the *Eighteenth Brumaire of Louis Bonaparte* (1852). Gramsci does not restrict his analysis to a retrospective glance at Italy. He has nineteenth-century Europe in mind but also, more importantly, the notion that Italian fascism, like the Risorgimento, bore the characteristics of what he termed 'a passive revolution'.

An acknowledgment of the failure to alter significantly the existing social and political structures is a necessary condition for learning from the past, and Sembène explores the ways immediate failure may, in the long run, be seen as intellectually and hence politically productive. This tracking of failure serves 'to displace discursive fields',[25] undermining linear views of history, challenging discourses of progress and bringing to the surface narratives of the defeated rather than of the victor that have been effaced, disfigured, or misrecognised by official history. Fascism was able through the 'legislative intervention of the State, and by means of the corporative organisation'[26] to produce economic reforms in the interest of traditional ruling classes (with the incorporation of friends and allies through economic concessions) and also through force to pacify or to control subaltern groups.

Le Camp complicates questions of revolution/restoration, dramatising the ways representatives of the French nation seek to cajole, and when all else fails, to coerce, the Africans at the camp in an attempt to maintain power. When the Africans finally revolt, brutal military force is brought to bear and the rebels largely annihilated. At stake in the film's political critique is a dramatisation and analysis of the historical links between nationalism and fascism. In the case of African countries, the national liberation struggles gave way to the replacement of the colonisers by an African bourgeoisie still attached in economic fashion to their former masters to advance their interests against those of the people.

In discussing the discursive elements of various nationalisms, Etienne Balibar describes how 'bourgeois formations passed one another reciprocally in a "process without a subject", by restructuring the state in the national form and by modifying the status of all the other classes. This process entails the simultaneous genesis of nationalism and cosmopolitanism.'[27] Furthermore, the narrative of nationalism is an 'already known', pre-given construction, which is presented to its audiences with its assumption of 'the continuity of a subject'.[28] Along with exporting its bureaucratic elites and its consumer commodities, France exported French culture to Africa, including French conceptions of ethnic, racial and gendered identity, and French notions of what constitutes the 'people', language, education, religion and history.

On the other hand and in less overt fashion than *Gelwaar* (the film suggests that the post-colonial struggle is, in Philip Rosen's term, 'inter-national'), *Le Camp* does not merely record events from the past but operates in proleptic fashion to encompass the present and to suggest a different future.[29] The emphasis on the need to detect and resist repetition, to evaluate the past in relation to the present, and, therefore, to resist all forms of reduction that have been part of a history of epistemic, economic and physical brutality, is necessary. However, also necessary is the critical awareness of obstacles to identifying those elements from the past that still exist in the present and inhibit new forms of thought and action.

In examining the films of Sembène, one notices how memory functions not to recover a lost moment in the past but to interrogate the role of history for the present. Hence, his structuring of time in narrative is not linear or unitary, but fragmentary and episodic. The past exists in the shape of ghosts, filled with secrets that are productive of dis-ease and ritualised violence. The melodramatic domestication of the world functions on the terrain of family, of body politics, and of the body politic. The lack of restraint that characterises many narratives of nation seems closer to descriptions of melodramatic excess than of comedy, what Gramsci has described as 'operatic'.

Le Camp provides no nostalgia for a lost tribal world, no common culture to which the men can adhere, but an exploration of the plethora of differences that have to be recognised. In his return to the past of the Second World War, Sembène probes the various ways in which the inability to distinguish sameness from difference, the familiar from the unfamiliar, are obstacles to learning about the present, guided as they are by past experience. What Gramsci describes as common sense, as in contradistinction to good sense, Gilles Deleuze describes as cliché. In the case of folklore or cliché, nothing intervenes to disturb and overcome habituated and automatic responses. In the face of this dilemma, Sembène does not offer relief. Nor does he propose a blueprint for the future. The Gods are silent, but the film's events are an intervention into habituated responses and an invitation to thought.

Sembène has violated expectations of what a conventional political film is as well as the role of history in film. The film is not a melodrama. It is not a 'biopic', exalting a single and exceptional individual. The characters are not triumphant: they do not overcome their enemy. Instead the film is an elegy, a memorial not merely to the men who were massacred but of the impossibility of their situation. In his discussion of *Le Camp* in the context of 'Marxist tragedy', Michael Wayne writes:

> The tragedy lies in the discrepancy between the necessity to revolt, to reaffirm their identity and integrity, and the historical conditions which give the dominant classes an overwhelming advantage. The massacre at the end of *Camp de Thiaroye* is rather like the shooting of the striking workers in Eisenstein's *Strike* (1924). The viewer is not drawn into the action to experience it cathartically, but instead views events from a distance angrily but with a measure of dispassion so that the historical conclusions can be drawn.[30]

The film's utilisation of narrative is not an end in itself but the pretext for an essay, a prolegomena and invitation to analyse the workings of historical narrative. While formally the film is not that of the Godardian modernist variety with its use of print on screen, an interview format, a montage of media memories and extensive theoretical quotations, the film shares certain similar theoretical objectives in its epistemological as well as formal concerns to question the status of the image, to recuperate images from memory, and to reconfigure and cast in a different context prescribed, institutionalised responses to narrative.

COMMON SENSE AND FOLKLORE

Through the complex, disjunctive and repetitive element of the style of *Le Camp*, Sembène rejects a familiar and transparent form of representation that would simplify the film's problematic or mitigate the failure of the attempts in the narrative to produce consensus, since the film's pedagogy concerning the complexity of difference would be blunted. Through the figure of Sergeant Diatta, the film sympathetically probes the contradictory nature of tradition and common sense and folklore. Common sense dictates a return to his family and a resumption of his life in the village or an assimilation into French culture, but the situation in the camp reveals the impossibility of either choice under the brutal circumstances of colonialism in the interests of inciting the spectator to consider an alternative understanding of the events.

The exposure of cliché, a form of common sense and folklore, seems central to the work of Sembène. By means of the reiterative slogan, word, prophecy and platitude resituated in an unfamiliar context, Sembène exposes the common sense valorisation of experience and the virtues of familiarity as propounded through cliché. Thus, the film juxtaposes African language and culture to Western, particularly French language and culture reminding its audiences that the narratives of colonialism and neocolonialism are not homogeneous. In the very form and structure of his films, Sembène calls attention to the need to disassemble, dismantle, the elements of historical thought and rethink them in critical fashion, assessing, even anticipating, and thus learning about, the likelihood of repetition.

Of folklore, Gramsci wrote in sympathetic fashion, identifying it with the philosophy of the people as a form of common sense that functions in relation to survival but also as an obstacle to new forms of thought and action:

> Folklore should instead be studied as a 'conception of world and life' implicit to a large extent in determinate (in time and space) strata of society and in opposition (also for the most part implicit, mechanical, and objective) to 'official' conceptions of the world … This conception of the world is not elaborated and systematic because, by definition, the people (the sum total of the instrumental and subaltern classes of every form of society that has so far existed) cannot possess conceptions which are elaborated, systematic, and politically organised and centralised in their albeit contradictory development.[31]

In contrast to ahistorical and disjointed common sense, Gramsci juxtaposes the notion of good sense that he defines as the effort to:

> Order in a systematic, coherent, and critical fashion one's own intuitions of the life and of the world, and to determine exactly what is to be understood by the word 'systematic', so that it is not taken in the pedantic and systematic sense. But this elaboration must be, and can only be, performed in the context of the history of philosophy, for it is this history which shows how thought has been elaborated over the centuries and what a collective effort has gone

into the creation of our present method of thought which has subsumed and absorbed all this past history, including all its follies and mistakes.[32]

Gramsci does not posit a stark cleavage between common and good sense. His objective, it would seem, is not to eradicate common sense but to indicate its limitations. In a sense, his emphasis on common sense bears a relation to such thinkers as Deleuze and Bergson who emphasise the importance of habituation and of sensori-motor responses to the world but seek to investigate other forms of memory, specifically, what Bergson calls 'attentive recognition' and Deleuze describes as 'jamming', a recognition of a clichéd response to images.

Gramsci's focus on common sense and folklore reveals the sway of the past as embedded in education and in the dissemination of existing forms of popular culture that do not offer alternative conceptions of the world or offer insights into the ways that de-familiarisation or de-habituation can induce a different sense of recognition, one that offers the possibility of seeing things differently. The object of this kind of analysis is to provide forms that might enable different insights to enter into the world of folklore. The attachment to figures and events in the past is not in itself pernicious. What is excessive in hegemonic historiography is its uncritical and affective investment in formulaic, sanctified versions of the past.

Gramsci has suggested that, as the repository of historical sediments from the 'Stone Age' to the present, and perhaps as the 'philosophy' of subalterns, common sense, as folklore, is not necessarily dysfunctional. The modes of forgetting and of rewriting the past endemic to common sense have their pragmatic value for safeguarding conditions of survival in the present. The trouble with common sense is not only its fragmentary and uncritical character, which militates against complexity and analysis, but its affective character, the feelings invested in the attachment to habits and beliefs, particularly as these are exhibited in religious belief. In order to provide a basis for understanding the past, common sense requires critical intervention to be made applicable for the present.

Gramsci sees common sense as the philosophy of the subaltern. He does not 'interpret' common sense or probe the mind of the subaltern but describes its conditions of possibility for producing change. In common sense, the sedimented layers of different experiences and forms of knowledge coexist, and the glue that holds these disparate and contradictory elements together is 'experience' with its penchant for affect, identity quests, crisis, catastrophe and salvation. Since assessments of history are constructed, and since these constructions are themselves historical, the role of intellectuals as cultural-political critics is integral to Gramsci's thought. Refining these assertions, Buttigieg writes that 'the critic is always situated in history, he always operates from within the context of a given culture'.[33]

As a film that critically explores common sense from the 'context of a given culture', Le Camp is invested in challenging monumental (that is, folkloric) national narratives that rely on a scenario in which the forces of light and darkness collide to produce an image of the enlightened and just nation. Even where melodrama as expressed as monumental history seems to transcend domestic circumstances, it turns out that its folklore expresses nostalgia for the nation, and religion. In melodrama, the family triumphs, since the language of the nation state is largely tied to melodrama and built upon discourses of the family with its versions of the prodigal son, the obedient daughter and the wise father lawgiver. Secrecy, divisiveness – the splitting of the good and bad siblings, and the identification of originary events (also arising from the family), are part of this 'folklore' that is fused with questions of loyalty, suffering and martyrdom. The face of the loyal subject is the mirror of this family bred from the 'family' of nations. Sembène's films seek to break this mirror and reject the inheritance of such a narrative through acknowledging important historical transformations.

LANGUAGE

By eschewing the melodramatic through dramatising the men's imperfect knowledge and the inevitability of the failure of their revolt, Sembène exposes the common sense valorisation of experience and the virtues of familiarity as propounded through cliché. Thus, the film juxtaposes African language and culture to Western, particularly French, language and culture reminding its audiences that the narratives of colonialism and neocolonialism are not isomorphic though they are related. In the very form and structure of his films, Sembène calls attention to the need to disconstruct the way elements of folklore and dominant historical thought confound important similarities and differences, and in Le Camp the question of language plays a key role in the film's complex texture through its constant play on questions of speech and silence, sameness and difference.

The treatment of the Africans by the French seems more brutal on African soil than their seemingly more 'benign' treatment on European soil, presenting a dilemma for the Africans in understanding their present plight. However, as it progresses, the narrative identifies similarities between Europe and Africa, indicating that differences between the Africans' experiences in Europe and here in the African camp are quantitative not qualitative. Recognition of this for the men (and for the audience) involves a lesson in sameness and difference that is the corollary to understanding the ways in which the men are beguiled by the words of the French, through repetition and familiarity.

Language enables people to perform, conform and survive in society but not necessarily to alter their conceptions of the world. The languages employed in the film are various – indigenous, European, and hybrid forms. The characters are European, indigenous, and Europeanised indigenous people. Of all Sembène's films – and all of them address issues of language and history – this film is preoccupied with language. From the multilingualism of the sergeant to the silence of the African soldier Pays, the film offers up a variety of silent, spoken and written forms of language as a means to dramatising that it is 'by breaking at any point the nexus between the existence of language, grammar, people, and state that thought and praxis will be equal to the tasks at hand'.[34] But this 'nexus' can be broken only through modes of jamming the production of the habitual and the repetitive, towards the ends of distinguishing the relationship between sameness and difference.

During the florescence of Gramscian enthusiasm in the 1960s and 1970s, critics paid particular attention to redefining education and the role of intellectuals, and to emphasising and focusing on the oppositional if not liberating dimensions of culture. In studying and accounting for the decisive and slippery role of language (verbal and cinematic) in the formation and deformation of the subaltern, Gramsci stressed the importance of working to create an oppositional culture to displace dominant political and social formations. From Gramsci's perspective, as from Sembène's, the creation of a new collective subject is achieved only through an effort on both cultural and political fronts, and in his pre-prison writings as well as in the *Prison Notebooks* Gramsci provided examples of their interconnectedness through his analysis of a wide array of cultural forms – theatre, opera, detective novels, Catholic popular novels and, to a slight degree, the cinema. Central to his enterprise is the seeking to unmask the 'common sense and folklore' of mass cultural production.

Gramsci was aware that in Italy there was in fact no popular culture but a dependency on foreign literary models of both canonical and popular character. In Italy the cleavage between North and South was a factor in the fragmentation of the nation and hence of social and regional classes, thus the creation of a popular culture was important to Gramsci as a major form in bringing about conditions conducive to transforming the subaltern, those exploited and dispossessed, into the dominant class. Gramsci examines how cultural artefacts (including cinema) are deeply imbued with 'the process of intellectual civilizing'.[35]

While allusions to cinema in his writings are sparser than those relating to literature, he sought, much like Sembène sought to do by turning from writing to filmmaking, to understand, reach and influence popular culture. Gramsci recognised how cinema vies with, even surpasses canonical literary, operatic and dramatic forms. His comments on opera, for example, suggest that the language of Verdian opera is 'responsible for a whole range of "artificial" poses in the life of the people, for ways of thinking, for a "style"'.[36] Under the rubric of the operatic and the melodramatic, Gramsci subsumed the uses of language, oratory, lecture, the theatricality of the law courts, and even 'sound films'. In relation to an analysis of the art of printing he writes that 'implicit in this research [is] that of the quantitative as well as qualitative modifications (mass extension) brought about in ways of thinking by the technical and mechanical development of cultural organization'. And specifically in relation to 'spoken communication', he wrote that it

is a means of ideological diffusion which has rapidity, a field of action, and an emotional simultaneity far greater than written communication (theatre, cinema and radio, with its loudspeakers in public squares, beat all forms of written communication, including books, magazines, newspapers and newspapers posted on walls) – but superficially and not in depth.[37]

Gramsci's comments on popular cinema are consistent with his comments on other popular forms such as theatre. For example, in 1916, Gramsci wrote:

They say that the cinema is killing the theater. They say that in Turin the theatrical firms have kept their doors closed during the summer because the public is deserting the theatre and thronging to the cinema ... There would be some basis to the sad observation that the audience's taste has degenerated and that bad times are around the corner for the theatre. We, however, are thoroughly convinced that these complaints are founded on a jaded aestheticism and can easily be shown to depend on a false assumption. The reason for success of the cinema and its absorption of former theatre audiences is purely economic. The cinema offers exactly the same sensations as the popular theatre, but under better conditions, with the choreographic contrivances of a false intellectualism, without promising too much and delivering too little.[38]

In the same vein, Gramsci focused on cinema's illusionism, its automatism, variety, machinic quality, and its role as escapist 'entertainment'. In his analysis of various cultural forms, Gramsci is attentive to the 'role of gestures, tone of voice ... a musical element that communicates the leitmotif of the predominant feeling, the principal passion, and the orchestral element; gestures in the broad sense, which scans and articulates the wave of feeling and passion'.[39] Cultural artefacts – the novel, drama, poetry, opera, painting and cinema etc. – are not easily contained in a progressive or regressive category.

Instead, as a caveat to reductive treatments of cultural artefacts that inhibit fundamental analysis of the complex and multivalent uses of language and their implications for assessing signs of cultural stasis or change, Gramsci wrote:

There are many 'conformisms', many struggles for 'new conformisms', and various combinations of that which already exists (variously expressed) and that which one is working to bring about (and there are many people working in this direction). It is a serious error to adopt a 'single' progressive strategy according to which new gain accumulates and becomes the premiss of further gains. Not only are the strategies multiple, but even in the most 'progressive' ones there are regressive moments.[40]

The conflict in Le Camp takes place on the terrain of culture (language, tradition, art) as manifest in the actions of the Africans and of the French, and the film is a parable that focuses on understanding the failure of the Africans to recognise the working of both consent and ultimately of force on the part of the French, and the treatment of language is revealed to be a major factor for distinguishing 'conformism' and its effects. The film has returned to the Second World War not merely to create a memorial to a forgotten but now recollected moment from the past, not merely to rethink the relationship of past to present but to probe the secrets and silences connecting fascism, war and colonialism, hence the emblem of the 'camp' has to be wrenched from its European context and understood within the African. Toward this pedagogical end, verbal communication serves to call attention to the limitations of language arising from the powerful residue of historical and cultural conditions that the film seeks to expose and undo.

Despite the differing linguistic groups among the Africans – and even between them and the African-Americans – the men organise to achieve certain pragmatic and immediate objectives. They organise to get food when they are outraged about the food they are being served. They are instrumental in returning Sergeant Diatta to the camp after he has been brutally assaulted by the American MPs who mistake him for one of their men, since he is wearing the uniform of the US Armed Forces and also speaks English. The men also cooperate to find sex for themselves out of frustration. They also make the general a captive, but they cannot discern the insidious linguistic manoeuvres of the French. In their communications with the French, the Africans understand when they are cheated, but they understand neither what underpins the French refusal to grant them their request for economic justice nor the duplicity of the Frenchman's uses of language that are an important key to their undoing. For example, their willingness to free the general and to accept his guarantee to meet their demands rests on the assumption that they share the same universe of discourse with the French colonisers.

Ultimately and tragically, the film foregrounds the question of language, since language is inextricably tied to the nation, hence to the state. The film, therefore, seeks to take into account that language is not merely linguistic but political and that it is expressive of subaltern and dominating social worlds. Of language, Gramsci wrote, 'What is called the "question of the language" has always been an aspect of the political struggle.'[41] On its preoccupation with language as culture, *Le Camp de Thiaroye* looks closely at collusions between universalism and racism. As Immanuel Wallerstein has argued,

Universalism and racism may seem on the surface strange bedfellows, if not virtually antithetical doctrines – one open, the other closed; one equalizing, the other polarizing; one inviting rational discourse, the other incarnating prejudice. Yet ... we should look more closely at the ways in which they may have been compatible.[42]

As a pivotal figure in the film's linguistic trajectory, Sergeant Diatta is a 'complex cross-border figure'.[43] He is responsible for the Africans in his unit and is the intermediary between the French officers and the men. He is proficient in French, English and Diola languages, a lover of classical music and jazz, a reader of Verlaine and other major French writers while the other men speak a form of pidgin French, 'Francite'. He is their 'translator' to the French and from the French to them. The sergeant as an African shares with Captain Raymond an admiration for the French language. The French officers have no great knowledge or esteem for their own intellectuals and none at all for African intellectuals, accusing them of being communists.

His knowledge of languages might put the French officers to shame but becomes a matter of annoyance to them. He is even refused entry to a house of prostitution when it is learned he is 'African', not African-American. Despite his linguistic capabilities, he is beaten and arrested by the Americans. He is a source of perplexity and dismay to his family who are not at all impressed by his Europeanisation, his marriage to a European woman and his adherence to Catholicism. According to them, by becoming a Francophile, he relinquishes his past, becoming the Europeanised African. The linguistic-cultural divide between himself and his family is evident in each of their encounters. They are separated by language, marriage custom and religion.

In becoming a Francophile, Diatta has loosened his cultural attachment to his family, village and the indigenous language. He is hybridised, expatriated, a European African who must learn that he has no nation. When confronted with the unambiguous evidence of French perfidy, he aligns himself with the Africans against the French, but it is too late. In a conventional film, Diatta and Captain Raymond would be the mediators of the conflict, thus validating the individual as a champion of justice and as a saviour, but this film is interested not in repeating these narrative conventions but in exploding them. In fact, among the many layers to this allegory, a major one concerns, in Gramscian terms, the breakdown of consensus, and the stark images of force that underpin attempts at consensus. For the spectator, though, the parable is not lost, since the film creates another text that involves another form of violence, epistemic violence, that can be discerned through language.

Language involves hearing and Sergeant Diatta, like the other men, and despite his linguistic skills, has some difficulty in hearing critically and making judgements. The numerous misunderstandings concerning language have ironic dimensions. When Diatta is asked to translate the American English for the French officer, he wisely omits whatever is derogatory to the French, particularly the comment of the American officer who asserts that the French are losing their empire. The episode reveals that subalterns are not completely unaware of their subjection and avail themselves when possible of expressing antagonism. Diatta uses his knowledge of French language and culture as a reproach to the cultural limitations of the colonisers and also as a means of exposing his blindness to his precarious situation where he is, in the eyes of the French, no different from the other men.

His role reveals that despite his learning, he is no better off than his colleagues. He is betrayed when his friend and assumed ally, Captain Raymond, is forced to take sides against the Africans, urging Diatta to counsel the men to desist from their demands for fear of the consequences. Through the examples of the various failures of translation, the French national culture is finally revealed to be something other than the romanticism Diatta has invested in his great books, music and love letters to an absent French wife, exposed in the film as contaminated by racism, fascism and colonialism.

Among the many languages in the film, American English also plays a role: as a clash of nationalities and cultures, as a way of dramatising differences and similarities between African-Americans and Africans. In the interchange between Diatta and the American soldier, Diatta's knowledge about Detroit and about jazz is revealed; however, the stilted conversation between the two men reveals limitations on both sides in understanding the political circumstances under which they meet.

The linguistic/cultural/political divide between the colonisers and colonised is also evident in the colonisers being constantly in need of translators, since they are unilingual (not having made an effort to learn the men's language). The role of translation signifies more than a paraphrase from one language to another. In Sembène's film the translator takes on the meaning of a cultural intermediary and raises numerous questions, on the one hand, about cultural knowledge and linguistic compliance and, on the other, about the potential of language for producing an awareness of difference. In writing about the function of language in Sembène's films, Philip Rosen asserts that the linguistic gift is double-edged and dialectical. Inevitably those who have journeyed spatially or linguistically may misuse or become blinded in some way by their privilege. As a result, they become separated from or oppose some of the key forces motivating the narrative. Those forces are associated with the needs of a less articulate populace. Thus silence and even inarticulateness can be both a mark of political oppression and a form of privileged refusal, a refusal of the privileges of language.[44]

In one sense, Diatta has become like his mentor, the captain, and as such threatens to become politically impotent, if not unwittingly a betrayer. It becomes evident that the traditional intellectual is faced with a situation in which he must identify with the coloniser, retreat to the past, or engage in forms of counter-violence. The prospect of recognising language and representation as instruments of struggle is only barely perceived, seen more in terms of immediate survival than of sustained critical insight. When the men agree to relinquish the general and celebrate their victory, suppressing the possibility that his promises are merely an evasion and a means for him to escape rather than a sign of his acquiescence to their demands, they reveal that they still do not understand their history and are doomed to repetition; however, the act of storytelling through the invention of memory aims at translating this 'failure' into pedagogy. In particular, the nature of 'awakening' involves more than negativity, more then the 'separation from colonialist domination' and will have to take place on an 'open terrain of forces with a positive logic'.[45]

Moreover, in the film's allusions to languages, another form of language becomes evident – cinematic language. Le Camp critically questions dominant forms of cinematic representation, calling attention to the forms of knowledge on which the characters' actions is based. The avant-garde cinematic text as a material object in its refusal of classical narrative forms, its intertextuality, and its 'reflexivity' as exemplified by the work of Jean-Luc Godard, seeks to destroy the narrative pleasure created by the mainstream cinema. Clearly, as we can see in the directions charted by Sembène, this mode of textual analysis is a challenge to inevitably compromised forms of ethnography and sanguine celebrations of the counter-hegemonic and hybrid dimensions of popular culture.

In its preoccupation with different orders of language, the film accords the role of silence a critical position. The one character that is set apart from the others is Pays, who is deprived of verbal language and can only communicate through gesturing to the other characters.

Though unable to speak, he attempts many times to warn the men of their situation. It becomes evident through his signalling that he can recognise similarities between European fascism and the men's present situation in the camp and can even foresee and signal the tragic outcome. He performs his appraisal of events. Yet, like the film itself, he can only communicate non-verbally through the use of his body and the sounds he emits as he seeks to avert the catastrophe. His 'silence' is not to be construed as a form of incoherence or refusal to communicate but as a sign of a different order of understanding that expresses as yet unspoken forms of knowledge and action. Nor is he finally the sole voice of truth. He is a reminder, however, of the limits of existing forms of speech and of the need to create new forms of speech-acts as knowledge in the interests of producing collective utterances on behalf of the people to come.

THE NATION AND THE PEDAGOGY OF SAMENESS AND DIFFERENCE

The pedagogy of the film for the spectator resides in the problem of how to detect difference in sameness, difference that masquerades as sameness, and difference as something new. The repetition of events in the mass slaughter of the men and their connection to life in the camps, the similarity of Thiaroye to Buchenwald, and the rhetoric of the French that focuses on sameness yet reveals profound difference – all are reminders of the folly of forms of thinking that are static and reductive. The film reveals that post-colonial analysis demands something other than compartmentalised and binary thinking. As Gayatri Spivak writes: 'You won't be able to dissolve everything into Black against White; there is also Black against Black, Brown against Brown and so forth.'[46] The Sembène film complicates cultural and political antagonisms, forcing a rethinking of difference against attempts at levelling or obliteration. The liberal humanist project of nominal equality presents the levelling of difference in the guise of benevolence. However, the liberal humanist rhetoric of universalism is exposed in Sembène's film as concealed European nationalism, relying on forms of racism and sexism, and on the concomitant violence to both mind and body inherent to them.

In Sembène's films, the role of nation is hydra-headed. It initially functioned in anti-colonial struggles to overthrow colonial domination and to function 'as a sign of the unity, autonomy, and power of the community ... the necessary vehicle for political modernisation and hence the ineluctable path toward freedom and self-determination'. Nevertheless, Michael Hardt and Antonio Negri ask,

> Is not the control exerted by the world market, however, the opposite of the nationalist dream of an autonomous, self-centered development? The nationalism of anticolonial and anti-imperialist struggles effectively functions in reverse, and the liberated countries find themselves subordinated in the international economic order.[47]

Thus a different form of domination becomes evident. The older forms of 'national liberation' have receded into folklore. *Le Camp*, in its backward glance at African history, complicates the question of the constitution and soundness of the nation, as Philip Rosen has indicated in his emphasis on the film's inter-national dimensions:

> From the perspective of colonised sub-Saharan Africa, the notion of the national citizen was at the origin of modern revolutionary politics. At the same time, the nation-state with its centers of modern power and capital tied to both domestic and international economic, military, cultural and administrative flows, was the political 'language', genre and/or 'technology' par excellence of colonialism.[48]

In relation to the French and the African intellectuals, it would appear that the French captain and the African sergeant share the same humane interests in their admiration of literary culture. Yet, in the end, these men are divided by forces that, while ironically giving lip-service to Enlightenment reason and individual agency, are actively engaged in using the state power to annihilate anyone who opposes their domination. The culture of the Enlightenment is in the final analysis an obstacle to the colonialists. They express their contempt for it by ostracising the Frenchman and by massacring the Africans who resist them in the name of reason.

Among other differences that are invisible to the French but evident to the film audience are religious differences. One is made aware of the groups of men praying toward Mecca. The followers of Islam constitute their own group. The sergeant is a Catholic. There is also evidence of residual, indigenous, ritual practices: the pouring off of a portion of the palm wine on to the ground before drinking, the ritualistic killing of the sheep, the 'victory' dances of the men, and the patterned mode of discourse in the African men's councils. The film builds further visual differences between the French and the Africans through the contrast between the camp facilities and the officers' club, between the men and the French officers. There is no doubt that the film marks differences among the men, attacking the French notion that French and African men were in the war with similar interests.

When the African men are first introduced, they are in American uniforms, which they must later change for French colonial uniforms, a signal of their change in status from Europe to Africa, and the sergeant's troubles begin with his being mistaken for an American by the Americans as a result of his uniform and his ability to speak English. The issue of exchanging uniforms is another way in which the film cues the audience to the problematic of confounding sameness and difference, relating finally to the African's confusion about repetition and change. The film's attention to the uniforms – American and African – serves allegorically to highlight its interrogation of the identity of the Africans: What is it to be an African? What are the delusory dimensions of identity? How and to what ends are such delusions fostered?

With the return to African uniforms, are the men returned to a more appropriate assessment of their situation or once again is this a delusion? Above all, the question of sameness and difference is germane to the film's visual treatment of history. The audience is given reminders of Buchenwald – Pays' helmet, the image of the camp with the close-up shots of the barbed wire, and the recurrent images of the watchtowers seen through Pays' perspective. And thus the questions arise: how different is Thiaroye from Buchenwald, the French from the Germans, fascism from colonialism, and how different is the situation under neocolonialism?

In one sense, despite their origins in different African countries, the men share a similar situation – going off and leaving African soil, being imprisoned in Europe, and returning to a situation that appears – but is not – the same as the one they left in Europe. The issue of sameness also functions, albeit towards different ends, for the colonisers for whom all the men are 'the same' – childlike, ignorant of the ways of the world, but also potential troublemakers (the French vilify the embattled Africans as communists). Yet it is evident as *Le Camp* unfolds that the men – Diatta, Diarra, Niger, Pays, Congo, Oubangui – are different, in terms of their countries of birth, their religion, levels of education, languages, social class, occupations, and behaviours, even if the French do not see differences.

The material conditions of the men's situation – their being behind barbed wire, their treatment as prisoners of war even to the diet they are given, their being deprived of their money and cheated on the exchange – are also designed to invite a questioning of sameness and difference, a necessary component of the critical analysis of history. The film is relentless in calling attention to the economic dimensions of the struggle between the Africans and the French, calling attention to the interrelation between economic and political dominance. On the level of monetary value, the French insist that there is little difference between the exchange rate they offer to the Africans and the official exchange rate. This act of levelling underscores how the value of the Africans for the French is purely a matter of exploiting the men and reducing the worth of the men's labour to the lowest common denominator of value. While the film focuses finally on how the men are exploited economically, it conjoins the emphasis on money, exchange and value to imperialism and colonialism, eschewing a strictly economic analysis but tying questions of economic exchange to the social, cultural and political conditions that are integral to the functioning of the existing order.

Gramsci too struggled against what he termed 'economism', the reduction of individuals and groups and events to 'mechanical causes', that is, to the inexorability of determinism associated with reductive forms of Marxist economism that rigidly adhere to a strict base-superstructural model and relegate economics to the base and culture to the superstructure. In discussing political analysis from the vantage point of history, stressing particularly the importance of identifying manifold connections between the economic and the cultural/political, and in distinguishing between different causes and effects, Gramsci wrote:

> A common error in historico-political analysis consists in an inability to find the correct relation between what is organic and what is conjunctural. This leads to presenting causes as immediately operative which in fact operate only indirectly, or to asserting that the immediate causes are the only effective ones. In the first case there is excess of 'economism', or doctrinaire pedantry; in the second, an excess of 'ideologism'. In the first case there is an overestimation of mechanical causes, in the second an exaggeration of the voluntarist and individual element.[49]

The film's allegory is geared to asking what, if any, are the alternatives to undergoing the same experiences again and again, and to the obstacles that obstruct the creation of a collectivity. The ending of the film returns to the beginning. Though instead of seeing the Senegalese troops disembarking on their return to African soil, another batch of recruits is headed out to Europe, thus underscoring powerfully the notion of repetition. However, there is a difference. Their departure is seen from the perspective of Bintum holding the sack of coffee that the captain had promised Diatta to take to his French wife and silently watching the men leave. In using the mode of allegory, Sembène seems to be resisting the tightly structured narrative on behalf of one that brings together a number of ostensibly different elements from the past and present. The ultimate failure of the men to understand their situation would seem to suggest that the film's focus is not on producing a familiar wholesome narrative of success, but on the audience's ability to work with the narrative of failure, to interrogate the nature of that failure and, even more, to create the possibility of recognition in the present and future for 'utterances which are already collective'.[50]

EPILOGUE

There is no reconciliation, no consoling moment – except the consolation of mourning offered through the film. There is no compensatory act, but there is the possibility for learning from the events. The film is a pedagogy of vast proportions. Its allegorical method contains different cultural and political strata – the possibilities for the creation of new types of intellectuals and of collective life, a critique of reductive forms for historicising as they affect subaltern life, an exploration of the power of memory, an essay into the political implications of assuming sameness, a misrecognition of repetition, a parable concerning changing conceptions of nation and of new international forms of domination, and, by example, an investigation into a form of filmmaking that challenges the folklore of melodrama. The film produces a form of cinema that, in the interests of change, does not provide programmatic answers to the problems it poses but instead proposes 'through trance or crisis, to constitute an assemblage that brings real parties together, in order to produce collective utterances as the prefiguration of the people who are missing'.[51]

NOTES

1. Françoise Pfaff, Lecture on *Guelwaar*, presented at Carnegie Museum, Pittsburgh, Pennsylvania, 3 March 1994.

2. Marcia Landy, *Film, Politics, and Gramsci* (Minneapolis: University of Minnesota Press, 1994), p. 10.
3. 'Introduction', Samba Gadjigo, Ralph H. Faulkingham, Thomas Cassirer and Reinhard Sander (eds), in *Ousmane Sembène: Dialogues with Critics and Writers* (Amherst: University of Massachusetts Press, 1993), p. 2.
4. See Lizabeth Malkmus and Roy Armes, *Arab and African Filmmaking* (London: Zed Books, 1991), pp. 53–62; Nourredine Ghali, 'An Interview with Sembène Ousmane', in John J. Downing (ed.), *Film and Politics in the Third World* (Brooklyn, NY: Automedia, 1987), p. 45; Claire Andrade-Watkins, 'Film Production in Francophone Africa 1961 to 1967: Ousmane Sembène – An Exception', in *Ousmane Sembène: Dialogues with Critics and Writers*, pp. 31–6; Manthia Diawara, *African Cinema: Politics and Culture* (Bloomington: Indiana University Press, 1992).
5. Françoise Pfaff, 'The Uniqueness of Ousmane Sembène's Cinema', in *Ousmane Sembène: Dialogues with Critics and Writers*, p. 14.
6. Frantz Fanon, *The Wretched of the Earth* (New York: Grove Press, 1979), p. 225.
7. Antonio Gramsci, *Selections from the Prison Notebooks*, ed. and trans. Quintin Hoare and Geoffrey Nowell-Smith (New York: International Publishers, 1978), p. 9, hereafter referred to as *SPN*; see also *Quaderni del carcere*, ed. Valentino Gerratana (4 vols, Turin: Giulio Einaudi, 1975): vol. 3, p. 1516.
8. Gramsci, *SPN*, p. 9; *Quaderni*, vol. 3, p. 1516.
9. Gramsci, *SPN*, p. 13; *Quaderni*, vol. 3, p. 1520.
10. Hussein Abdulahi' Bulkan, 'Black Psyches in Captivity and Crisis', *Race and Class: A Journal of Black and Third World Liberation*, vol. XX, no. 3 (Winter 1979), p. 245.
11. Fanon, *The Wretched of the Earth*, pp. 222–3.
12. Philip Rosen, 'Nation, Inter-nation, and Narration in Ousmane Sembène's Films', in Sheila Petty (ed.), *A Call to Action: The Films of Ousmane Sembène* (Westport, CT: Greenwood Press, 1996), p. 42.
13. According to Sembène, 'For me, the problem over whether it's De Gaulle or Pétain, is a problem of which horse's ass you are talking about.' Ghali, 'An Interview with Sembène Ousmane', p. 49.
14. Ghali, 'An Interview with Sembène Ousmane', p. 45.
15. Mbye Cham, 'Official History, Popular Memory: Reconfiguration of the African Past in the Film of Ousmane Sembène', in *Ousmane Sembène: Dialogues with Critics and Writers*, p. 24.
16. Cham, 'Official History, Popular Memory', p. 26.
17. Gayatri Chakravorty Spivak, 'Introduction, Subaltern Studies: Deconstructing Historiography', in Ranajit Guha and Gayatri Chakravorty Spivak (eds) *Selected Subaltern Studies* (New York: Oxford University Press, 1988), p. 18.
18. Ousmane Sembène, 'Remarks After the Showing of His Film *Camp de Thiaroye*', in *Ousmane Sembène: Dialogues with Critics and Writers*, p. 85.
19. Gilles Deleuze, *Cinema 2: The Time-Image*, trans. Hugh Tomlinson and Robert Galeta (Minneapolis: University of Minnesota Press, 1989), pp. 222–3.
20. Gramsci, *SPN*, p. 260; *Quaderni*, vol. 3, p. 2302.

21. Anne Showstack Sassoon, *Gramsci and Contemporary Politics: Beyond Pessimism of the Intellect* (London: Routledge, 2000), pp. 69–70.
22. Gramsci, *SPN*, pp. 56–106; *Quaderni*, vol. 3, p. 2302.
23. Gramsci's conception of the relations between civil society and the state has become a major source of critical contention today for those who would argue that the state has eroded all forms of private life as well as for those who see the necessity for reinvigorating civil society by creating non-governmental institutions. While in the normative context, Gramsci may not offer a panacea, his comments on the relations of the two spheres have been productive for an understanding of totalitarianism. In one context, he sees relations between civil society and the state as reciprocal; in another as conflicting. These differing positions would suggest that he saw them at the time he was writing as unstable and dependent on specific economic, historical and social conditions, particularly in relation to the invasive and corrosive role of fascism.
24. Gramsci, *SPN*, p. 112; *Quaderni*, vol. 3, p. 1773.
25. Spivak, 'Subaltern Studies', p. 9.
26. Gramsci, *SPN*, p. 120; *Quaderni*, vol. 2, p. 1228.
27. Etienne Balibar and Immanuel Wallerstein, *Race, Nation, Class: Ambiguous Identities*, trans. Chris Turner (London: Verso, 1991), p. 89.
28. Balibar and Wallerstein, *Race, Nation, Class*, p. 86.
29. Rosen, 'Nation, Inter-nation, and Narration', p. 32.
30. Michael Wayne, *Political Film: The Dialectics of Third Cinema* (London: Pluto Press, 2001), p. 68.
31. Antonio Gramsci, *Selections from the Cultural Writings*, ed. David Forgacs and Geoffrey Nowell-Smith, trans. William Boelhower (Cambridge, MA: Harvard University Press, 1985), pp. 188–9, hereafter referred to as *SCW*; *Quaderni*, vol. 3, pp. 2311–12.
32. Gramsci, *SPN*, p. 327; Quaderni, vol. 2, pp. 1379–80.
33. Joseph A. Buttigieg, 'The Exemplary Worldliness of Antonio Gramsci's Literary Criticism', *boundary 2*, vol. 11, no. 1–2 (Fall-Winter 1982–83) p. 27.
34. Giorgio Agamben, *Means Without End: Notes on Politics*, trans. Vincenzo Binetti and Cesare Casarino (Minneapolis: University of Minnesota Press, 2000), p. 69.
35. Gramsci, *SCW*, p. 377; *Quaderni*, vol. 2, p. 989.
36. Gramsci, *SCW*, p. 382; *Quaderni*, vol. 3, p. 1891.
37. Gramsci, *SCW*, pp. 382–3; Quaderni, vol. 3, pp. 1891–2.
38. Gramsci, *SCW*, pp. 54–5. See this passage quoted in Italian in Gian Piero Brunetta, *Buio in Sala: Cent'anni di passioni dello spettatore cinematografico* (Venice: Marsilio, 1989), p. 22.
39. Gramsci, *SCW*, p. 123; *Quaderni*, vol. 3, pp. 2194–5.
40. Gramsci, *SCW*, p. 101; *Quaderni*, vol. 3, p. 1821.
41. Gramsci, *SCW*, p. 187; *Quaderni*, vol. 3, p. 2350.
42. Immanuel Wallerstein, *Historical Capitalism* (London: Verso, 1984), p. 85.
43. Rosen, 'Nation, Inter-nation, and Narration', p. 32.
44. Rosen,'Nation, Inter-nation, and Narration', p. 34.

45. Michael Hardt and Antonio Negri, *Empire* (Cambridge, MA: Harvard University Press, 2000), pp. 132–3.
46. Gayatri Chakravorty Spivak, *The Post-Colonial Critic: Interviews, Strategies, and Dialogues* (New York: Routledge, 1990), p. 65.
47. Hardt and Negri, *Empire*, pp. 132–3.
48. Rosen, 'Nation, Inter-nation, and Narration', p. 52.
49. Gramsci, *SPN*, p. 178. See *Quaderni*, vol. 3, pp. 1560–1.
50. Deleuze, *Cinema 2*, p. 224.
51. Deleuze, *Cinema 2*, p. 224.

3

The Althusserian
Moment Revisited (Again)

Deborah Philips

The concept of ideology was a field of contestation throughout left cultural circles in the 1970s – debated in political groups, cultural studies events, journal issues and among film critics and practitioners, it was the buzzword of conferences and meetings, and the unavoidable issue of contemporary Marxist thinking.

The debate centred around a key essay by Louis Althusser; 'Ideology and Ideological State Apparatuses: Notes Towards an Investigation', first published in French in 1970 and translated into English in 1971.[1] Althusser was, in the mid 1960s, a leading Marxist philosopher, born in Algeria, and based at the École Normale Supérieure in Paris. In this essay Althusser investigates an ambiguity in Marx's own use of the term, and proposes that rather than understanding ideology as a form of 'false consciousness', ideology is *material* sets of social practices, that is, it assumes material forms in lived cultural practices. What made the essay so critical to Marxist thinking was its challenge to the classical Marxist reading of the term, manifest in the writings of Jean-Paul Sartre and of the Frankfurt School. Althusser's philosophical background brought Marxist theory together with the structuralist thinking that was so prevalent in Paris at the time to challenge any straightforward account of the term.

Interspersed with gnomic sub-headings Althusser's essay on ideology remains a dense philosophical study, but what made it crucial to those involved in questions of cultural representation was that it introduced a shift in the understanding of the term. Its major formulation was that ideology made the imaginary relations of capitalism 'real' – that is, that ideology was formulated, circulated and reproduced in material forms. The essay presents itself in the form of notes, and the argument is rooted in and constantly refers back to Marx's *Capital*. The argument is concerned with the question of how it is that the material conditions of production, the interlocking system of capital, production, consumption, wages and labour power, are reproduced, and the concept of ideology is made central to the workings of that system.

The essay's argument is a direct development of Marx's analysis of the structure of a capitalist economy outlined in *Capital*, in which Marx formulated the model of the capitalist system as made up of an economic base – the infrastructure, which (for Althusser, in the 'last instance') determines the superstructure – the institutions and culture of a society. Acknowledging that he is borrowing from Gramsci (in taking on Gramsci's distinction between rule by consensus and rule through coercion), Althusser defines two levels of the superstructure. The first, the 'Repressive State Apparatus' (RSA) comprises the state institutions of direct political and legal coercion (these include the institutions of government, the police force, the army, and the judicial and prison systems). There is another level which operates through apparent consent, which Althusser identifies as the 'Ideological State Apparatus' (ISA). This level produces an ideological consensus through the production of religious, ethical, legal, political and cultural ideologies by institutions which are voluntarily participated in, such as religion, cultural life (including the media) and education. Both these levels function together to sustain state power for the ruling class, and to maintain the status quo. While there is a single Repressive State Apparatus which operates in the public domain, there is a plurality of Ideological State Apparatuses, which operate in the private sphere (private in the sense of civil society), and therefore do not appear to be political. These promote forms of ideology which appear to be personal and disparate, but which function together to promote a ruling (or 'dominant' ideology) and to sustain (in Gramsci's term) a hegemony in which the ruling order appears as 'natural' and unified. Althusser formulates this principle under the heading: 'Ideology is a "Representation" of the Imaginary Relationship of Individuals to their Real Conditions of Existence':[2] the real conditions of existence are the relations of exploitation in a capitalist economy, and ideology serves to reproduce that economic base in the interests of the ruling class and the capitalist system.

The ideological mediations of the ISAs thus present a distortion of the 'real' (economic) relations of individuals to the world; these 'ideologies' are, however, (and this was among the most controversial aspects of Althusser's essay) understood as a new 'reality'; that is, they assume material form. The ideology of 'justice', for example, may be an abstract concept, but the legal demands of respect for property and loyalty to the ruling order assume material proportions in the actual bricks and mortar of prison cells and courtrooms. This argument represented a major shift in the use of the term; in the classical Marxist formulation, ideology had been taken to mean a system of illusory ideas which served to maintain the capitalist mode of production.

Ideology for Althusser is reproduced through the repetitions of ritual; the 'lived practices' of everyday life. Ideology (and this was one of the reasons many Marxist thinkers balked at the theory) was, according to Althusser, inescapable: everyone lives within and reproduces ideological positions, in attending schools and colleges, living within families, and consuming commodities, culture and the media. Althusser argues that the ideological level of the superstructure is determined in the 'final analysis' by the economic base, but claims that it has a 'relative autonomy'; that is, that ideology cannot be understood as a direct reflection of the economic base, but is constantly mediated and reproduced through the workings of the ISAs. So, in Althusser's argument, the educational system is in part structured by the needs of the infrastructure, to teach the skills required for the production of commodities. However, along with the requirements for employment and for social survival (such as literacy and numeracy), children are educated into the ethos and rules of 'good behaviour', and so are trained into the dominant ideology.

The centrality of culture, the media, and education to Althusser's analysis of ideology made his theory of immediate relevance to those involved in higher education, and particularly those concerned with popular culture and media analysis. Althusser had shifted the concept of ideology as a system of false ideas which mask the material and economic realities to one in which ideology actually constructs our experience and reception of the world, a theoretical development which was embraced by many left academics.

The anti-humanist aspect of his thinking, which was to prove most difficult for many Marxist thinkers, was focused around the concept of the 'subject' (a pun, in which the individual is understood as both subject to the processes of ideological formation, and the subject of their own life). This was a concept (derived from the psychoanalytic theories of Lacan) which was to prove problematic for those classical Marxists who believed in the potential of free will. This concern with the structures of subjectivity was later developed by a number of Marxist thinkers concerned with Freudian psychoanalytic theory, many of them feminist thinkers. The notion of the 'subject' became central to feminist theory and to feminist work in film and cultural studies.

The defining function of ideology for Althusser was the way in which ideology categorises people as individual 'subjects' and so disguises the class basis of a capitalist society, and distorts our sense of our place in the world. The notion of ourselves as free agents with individual consciousnesses and choice is, for Althusser, in itself an ideological construction, which prevents us from recognising the economic and class determinants of our decisions and potential. Althusser terms the process by which we recognise ourselves as subjects as 'interpellation'; the act of recognition in the response to an advertising hoarding with the slogan 'Hey – you there!' (or in Althusser's example, a policeman calling out in the street) constitutes a process of ideological interpellation. It is through this interpellation that people are inserted into and engage in ideological practices, without recognition of their ideological nature. The acceptance of social practices as 'natural', 'inevitable' and unchangeable is to be trapped within ideology; the only means of penetrating and challenging these ideological constructions is to have a theoretical understanding (Althusser uses the term 'scientific', by which he means a rigorously Marxist analysis) of the 'real', that is, of the economic and class relations, of the structures of culture and society.

It is through ideology that the rules of the established (capitalist) order are submitted to, sustained and reproduced. The field of ideology thus becomes a crucial site of class struggle; Althusser's concept of 'theoretical practice' proposed that the struggle in the arena of ideas is as central to the fight against capitalism as are the more obviously campaigning issues such as the fight for rights, wages and equality in the workplace. The argument that Marxist intellectuals were in the vanguard of political struggle was to prove attractive to many left academics working in universities in the politically heady days following May 1968 in Paris, and the contemporaneous anti-war, student and political actions across America and Europe.

Althusserian thinking was for a moment embraced by a generation of Marxist intellectuals in Britain, among whom were the first graduates to have studied cultural and media studies at degree level. This was a generation that was too young to have experienced directly the political action of May 68, but who were informed by the debates and intellectual thinkers who emerged from Paris; among them Barthes, Althusser, Kristeva and Lacan. The impact of May 68 also involved a focus around French intellectual life, in which gender relations, the hierarchical nature of education, and media representations of resistance were all the subject of fervent debate, both inside and outside the academy. Althusser's arguments, along with his emphasis on education and culture, had clear attractions to contemporary Marxist academics, justifying as it did their significance and political place in the academy, and validating as political activism the enterprise of refining and developing theoretical models.

Althusser's assertion that the individual was itself an ideological construction, and the implication that human agency could not be free from ideological constraints, prompted widespread dissension in political circles, and furious responses from some key Marxist thinkers. Althusser's position that ideology had its own autonomy, and the implication that there was nothing *but* representation (and the abstruseness of his language) had many materialist thinkers reeling. Most notable of these was E.P. Thompson. Thompson's title essay in *The Poverty of Theory*,[3] threw down a gauntlet to those who advocated theoretical practice as politics; the 'theory' of the title was clearly directed at Althusserian defenders. Althusserianism, Thompson fulminated, had:

> lodged itself firmly in a particular social *couche*, the bourgeois *lumpen intelligentsia*: aspirant intellectuals, whose amateurish intellectual preparation disarms them before manifest absurdities and *practice* leaves them paralysed in the first web of scholastic argument which they encounter, and *bourgeois*, because while many of them would *like* to be revolutionaries, they are themselves the products of a particular 'conjuncture' which has broken the circuits between intellectuality and practical experience.[4]

This intemperate outburst is an onslaught less on the theory itself than on the generation of those who espoused it. He does not name names, but the intellectuals of this historical 'conjuncture', the 'lumpen intelligentsia' that he attacks here would at the time have included members of the Communist Party, Trotskyist groups, elements of the Birmingham Centre for Cultural Studies, of History Workshop and the board of *Screen* and *Screen Education*. Among those he is attacking are Rosalind Coward and John Ellis, whose championing of Althusser, Lacan and French semiological theory in their book *Language and Materialism*[5] had become key reading for any Marxist with philosophical and intellectual pretensions.

'The Poverty of Theory: or an Orrery of Errors' was in its title and argument deliberately provocative and combative. Thompson prefaces his series of essays with an admonitory quote from Marx: 'To leave error unrefuted is to encourage intellectual immorality'; with the clear implication that Althusserian thinking was among those errors, and that Thompson saw it as his responsibility to refute him. From a Marxist historian, with a firm belief in the power of reason, Thompson's acerbic riposte was fuelled by what he saw as an attack on the value of history, and on rationality. He characterises Althusserian thinking as 'claiming to be more Marxist than Marx. From the quarter of Louis Althusser and his numerous followers there has been launched an unmeasured assault upon "historicism"'.[6] In the foreword to the collection Thompson expresses a painful sense of distance between his generation of Marxist thinkers and the next generation of left intellectuals – and articulates the bafflement and threat felt by many of the previous generation:

> much of this Left did not want our arguments and was developing ideas, attitudes and practices inimical to the rational, libertarian and egalitarian principles to which we were committed. If one offered to argue, one was answered, not with argument but with labels ('moralism', 'empiricism', 'liberal illusions'), or, commonly, with a biological dismissal (the 'generation game') which foreclosed further argument.[7]

Thompson did indeed 'attend to' Althusser, as he put it, in the course of this essay; 'And then I have *argued back.*'[8] But his elegant and impassioned argument finally takes recourse to an abstracted concept of 'reason'; Thompson was not prepared for or willing to accept a new emphasis on theories of subjectivity. The growing impact of feminist theory and of psychoanalytic thinking on Marxist thought had shifted the territory from an old left reliance on empirical reasoning.

Language and Materialism was one of the first published books in the debate, and an important intervention because it attempted to take the theoretical developments around language and psychoanalysis out of the academy and into the realm of European politics. In the introduction, Coward and Ellis sternly impress on their readers the significance of ideology for Marxist thought, and make great claims for theoretical correctness:

> The articulation of language and ideology is the single most important area for materialism to develop. Its failure to do so has become increasingly a political lack as well as a theoretical absence in the years following 1968: such

an absence has been exposed in the political and intellectual developments in Europe over the last decade.[9]

Coward and Ellis are here clearly employing 'ideology' as a concept informed by readings of both Althusser and Lacan, a position they set out early in their text. Their rallying cry is: 'an attempt to fight against the crude economism of early Marxism, which is still inhibiting political development, and its concomitant mechanistic versions such as dogmatism, idealist humanism, etc.'.[10] The language employed here: 'crude economism' (this is relatively polite, the phrase 'vulgar Marxism' was an equivalent much in use at the time), 'dogmatism', 'idealism' and 'humanism', became (as Thompson had identified) terms of abuse at political meetings and academic seminars directed at those who were seen not to have embraced the Althusserian project. 'Stalinist' was an accusation hurled at both sides (although this was often employed by those who had not actually read Coward and Ellis, Thompson or even Althusser).

The uncompromising tone of the injunctions from Coward and Ellis is indicative of the certainties and political assurance that in some cases typified those who were involved in these debates. There is in hindsight a stubborn belief in Coward and Ellis's argument, that if only the theory was right, then the correct politics would inevitably follow. In practice, the abstracted nature of the theory and its lack of relation to the contemporary political base allowed for a series of increasingly arcane wrangles. The work of Barry Hindess and Paul Hirst made their names synonymous with abstruse academicism.[11] These arguments, internal and intricate though they might have been, were nonetheless seen at the time as crucial to the advance of the fight against capitalist ideology. While the justification for this academic theory was a point taken from Althusser, that theory and practice were both necessary for political struggle, theoretical struggle could all too easily become an end in itself.

This was a debate that was in fact often available only to those in the academy, and among those, only to those with very good French. Coward and Ellis pursued their discussion of the importance of the subject in an analysis of Barthes' writings on Balzac in S/Z.[12] Stephen Heath, translator of Barthes[13] and a key figure among those who took these theoretical debates into film and cultural analysis (much cited by Coward and Ellis as a model of theoretical rigour), initially wrote about the French nouveau roman.[14] While these ideas were filtering into and gathering pace in cultural, film and media studies, the arguments were originally honed in the more traditional discipline of literary criticism.

Not much of the original French material was available in English at the time of these debates, and the theoretical high ground always lay with those who had read the latest incursions in the original. Coward and Ellis's reading of Althusser, that in ideology 'the subject' was a construction, was to become the most contentious part of the debate – but this point was crucial in its bringing together of the key theoretical strands then developing in the analysis of media and cultural representations. Althusser's notion of 'interpellation' had drawn on a Lacanian theory of the 'subject' and took the political and philosophical arguments into the realms of Freudian psychoanalytic theory. As Coward explained:

> [as] a result of the coming together of linguistics and Freudian psychoanalysis ... this moment has provided for perhaps the first time a theory of representation which avoids idealist assumptions and which has been able to specify signification as a practice with its own level of determinacy and definite effects.[15]

This 'moment' was a coming together not only of linguistics and psychoanalysis, but also of a preoccupation with subjectivity in feminist and queer theory. It is in the context of this brew of divergent Marxist positions on Althusser and history, and in gender and sexual politics, that 'theories of representation' became politically significant. It was historically inevitable that the emerging fields of cultural, film and media studies should be the sites in which these battles were waged most fiercely. Both film theorists and practitioners were embroiled in argument (that dated from the debate between Brecht and Lukács) as to the relative merits of realist forms and the avant-garde in filmmaking, a debate that clearly involved a collusion between theory and practice. As Hall put it at the time: 'The area of film and Media Studies has become a privileged one for the construction of new theoretical approaches.'[16]

Charlotte Brunsdon has described the experience of arriving to study at the University of Birmingham Centre for Cultural Studies in 1975, to find: 'The engagement of the Centre as a whole with Marxism was in a fiercely Althusserian moment, with passionate argument about the determinants – or otherwise – of the "last instance" and a correlative commitment to the study of theories of the State.'[17]

Stuart Hall, then the Director of the Centre for Cultural Studies in Birmingham (originally started by Richard Hoggart), the founding department of cultural studies in Britain, has given his own account of what the Birmingham Centre was about, in a manifesto for the work at the Centre. He situates the notion of ideology at the heart of the project, citing:

> a framework which drew on what can broadly be defined as the 'ideological' role of the media. This latter approach defined the media as a major cultural and ideological force ... This 'return' to a concern with the media and ideologies is the most significant and consistent thread in the Centre's media work.[18]

Nonetheless, the published volume of the Birmingham Centre's working papers includes an essay from Hall[19] that sounded a warning note and distanced the Birmingham Centre from some of the more abstruse and abstract tendencies of contemporary Marxist thinking. Hall refers to this tendency as 'screen theory', in reference to the then current debates in the journals *Screen* and *Screen Education*. The term 'screen theory' was apt, as it was in the field of film studies and in the pages of *Screen* that the debates were most publicly articulated and at their most furious. As Charlotte Brunsdon has explained: 'Film studies, while institutionally marginal, was one of the most overtly politicised and theoretically engaged disciplines in Britain in the 1970s, symbolised through the reach and reputation of the journal *Screen*.'[20]

Writing in *Screen* herself, Coward also acknowledged the importance of *Screen*, and the centrality of the journal to current arguments in film, media and cultural studies:

> The first appearance of this journal in 1970 coincides with the shift in the work of the Centre for Contemporary Cultural Studies towards a closer involvement with Marxist theory. The journal is widely used in media studies and has played a central role in the dissemination of Marxist 'cultural' political theory in this country.[21]

One of the most important of the debates featured in consecutive issues of *Screen* was that between Rosalind Coward and representatives from the Birmingham Centre (of which she had once been a part). Geoffrey Nowell-Smith's editorial for a 1977 issue introduces the 'epistemological critique of realism' and rather optimistically suggests:

'We hope that the clarification of differences in epistemological position will lead to a productive interchange of ideas in this important area.'[22] The articles that followed were less a productive interchange than a declaration of ideological warfare.

Coward's long (and very dense) essay 'Class, "Culture" and the Social Formation' was a major salvo from the Althusserian and Lacanian lobby against 'liberal humanism' and 'idealism' in film and cultural studies, and an attack on those Marxist thinkers who had failed to embrace contemporary French theory. Coward attempts in this essay to give a rundown on Saussurian semiology, Lacanian analysis and Althusserian and Marxist theory. As such, it is thick with references, many to untranslated French texts, and is hardly an accessible introduction to the debates. The argument is couched in terms of the need for a politics that took account of the dissenting voices that had emerged after 1968 and that was properly inclusive of feminist and sexual politics (Coward was hardly alone in this). It is, however, also a coruscating attack on certain forms of Marxist thinking; she admonishes the current work emerging from the Birmingham Centre for not sufficiently engaging with new theoretical developments:

> I wish to argue that the sort of theories of representation which *Screen* has drawn on also have consequences at the level of class analysis and indeed at the level of conceptualisation of the social formation which make untenable the sort of analysis in the WPCS[23] texts where the ideological and political are finally reduced to being an expression of a class interest or position.[24]

Throughout the essay, the Birmingham Centre's working group on subcultures (which numbered Dick Hebdige among its members) and the working group on Current Affairs and Television (which included Charlotte Brunsdon and David Morley) are aligned together with Lukàcs, Richard Hoggart and Hegel as inveterate humanists and idealists. The *Screen* editorial position is chastised, although Coward does grudgingly acknowledge the *Screen* work on representation 'as illuminating'. The Glasgow Media Group fares slightly better, although it too is tainted through association with the Birmingham Centre as 'evidently influenced by some of the assumptions of cultural studies'. Even the use of Althusser is not enough: she berates the writers of 'Sub-cultures, Cultures and Class',[25] for its employment of Althusser in 'its most functionalist form'.[26]

Coward centred her argument around the published work of the Birmingham Centre in their Working Papers in Cultural Studies (later published as a series of books by Hutchinson). Coward accuses the Birmingham project of working with a notion of the 'subject' that is effectively 'no different from the classical humanist subject',[27] the humanist subject that Althusser set out to critique. This very prescriptive assessment of her colleagues' work at the Birmingham Centre leads to the accusation that in the Birmingham project: 'the idealist notion of "culture" is much in evidence. It is seen as a specific area, and above all, an area whose operation is the production of meanings by individual consciousness.'[28]Against these failings, Ben Brewster (the translator of Althusser into English) and Paul Hirst are invoked as the models of properly rigorous analysis, as is her partner, and co-writer of *Language and Materialism* (published in the same year), John Ellis. Feminist theorists cited with approval in the article are Parveen Adams and Elizabeth Cowie (a member of the editorial board of *Screen* at the time), both of whom were involved with the theoretical feminist journal *M/f*.

It is not clear from the article quite what Coward is arguing for politically – apart from a more sophisticated theoretical approach which took more account of psychoanalytic thinking, and particularly of Lacan. However, there is also an implicit critique here of an understanding of materialism as dialectical progression. Coward here refutes a concept of Marxism as 'a logical, linear and hierarchical dialectical process in which the proletarian class is seen as the necessary bearer of progress'.[29] This challenge to the grand narrative of progress, explicit in Marx, was later to become the mark of postmodern arguments with Marxism.[30]

Representatives of the Birmingham Centre riposted to Coward's attack in the winter 1977/78 issue of *Screen*. Nowell-Smith's editorial[31]devoted this issue to the 'revival of interest in history' and approvingly cited the films of Ken Loach and Tony Garnett. These were both statements likely to inflame the Althusserian critics; Loach and Garnett were both filmmakers who insisted on working within the realist form, and who firmly resisted the critiques of a more avant-garde position. Nowell-Smith nonetheless acknowledges the urgency and fierceness of the debate, and recognises that there is 'a crisis of confidence in the term "history" itself'. He adds hopefully:

While accepting that at the moment there is something of an uneasy fit between classical Marxism and contemporary theories of discourse and the subject, we do not see this as unproductive, far from it. The danger comes when Procrustean attempts are made, on whichever side, to compress one set of problems into the other.[32]

Having thus attempted to square the circle of conflicting positions, Nowell-Smith left the stage, and announced his retirement from the editorship of *Screen*.

The Birmingham Centre's reply to Coward was flagged under the title 'Debate', and Coward was given space to reply in the same issue. Six members of the Birmingham Centre, including Stuart Hall (then Director of the Centre, and, with Tony Jefferson, one of the editors of the collection that had invoked Coward's particular disdain), penned a collective response to Coward's article. The authors point out that the published work from the Centre referred to in Coward's piece explicitly works with Althusser's work on ideological state apparatuses. They accuse her of constructing a 'single, monolithic Centre line, which provides her with an all too easy target'.[33] There was some justification for this: the working papers, journals, and the series of books published both by groups of individuals and under the Centre's collective authorship had all emerged out of a hotbed of discussion and debate, and never posited a united line.

Their response does not pull its punches, and attacks Coward (again, with some justification) for her uncomradely political tone: 'the sectarian manner in which this attack is conducted ... undermines the possibility of constructive debate'.[34] The authors are not themselves innocent of sectarian language; they go on to accuse Coward herself of 'an unmediated and abstract theoretical purism', and pointedly ask: 'whether or not she does envisage herself as working within a Marxist problematic; and, if so, what the status is of a "reworking of Marxist theory" which lacks any pertinent, substantive reference to class practices and class struggle'.[35]

The Birmingham group do acknowledge the Althusserian theory of ideology as a useful tool in their explicitly Marxist project, but it is the Lacanian aspects of Coward's argument that they find hard to take on board, understanding Lacanian theory to be ahistorical and universalising. The Birmingham Centre's estimation of Althusser's intervention was that, while the theory of the subject may have 'some importance' in the understanding of the workings of ideology, Lacan himself had never claimed to be working within a Marxist framework. They maintained that Lacan could not be understood as a materialist, and so conclude that Althusser's attempts to integrate a notion of the Lacanian subject with a Marxist theory of ideology were not 'entirely successful'. The Centre group's argument is that Coward's advocacy of Lacanian theory does not take the Marxist project any further: 'The theory of signification she offers, far from taking us into the specificity of specific discourses, advances a very general, universalising, historically – or mode-unspecific – theory of the operation of Language, based on a particular reading of Lacan'.[36]

The Birmingham Centre's response ends with a theoretical flourish, aimed not only at Coward, but at Hindess and Hirst, Stephen Heath, Ben Brewster and all those who they perceived to be taking flight into a theory of language:

> We cannot simply borrow and ditch and conflate at will, nominating the resulting porridge 'Marxist' as we go ... A theory of the positioning of 'the subject' in-general, in ideology in-general, through Language in-general, with no further reference to mode of production or social formation or conjuncture can be declared to be 'Marxist' only if theory production consists wholly of successive acts of faith.[37]

Coward responded in the same issue of *Screen*, and, predictably, accused the Birmingham group of failing 'to engage fully with the central argument of that article'.[38] She also suggested that the work of the Centre was dismissive of feminist theory. This was not strictly fair, many of those working at the Centre at the time were (or were about to become) significant feminist theorists in cultural and media studies, and the Centre's work was very much informed by feminist ideas.

There was at this point a tendentious relationship between feminism and psychoanalytic and Marxist theory; Althusserian and Lacanian theory were by no means welcomed by all feminist political groups. Feminism had, in the early stages of the women's movement, been hostile to Freud, following Kate Millett's characterisation of his patriarchy in *Sexual Politics*.[39] By the early 1970s, however, the experience of women's consciousness-raising groups, and the exploration of the slogan 'the personal is political' had engendered an interest in theories of subjectivity and in psychoanalytic theories of gender difference, which led many to Freudian theory, and on to Lacan. The appearance of Juliet Mitchell's *Psychoanalysis and Feminism*[40] in 1974 was important in arguing that feminist theory dismissed Freud at its own peril. While this was a position taken up by many feminist academics and activists, it was by no means characteristic of the women's movement as a whole.

What marks the difference between the Birmingham Centre and Coward is less their position on feminist theory than in their different modes of writing. Hall's account of media studies uses a collective 'we' to describe the enterprise at Birmingham. There is a collective spirit in the work of the Birmingham group; not only in this collectively authored response, but also in the clear commitment to collaborative work that informs their argument.

The vitriol and intellectual energy produced by the debate around Althusser is apparent from the number of responses these articles generated, evident in the letters in the 'Correspondence' section of *Screen*, but also in the number of advertisements for discussion groups and meetings at film centres and academic conferences around the country. Almost all of these feature the term 'ideology' among the topics of debate. There was an expectation from *Screen* that readers should become engaged with the arguments; the 1977 issues advertised 'readers' meetings' at the *Screen* offices in London. The extent and range of the discussion is also suggested by the subject areas and range of political and intellectual groups confronting the debate: the ninth Summer Communist University of that year stated its objective to 'open up new areas of debate and discussion' and included a specialist course on 'Culture and Ideology', and another on semiotics. The 1978 British Sociological Association conference on 'Culture' included a session on culture and ideology (at which Hindess and Hirst spoke).

Journals and books explicitly concerned with the Althusserian debate followed. *Ideology and Consciousness* ('a Marxist journal in psychology-psychoanalysis-linguistics-semiotics') announced its first issue in the same issue of *Screen* as Coward's article. The next collection of Working Papers in Cultural Studies from the Birmingham Centre was titled 'On Ideology' and published under the collective authorship of the Centre.[41] A new Open University course in popular culture included two obligatory lectures – one on Gramsci and the concept of hegemony, and one on Althusser and ideology. As the discussion moved into arenas beyond the confines of academic cultural and film studies, the language of the debates entered more widely into the discourses of political and critical theory.

Translations of much of the material that Coward and others had discussed became available in the latter half of the 1970s; more of Barthes' work, of Lacan, and Pierre Macherey, a collaborator with

Althusser. Also translated were the works of feminist theorists styled as the 'New French Feminists', among them Cixous, Irigaray and Kristeva. By the early 1980s, these names and theoretical developments had become part of the undergraduate experience of critical theory, and extended beyond the disciplines of film, cultural, media and women's studies. Terry Eagleton's *Literary Theory*[42] and Toril Moi's *Sexual-Textual Politics*,[43] gave sophisticated but popularised accounts of the Marxist and feminist theories, which finally made them relatively accessible (both texts are still in print and in use in academic departments).

The high Althusserian moment had, however, by this time passed its peak. The precision and rigour of the earlier debates had relied on a commitment to a philosophical reading of Marx. Althusser's predecessor, Antonio Gramsci, appeared to offer an analysis of culture that addressed and came out of direct political engagement. The Birmingham Centre characterised this shift from Althusserian ideology to Gramscian hegemony. Charlotte Brunsdon explains that by the time she arrived as a postgraduate student in the late 1970s at the Birmingham Centre: 'Antonio Gramsci ... was rapidly replacing Althusser as top CCCS theory man – with his stress on the significance of common sense in the securing of hegemony.'[44] Dick Hebdige, another Birmingham Centre postgraduate, also identified and endorsed the shift from Althusser to Gramsci in cultural studies thinking:

> the concept of hegemony remains distinct ... from the ascription of class domination which is implied in the Althusserian model of a contradictory social formation held in check eternally (at least until 'the last (ruptural) instance') by the work of the RSAs and the ISAs.[45]

The tragedy of Althusser's final years left many of both his critics and his champions silenced. His mental decline (he had suffered from a bipolar disorder for much of his life), the murder of his wife and his subsequent incarceration allowed many Marxists to dismiss him entirely, and those who had espoused his theories to veer away from direct association with the man himself. While ideology continued to be a much used term, Althusser's name was not. Althusser himself became a constitutive absence in Marxist and cultural theory until his death in 1990.

In retrospect, it is hard to understand how these bitter and recondite debates could have been taken at the time as serious political practice, but they were. It took the shock of Thatcherism in Britain, and the rise of the right across Europe and America to recognise that theoretical practice could not in and of itself change the political agenda. Nonetheless, Althusser's essay and the debates that followed have left an indelible mark. Without him, cultural and media studies and film theory would not be using the language that has now become familiar, and semiology and deconstruction would not be as integral to the analysis of media and cultural representations as they have become. Many of the most prominent contemporary feminist and radical thinkers in the fields of cultural, film and media studies were intellectually formed by an awareness of these debates, whatever their position might have been at the time.

E.P. Thompson finally lost the battle against the 'freak of intellectual fashion',[46] as he described Althusserianism. 'Economism' and 'empiricism' remain derogatory terms within cultural and media studies circles, if few can remember quite why. Foucault, Derrida and Baudrillard are now more likely to be invoked as theorists than Althusser, but all forged their work in the context of his interventions into Marxist theory. If Marxist intellectuals are now more inclined to talk about hegemony and discourse theory than to discuss ideology, in the context of European and American media and cultural studies these are terms that are inescapably inflected through the Althusserian concept of ideology (although this is rarely admitted), and through the history of the subsequent debates.

NOTES

1. Louis Althusser, 'Ideology and Ideological State Apparatuses: Notes Towards an Investigation', in Lenin and Philosophy, and Other Essays, trans. Ben Brewster (London: New Left Books, 1971), pp. 127–86.
2. Althusser, 'Ideology and Ideological State Apparatuses', p. 162.
3. E.P. Thompson, The Poverty of Theory & Other Essays (London: Merlin Press, 1978).
4. E.P. Thompson, 'The Poverty of Theory: or an Orrery of Errors', in The Poverty of Theory & Other Essays, p. 195.
5. Rosalind Coward and John Ellis, Language and Materialism: Developments in Semiology and the Theory of the Subject (London: Routledge and Kegan Paul, 1977).
6. Thompson, 'The Poverty of Theory', p. 194. Historicism is the study of texts as sets of discourses located in their historical contexts.
7. E.P. Thompson, Foreword to The Poverty of Theory, p. ii.
8. Thompson, Foreword to The Poverty of Theory, p. iv.
9. Coward and Ellis, Language and Materialism, p. 9.
10. Coward and Ellis, Language and Materialism, p. 9.

11. Hindess and Hirst wrote a book which revised their earlier work in the light of their reading of Althusser: Barry Hindess and Paul Hirst, *Mode of Production and Social Formation: An Auto-Critique of Pre-Capitalist Modes of Production* (London: Macmillan, 1977).

12. Roland Barthes, *S/Z* (Paris: Editions du Seuil, 1976).

13. Roland Barthes, *Image/Music/Text*, trans. Stephen Heath (London: Fontana, 1977).

14. Stephen Heath, *The Nouveau Roman: A Study in the Practice of Writing* (London: Elek, 1977).

15. Rosalind Coward, 'Class, "Culture" and the Social Formation', *Screen*, vol. 18, no. 1. (Spring 1977), p. 77.

16. Stuart Hall, 'Introduction to Media Studies at the Centre', in Stuart Hall, Dorothy Hobson, Andrew Lowe and Paul Willis (eds), *Culture, Media, Language* (London: Hutchinson, 1980), p. 12.

17. Charlotte Brunsdon, *The Feminist, the Housewife and the Soap Opera* (Oxford: Clarendon Press, 2000), p. 8.

18. Stuart Hall, 'Introduction to Media Studies at the Centre', p. 117.

19. Stuart Hall, 'Recent Developments in Theories of Language and Ideology: A Critical Note', in *Culture, Media, Language*, pp. 157–63

20. Brunsdon, *The Feminist, the Housewife and the Soap Opera*, p. 20, fn. 1.

21. Coward, 'Class, "Culture" and the Social Formation', p. 76.

22. Geoffrey Nowell-Smith, 'Editorial', *Screen*, vol. 18, no. 1 (Spring 1977), p. 6.

23. Working Papers in Cultural Studies from the Birmingham Centre.

24. Coward, 'Class, "Culture" and the Social Formation', p. 76.

25. Later published in book form as *Resistance through Rituals*, ed. Stuart Hall and Tony Jefferson (London: Hutchinson, 1976).

26. Coward, 'Class, "Culture" and the Social Formation', p. 83.

27. Coward, 'Class, "Culture" and the Social Formation', p. 87.

28. Coward, 'Class, "Culture" and the Social Formation', p. 85.

29. Coward, 'Class, "Culture" and the Social Formation', p. 89.

30. Jean-François Lyotard, *The Postmodern Condition: A Report on Knowledge*, trans. Geoff Bennington and Brian Massumi (Manchester: Manchester University Press, 1984).

31. Geoffrey Nowell-Smith, 'Editorial', *Screen*, vol. 18, no. 4 (Winter 1977/78), pp. 5–7.

32. Nowell-Smith, 'Editorial', p. 5.

33. Iain Chambers, John Clarke, Ian Connell, Lidia Curti, Stuart Hall and Tony Jefferson, 'Debate', *Screen*, vol. 18, no. 4 (Winter 1977/78), p. 109.

34. Chambers, Clarke, Connell, Curti, Hall and Jefferson, 'Debate', p. 109.

35. Chambers, Clarke, Connell, Curti, Hall and Jefferson, 'Debate', p. 113.

36. Chambers, Clarke, Connell, Curti, Hall and Jefferson, 'Debate', pp. 114–15.

37. Chambers, Clarke, Connell, Curti, Hall and Jefferson, 'Debate', p. 119.

38. Rosalind Coward, 'Response', *Screen*, vol. 18, no. 4 (Winter 1977/78), p. 120.

39. Kate Millett, *Sexual Politics* (London: Hart-Davis, 1971).

40. Juliet Mitchell, *Psychoanalysis and Feminism* (London: Allen Lane, 1974).

41. University of Birmingham, Centre for Contemporary Cultural Studies, *On Ideology* (London: Hutchinson for Birmingham Centre for Cultural Studies, 1978).

42. Terry Eagleton, *Literary Theory* (Oxford: Blackwell, 1983).

43. Toril Moi, *Sexual-Textual Politics: Feminist Literary Theory* (London: Methuen, 1985).

44. Brunsdon, *The Feminist, the Housewife and the Soap Opera*, p. 8.

45. Dick Hebdige, 'Staking Out the Posts', in *Hiding in the Light: On Images and Things* (London: Routledge, 1988), p. 206.

46. Thompson, 'The Poverty of Theory', p. 195.

4

Jameson, Postmodernism and the Hermeneutics of Paranoia

Mike Wayne

In 1984, the Marxist cultural theorist Fredric Jameson published his long essay, 'Postmodernism, Or The Cultural Logic of Late Capitalism', in *New Left Review*, marking an early and hugely influential intervention into debates around postmodernism.[1] Primarily known as a literary theorist in the 1970s, Jameson was the first critic to tackle postmodernism across the spectrum of the arts. Given the prominence of the image in postmodernism, the visual arts (including film) were accorded a particular significance in his essay.[2] It was an apposite year in which to sally forth with an agenda-setting framework which proposed that we in effect live in a world frighteningly controlled by vast forces which radically decompose individual agency and autonomy, neutralise and absorb all criticism, stultify our capacity to represent history, and manipulate knowledge and information to the extent that the boundaries between what is real and what is not, what is true and what is false, effectively disappear.[3] But the shades here of George Orwell's classic vision of totalitarian control in *1984* have undergone an important shift in Jameson's dystopian analysis, away from the state and bureaucracy generally (the central locus of power in Orwell's text as well of course in the theoretical work of Max Weber and Michel Foucault) to multinational corporate capital generally and media capital specifically; a shift from 'hard' (coercive) to 'soft' (cultural) forms of control, as Jameson himself has noted.[4] Among the first things we see and hear in *The Matrix* (Andy and Larry Wachowski 1999 US) are a blinking cursor on the computer screen and the tracing of a telephone conversation as we watch the numbers locating the call locking into place. These are the new, literally soft(ware) forms of control. Yet the central role of film itself within the synergistic strategies of media capitalism tends to get displaced on to the cultural, political and economic power of television or other communication systems, as in *Enemy of the State* (Tony Scott 1998 US), *The Net* (Irwin Winkler 1995 US),

Ed TV (Ron Howard 1999 US), *The Truman Show* (Peter Weir 1998 US), *Pleasantville* (Gary Ross 1998 US) and *Series 7: The Contenders* (Dan Minahan 2001 US). This is not a hangover of cinema's early attempts to disparage its new competitor back in the 1950s and 1960s. Despite the importance of film within the culture industries, it is the sheer real-time coextensiveness with the everyday that gives television and other communication technologies an emblematic power that the film medium does not have when it comes to representing conspiracies. In such films we observe the formation of paranoid media totalities, where media representations and information technologies facilitate massive social control. Paranoia is, on the one hand, a response to the postmodern scenario in which capital, technology and cultural representation converge but, on the other hand, a profoundly anti-postmodern sensibility insofar as it insists that *everything is connected*. In joining the dots together and reading apparently discrete signs as fragments of a larger set of invisible forces determining our lives, paranoia has some affinities with the Marxist concept of the social totality. By contrast, the philosophy of postmodernism (articulated by thinkers such as Jean Baudrillard, Jacques Derrida, Jean-François Lyotard, Michel Foucault and Richard Rorty) eschews such 'big thinking' or grand narratives. The tension within Jameson's distinct version of the postmodern is that he tries to combine the postmodern emphasis on the fragmentary, heterogeneous and relativistic nature of today's world with a Marxist insistence that all these different impulses ultimately have to be related to such totalising concepts as the capitalist mode of production, if they are to be understood. In practice, as we shall see, capitalism also has a similar ambivalence, frustrating our capacities to situate ourselves in time and space within the larger socioeconomic relations around us, while also developing the possibilities of doing exactly that. The impetus towards a ferocious connection in paranoia is one reason why this cultural phenomenon should be of interest to a Marxist cultural analysis of popular culture. Yet as we shall see, ultimately, paranoia is a symptomatic, not a Marxist, response to the crisis of capitalism.

AFTER MODERNISM?

The title of Jameson's 1984 essay summarises his central thesis: that postmodernism does not designate merely an aesthetic style or set of aesthetic characteristics; rather it describes the interface between culture and capital, the penetration of culture by the logic of profit accumulation to a degree and extent which is (arguably) historically unprecedented. Jameson's Marxist emphasis on the socioeconomic conditions of a style is particularly important today when debates about the postmodern do casually invoke it as merely a style (self-reflexive intertextual referencing for example). However, the question of how distinctive the integration of culture and capital is in the postmodern era (usually dated from the 1960s at the earliest) is contentious. An earlier critique of the culture industry by Theodor Adorno and Max Horkheimer also famously diagnosed it as a more or less seamless integration of culture into the logic of industrial capital.[5] Such critiques tend to require some aesthetic standard against which to measure the decline in the autonomy of culture. Jameson measures the integration of culture into late capitalism primarily against a prior *modernist* autonomy.

'Modernism' is the term ascribed to the avant-garde of the early twentieth century where experiments in film (e.g. Eisenstein, Vertov, Buñuel), painting (e.g. Picasso, Rivera, Kandinsky) and literature (e.g. Joyce, Elliott, Woolf, Dos Passos) broke with established (nineteenth-century) conventions of representation and constructions of time, space and causality. A modernist-inspired theoretical critique of such 'realist' representations in literature and film was mapped out famously by Colin McCabe, who argued that the strategy of narration of what he called the classic realist text progressively and ultimately offered the spectator a position of knowledge about the story world as incontestable truth and one which the narration assembles (invisibly) for the spectator.[6] Modernist practices, by contrast, offer the spectator a much more problematised multi-perspectival experience in which meaning-making is more relativised, not least because the process and act of it is foregrounded and therefore open to dispute, at least potentially. In the classic realist text one cannot, however, call into question very easily the narration's unfolding of the story world as 'objective' reality. Although postmodern at the level of content, *The Matrix* is strikingly classical in its narrative strategies. When Neo finds out that what he took to be the real world is in fact a simulated illusion, we trust the narration that *this* is the truth about Neo's world. There is no modernist problematising or foregrounding of this perspective, or, as in political modernism, explicit anchoring of the narration from a political perspective (itself a kind of relativisation).

In the early decades of the twentieth century modernist practitioners worked outside the core centres of the capitalist media, a marginality that afforded an authentic capacity to shock and scandalise a traditional and conservative bourgeoisie with attacks on accepted conventions of art and/or society. The era of the postmodern, by contrast, is characterised by the effacement of the boundary and distinction between high culture and the avant-garde on the one hand and mass culture on the other, while the term 'bourgeoisie' no longer conjures up a unified set of conservative cultural values waiting to be shocked.[7] The postmodern is characterised by similar experiments in time, space and perception that modernist culture developed, but now it is crossed with popular genres – e.g. *Pulp Fiction* (Quentin Tarantino 1994 US), *The Usual Suspects* (Bryan Singer 1995 US), *Sliding Doors* (Peter Howitt 1997 UK/US), *Memento* (Christopher Nolan 2000 US) – made in the centres of corporate media capital and distributed to global audiences. Perhaps in this sense the postmodern does represent some new phase in the commodification of culture now that no space or area of practice exists for long outside the reach of multinational capital. Given the colonising logic of capital, its expansionary drive was bound at some point to breach the very divisions of cultural production and consumption (between mass culture and the avant-garde) established in an earlier phase of its own development. Yet whether we have moved beyond modernism (or indeed the more comforting assurances provided by classical realism) in the definitive sense that the prefix 'post' implies, is open to question. Rather, classic realist, modernist and postmodernist strategies mingle together in new combinations and mutations.

CLASS-CONSCIOUSNESS AND SYMPTOMATIC READINGS

Jameson's decoding of culture is a relentlessly symptomatic one. This means he fastens above all on what is *repressed* in the text, its strategic silences and aversions to social content too problematic, too profoundly disturbing to the very basis on which life (as the text conceives it) is constituted. The text senses this problematic content just *beyond* the range of its language and forms and which it must then recoil from, inscribing that absence and omission within its very expression. This sort of 'decentring' of the text marked a hard-fought victory against liberal humanist conceptions which tend to evaluate cultural texts in terms of their harmonious integration of their forms and themes. Within Marxist theory the work of the philosopher Louis Althusser and the literary theorist Pierre Macheray was instrumental in developing symptomatic readings of texts, seeking out their silences and contradictions. For Jameson, all texts, aesthetic theories as much as aesthetic practices, are essentially narratives which form themselves around an unresolved and possibly irresolvable problem. The main problem, Jameson argues, is the problem of grasping the social totality, relating this or that part of social life to the very mode by which social life as a conflictual whole (the mode of production) is produced and reproduced and grounding concrete places in their relations to the vast abstract space of global capitalism. Modernism, which for Jameson, as we would expect, is about rather more than just a set of aesthetic characteristics, is characterised precisely by its *formal* responsiveness to this question of the social totality or mode of production in the age of settler colonialism and extensive political and economic control by the West of the rest (imperialism). This is how Jameson poses the dilemma which this extensive social totality (now much larger than national life) poses:

> For colonialism means that a significant structural segment of the economic system as a whole is now located elsewhere, beyond the metropolis, outside of the daily life and existential experience of the home country, in colonies over the water whose own life experience and life world – very different from that of the imperial power – remains unknown and unimaginable for the subjects of the imperial power, whatever social class they may belong to. Such spatial disjunction has as its immediate consequence the inability to grasp the way the system functions as a whole ... daily life and existential experience in the metropolis, which is necessarily the very content of the national literature itself, can no longer be grasped immanently; it no longer has its meaning, its deeper reason for being, within itself.[8]

Thus Jameson finds in E.M. Forster's *Howard's End* a proto-modernist impulse to register this space *beyond* representation in a passage describing the train journey of Mrs Munt. The literary text suggests an absolute disjunction between the concerns of Mrs Munt, which are focused only on rescuing 'poor Helen from this dreadful mess', and the signs of historical change and transformation that flash past the train window, one of which is the Great North Road, which at times runs along the track and which is 'more suggestive of infinity' than the older technology of the train. Jameson latches on to the signifier of 'infinity' as gesturing towards that larger imperial space that lies outside the scope of *Howard End*'s capacity to figure (despite its ironic undercutting of Mrs Munt's narrowly private concerns). The tension between a part or fragment of social experience which comes into view in an almost accidental or contingent manner (the

Great North Road) and some larger, ungraspable set of socioeconomic determinants which are very far from being accidental, is marked by Forster's weak philosophical abstraction (the signifier 'infinity').[9] As Jameson notes: 'It is Empire which stretches the roads out to infinity, beyond the bounds and borders of the national state.'[10] The significance of modernism proper is that while it is no more able to represent the unrepresentable social totality than any other aesthetic strategy, it is uniquely aware of its *incompleteness* and the vastness of the spatial scale at which it must operate if it is to at least register this ineffable, sublime space of international capitalism (hence its predilection for fragmentation and montage which can stretch across space and time). Elsewhere, and in relation to a more properly modernist practitioner, Jameson writes of 'the interpretative lust of Dali's "paranoiac-critical" method, where the very grain of gold sand, the individual beads of perspiration on the limp watches, promise an impending revelation'. [11]Again we find this characteristic feature of Jameson's hermeneutic approach where some signifying fragment quivers with a social significance and portentousness, an almost 'paranoid' sensitivity to some larger meaning or set of determinants just beyond reach and yet symptomatically present (as an 'impending revelation', always deferred).

JAMESON ON *DOG DAY AFTERNOON*

A number of these features of Jameson's approach to cultural critique can now be fruitfully reviewed in relation to film in his influential 1977 essay 'Class and Allegory in Contemporary Mass Culture: *Dog Day Afternoon* as a Political Film'. This essay also usefully identifies the proto-postmodernist social and cultural trends that Jameson was to theorise more substantially in the 1980s. There are, however, some crucial ambivalences (and we may say repressions) evident in his brilliant and complex reading that also continue on through into his later decodings of the postmodern. We can note to begin with that the proto-postmodernist trends which Jameson detects in Sidney Lumet's 1975 (US) film of a bank robbery that turns into a hostage scenario, are a continuation under new conditions of the same international trends in which he located modernism. Specifically Jameson will (in modernist fashion) once again fasten on to some 'narrative fragment' which then resonates with the repressed social content of a larger set of socioeconomic determinants. As Jameson notes in his 1992 book *The Geopolitical Aesthetic*, 'the message of the fragment, in late capitalism, always being the totality itself and the world system'.[12]

If under modernism 'a significant structural segment of the economic system as a whole is now located elsewhere, beyond the metropolis, outside of the daily life and existential experience of the home country', that global economic system has become so large, so powerful, so mobile, that it now turns on significant areas of the metropolis itself, firstly gutting and ghettoising 'the older urban neighbourhoods'[13] and then removing the last shreds of independent small businesses and replacing them with 'parking lots or chain stores'.[14] The fate of the petit bourgeoisie is a recurrent concern of Jameson's,[15] largely because he sees it as mirroring the demise of independent cultural production.[16] In *Dog Day Afternoon*, the significance of the narrative fragment of the airport (a zone where national place meets global space) at the film's night-time conclusion is that it represents the most advanced trends within a global 'post-national' capitalism, thoroughly remote and abstract, an

> eerie and impersonal science fiction landscape ... a corporate space without inhabitants, utterly technologized and functional, a place beyond city and country alike – collective, yet without people, automated and computerized, yet without any of that older utopian or dystopian clamour.[17]

This reading of the airport as a signifier of multinational capital's indifference to the human, the concrete and the local, also seems remarkably apposite to the conclusion of the Michael Mann film, *Heat* (1995 US). Here Al Pacino (the star of *Dog Day Afternoon*) confronts his antagonist played by fellow method actor Robert De Niro one last time, where their displaced homoerotic masculine understanding seems a hopelessly anachronistic and impossible gesture of human connection (as indeed do all relationships in the film) amongst the airport's steel containers, runways and impassive overhead planes arriving and departing from distant locations in a global economy. That the planes unknowingly affect the outcome of the contest between the protagonists by periodically bathing the terrain with light, merely underlines the impassive causal relations between a global system and the people occupying local places on the ground, as it were. The emptying out of human relationships of any substantive bonds is central to Jameson's analysis of *Dog Day Afternoon* which turns on the juxtaposition he sets up between Al Pacino's bank robber, Sonny, and the FBI agent, Sheldon (James Broderick). For

Jameson these characters represent two different kinds or models of the subject, that is, two conflicting models of what it means to be an individual within advanced capitalism. The FBI agent represents a new character type, functionally more congruent in many ways with capitalism at the leading edge of its developments and one which is dominant over the 'antiquated paradigm of the anti-hero and the method actor' represented by Al Pacino.[18]

Al Pacino was of course, and perhaps still is, the leading exponent of the method school of acting (which finds its newest generation in such stars as Ed Norton and Daniel Day-Lewis) and the authentic inheritor of the crown worn by Marlon Brando, who was the leading exponent of the method back in the 1950s when it first broke into Hollywood films as a legitimate style. In an anticipation of a later theme, Jameson sees the return to the 1950s as an example of a pervasive nostalgia within consumer culture, 'the deliberate substitution of the pastiche and imitation of past styles for the impossible invention of adequate contemporary or post-contemporary ones'.[19] The notion of a nostalgic return is certainly problematic here given that there had in fact been no *break* in the developing and expanding influence of the method style. Indeed the careers of Brando and Pacino overlapped in the 1970s. Whether we are dealing with the imitation of past styles or the continuation of established ones is in fact a crucial point. If the latter, as seems the case here, then we have to engage with the very *uneven development* of cultural formations, and that ought to caution us against the notion of clean breaks, nostalgic returns, and new dominant formations often associated with the term 'postmodernism'. Nevertheless, returning to Jameson's argument we find him recovering a political allegory in the *formal* contradiction between Al Pacino's method school of acting and the acting codes deployed by James Broderick as Sheldon. Pacino's style belongs to what Jameson sees as an 'outdated' paradigm (although even today still culturally influential) because of its individualism, its attempts to portray psychological depth and complexity as something welling up from *within* the individual themselves, and the investment it makes in the expression of emotion. By contrast, the collective forces of capitalism at work in the social environment bypass such an acting style, indicating its essential impotence and instead find their dominant and adequate expression in the relatively anonymous and resolutely unhistrionic performance by James Broderick, a television contract player. This is significant because of the role television was to subsequently play not only in representations of the postmodern but in postmodern theory, which often sees television as the postmodern medium par excellence. Sheldon's 'technocratic expertise' and professionalism represent the 'essential impersonality and post-individualistic structure' of late capitalism.[20] Thus the film makes self-reflexive use of the grammar of acting as it has been institutionally produced by film and television, to underline the struggle between the old, individualistic, apparently autonomous model of the human subject represented by Pacino/Sonny and the equally emotional hot and flustered local police chief Maretti (who is subsequently displaced by the FBI) and the new model (Sheldon) who is a component of a network, a system unable to accommodate anything as remotely unpredictable as human feeling, conscience, compassion, hate, guilt and so forth. In his 1984 essay, Jameson will use juxtaposition again to illustrate the shift from an older model of the individual (one which invests in psychological depth and uniqueness) to the new postmodern subject, evacuated of emotion, psychological depth and individuality. Here his examples are Edvard Munch's painting *The Scream*, 'a canonical expression of the great modernist thematics of alienation, anomie, solitude, social fragmentation, and isolation',[21] and the postmodern gestures of Andy Warhol, such as his prints of Marilyn Monroe, which emphasise the media reproduction of the human figure. Warhol's Monroes bear no sign of the troubled individual that was Monroe; it is pure image or rather the playful differentiation of multiple images in which the 'unique' individual or referent, Monroe, recedes from view.

But to return to film and Jameson's reading of *Dog Day Afternoon*, we have seen how Jameson extracts a nugget of class consciousness from a popular culture text, fastening on to narrative fragments such as the airport or the figure of Sheldon (who is narratively marginal until the last third) to hint at the outlines of multinational capitalism. This reading of the FBI is virtually reprised, albeit rather more self-consciously, in *The Matrix*, where in an early scene Agent Smith and his similarly suited FBI colleagues arrive on the trail of Trinity, and promptly take over from the local police. Smith's earpiece is the visual signifier of his role as a component of a larger system, which feeds him information and instructions. Of course, one difference between *Dog Day Afternoon* and *The Matrix* is that in the latter there is no rich, individuated, psychologically complex hero to be juxtaposed against the hollowed out subject/agent of the system, just the almost equally blank, 'empty' hero played by Keanu Reeves. The formal contradiction between the investment the film puts into the *individual* as narrative agent and, at a thematic level, Neo as new Messiah, and the utter vacuity of the very character supposed to represent the triumph of the individual against the system, is indicative of an important fault line within contemporary capitalist culture and its continuing uneven development.

CAPITALISM AND REIFICATION

At this point it is worth just drawing out a little what it is about the capitalist mode of production that makes consciousness of its class nature difficult to grasp while also, paradoxically, making it possible, even if within Jameson's work such class-consciousness is recovered only through rather clever symptomatic readings. I have above quoted Jameson arguing that modernism as a form marks both an increasing awareness that the national space is constituted within a larger international system and a recognition of the difficulties of concretely bringing that enlarged frame of reference into representation. The difficulties, though, do not arise simply because of the international scale at which capitalism operates, but because of the *specific* qualities which capitalism has as a mode of production. The crisis (and the possibilities) of representation derive from these qualities. The concept of the mode of production is composed of a master couplet: the social relations and forces of production. Accumulated and inherited knowledge, wealth and technology in conjunction with human labour power constitute the forces of production; their mobilisation according to definite relations between owners of the means of production (capital) and workers of those means (labour) constitutes the social relations of production. In its restless search to accumulate capital, this mode of production constantly revolutionises the means of production, expanding the power and reach of capital. As Marx notes:

> The need of a constantly expanding market for its products chases the bourgeoisie over the whole surface of the globe. It must nestle everywhere, settle everywhere, establish connexions everywhere.[22]

Here we come to the great contradiction of the capitalist mode of production. The development of 'more massive and more colossal productive forces'[23] requires an immense coordination, cooperation and forging of connections, of drawing peoples and places into ever more elaborate *interdependence*; in short, it requires the *socialisation of the mode of production*. Here lies the material basis of a class-consciousness that stretches as widely as the global market itself. And as we shall see later, Jameson argues that conspiracy theories are a *distorted* version of that socialised consciousness. And yet, of course, this socialisation of production, while absolutely indispensable for capitalism, is the very thing which it fears and recoils from, which threatens the very existence of class society and which must be repressed, contained within narrow parameters and channelled into activities that do not threaten capital (such as war, which is the only form of public expenditure supported enthusiastically by the tabloid press and which requires, despite its destructiveness, awesome collaboration). The socialisation of production thus comes into contradiction with the *de-socialisation* which dominates the capitalist mode of production: the hierarchical arrangements within the production process, the lack of popular control over the means of production generally, the lack of accountability over elites (political and economic), the competition (which cuts across and undermines cooperation) which the unquenchable thirst for profit requires, and the everyday exchanges in the market which take place as discrete *isolated* acts between buyers and sellers (denying that those exchanges impact on others). This de-socialisation penetrates deep into our culture and consciousness. Jameson argues that under late capitalism our capacity to think historically is jeopardised. What Jameson calls the nostalgia film, for example, is saturated with pop images and stereotypes of history rather than a more authentic engagement with history and temporality.[24] Cosmetic surgery, once the exclusive choice of film stars but now a part of popular culture, enacts a similar denial of history at the level of individual biology, seeking as it does, most notably in facelifts and Botox, to erase the evidence of age and life experiences that make us the people we are. It has been said that within Hollywood, top-name directors are finding it difficult to cast actresses (men are allowed more leeway to grow old) who can display facial expressiveness due to extensive surgery. It may be an apocryphal story, but it does nicely illustrate at the level of the body itself the waning of affect or emotional expressiveness which Jameson also associates with the death of the monadic subject and their integration (including their very skin) into commodity capitalism.

Just as our ability to appreciate and value the temporal process declines, so our capacity to be attuned to the spatial connections between different aspects of the social process at any one time also petrifies. It is only with considerable intellectual effort that one can re-establish the connections or 'secret affinities between those apparently autonomous and unrelated domains'[25] that make up the social whole. Such an intellectual effort must confront the liberal-empirical mode of thought which

> in its various forms and guises, consists in separating reality into airtight compartments, carefully distinguishing the political from the economic, the legal from the political, the sociological from the historical, so that the full implications of any given problem can never come into view.[26]

Marxists describe this fragmentation of thought (and of practices) as *reification*. The politics dedicated to bringing the cooperation, coordination and collaboration latent within capitalism to a more fully developed and conscious form is usually known as socialism. We have seen how within literary and film analysis, Jameson will attempt to *reconnect* the reified textual fragment to that larger social totality that hovers beyond our daily compartmentalised experience, a totality which sometimes metonymically comes crashing unexpectedly and disastrously into routine life, as it does (to once more invoke a signifier of travel) when the wing engine of a jet plane smashes through the roof of the protagonist's house in *Donnie Darko* (Richard Kelly 2001 US). This incident in turn inaugurates (by the fact that Donnie survives) a sequence of events, which, through a series of accidents, chances and misfortunes, ends in the death of Gretchen, Donnie's girlfriend, and Frank, the young man who accidentally runs Gretchen over. A narrative predicated on random chance inevitably invokes within the film itself a metaphysical discourse on Fate or God, which seeks to impose some order or meaning on this chronology, as well as ruminations on the scope for individual choice and agency. These concerns converge when Donnie, having figured out how his premonitions of doom come to pass inexorably, rewinds time and cancels out the whole sequence, sacrificing himself (Jesus-like) by making sure he is in his bed when that jet engine comes calling. And yet that jet engine, although a bizarre and eventually fatal intrusion from somewhere 'beyond' the small town of Middlesex, also straddles another discourse and is indeed the most potent symbol of some larger *human-made* socioeconomic system. This is buttressed by the 1988 presidential elections playing itself out on the TV screen in Donnie's home and the appearance after the accident of air industry regulators who give off a bad smell of cover up. And yet, while the subsequent plot, complete with accidents, allows for a wonderful critique of right-wing small-town values, the *socioeconomic determinants* gestured to obliquely by the appearance of the jet engine are in some conflict (the text, in other words, is a tissue of contradictions) with the subsequent plot turning on chance or metaphysics. Perhaps all this confirms the profound difficulties of bridging the gulf between private and public, local place and global system under advanced capitalism.

Yet perhaps symptomatic readings are themselves guilty of repressing something: namely that the real protrudes rather more than Jameson's insistence on symptomatic decodings suggests. After all, one could read many American films made during the 1970s in terms of the emergence into representation of powerful corporate capitalist agents – it is hardly something that can only be extracted – albeit with great hermeneutic skill – from *Dog Day Afternoon*.[27] For of course the late 1960s and subsequent decade was a period of considerable crisis at both an industrial/economic level for Hollywood and a political/cultural level for the dominant social order generally which saw a substantial politicisation amongst wide layers of the population. Jameson has nothing to say about Hollywood's industrial crisis and relatively little positive to say about the general political conjuncture, suggesting that most of the left, liberal and progressive forces in this period had more or less abandoned class as a significant category for analysis and critique. Jameson is relatively uninterested in these levels of social analysis and their vicissitudes. For Jameson the industrial and the political, as methodological categories, are one feels too 'local', too diachronic,[28] too prone as objects of analysis to collapsing back into the separate disciplines or 'airtight compartments' of analysis (political economy or political history) to be able to grasp the social totality.[29] And yet, while reification does indeed present methodological difficulties, unless analysis can track back and forth between the industrial, the political and the mode of production the latter tends to acquire in the mind a certain functionalist quality, in which its inner tendencies play themselves out inexorably. A greater attention to the workings of the culture industries, the specific conditions of production for given (film) texts and wider political contexts would sensitise analysis to the constantly shifting scope and points of intervention for progressive media practices.

It is not so much that the mode of production has no human agency in Jameson's use; it is just that all the agency seems to belong to the personifications of capital. For Jameson, what makes class visible or figurable in his analysis of *Dog Day Afternoon* are the activities (or mutation) of the dominant class rather than any agency of the dominated. And yet it is precisely Sonny's attempts to politicise a routine bank robbery through his orchestration of the crowd, his reminder to them of recent police brutality, that sees several cuts between the main action and the FBI man Sheldon, watching events from the background while the local police chief tries to resolve the hostage situation. That the FBI man is rather more interested in the latent politics of the crowd's identification with Sonny than Jameson, derives from the latter's preferring to hook cultural objects up to the fundamentals of the mode of production while bypassing such superstructural activities as political contestation and events.[30] Yet the political conjuncture plays a crucial mediating role in defining the possibilities for reading or decoding the mode of production. If the latter establishes the real conditions of production, the nature of the political conjuncture, whether it is dominated by a confidant ruling-class hegemony or whether that hegemony (meaning intellectual and moral leadership) is under substantial challenge, sets the terms in which cultural texts can penetrate to the real class forces at work. It is thus significant that in the early 1990s Jameson returned to the turbulent 1970s and used the trilogy of paranoid films made by Alan J. Pakula for particularly lucid articulations of the global system.[31]

It should be noted that our present political conjuncture is rather different to the one in which Jameson first wrote his 1984 essay on postmodernism, since that saw a neat fit between a new multinational phase of advanced capitalism and a seemingly unchallengeable political hegemony of the New Right (Reaganism, Thatcherism). And, indeed, perhaps that political conjuncture shaped the implicit pessimism of Jameson's account of postmodernism in unacknowledged ways. By contrast, the late 1990s saw the first signs of new forces emerging to contest the ascendancy of the New Right. If, for example, one compares the international solidarity generated by the struggle of the Vietnamese against American imperialism in the 1960s and early 1970s, with contemporary emergent critiques of global capitalism, it seems that the former was in fact the last hangover from an older era, being essentially a struggle for *national* liberation, while today the scale at which critiques of capitalism must operate are truly and instantly global and profoundly engaged with economic relations and organisations (the International Monetary Fund, the World Bank, the General Agreement on Tariffs and

Trade (GATT) the General Agreement on Trades in Services (GATS), structural adjustment programmes and the like) and not just primarily (as with the anti-colonial national struggles) questions of political representation. Here then is an example of the multinational nature of global capitalism generating an emergent, still embryonic class-consciousness in antagonism with global capital and its works.

Within Jameson's work the question of whether the postmodern is a moment when the real relations of capital become visible or a moment when those real relations are pushed even more thoroughly beyond representation, is resolved by hermeneutic methods which acknowledge and extract critical possibilities, but only after elaborately clever readings have levered the repressed nature of the global capitalist mode of production into the light of day. As Sean Homer argues, within Jameson's work

> the concept of totality functions as a methodological standard, an unrepresentable horizon which marks the limits of our thought rather than a possibility to be realized. The concept of totality, therefore, is always already inscribed within our discourse as a limit.[32]

The idea of the social totality functioning as an 'unrepresentable horizon' marking the symptomatic silences and repressions in all discourse (theoretical as much as cultural) certainly has a valuable role in keeping our critical faculties alive to the incompleteness of our representations. Yet we must be careful not to follow the road of much contemporary cultural theory influenced by Lacanian psychoanalysis (including Jameson, unfortunately),[33] and make such repressions into a homogeneous blanket fact always and everywhere inscribed into representation as an ontological condition of signs and meanings *themselves*. Rather, the limits of any discourse are a historically variable product of social relations and locations and this means that some representations will reveal considerably more of the social totality than others. The problem with Jameson's emphasis on the *limits* of representation is that it tends to play down the political significance or possibilities of what is *actually* represented *within* the limits of representation. *Bladerunner* (Ridley Scott 1982 US), an early example of a *critical* postmodern text[34] (probably a last-gasp articulation of the residual radicalism of the 1970s) and the more recent films emerging in the new political conjuncture, suggest that such 'symptomatic' readings of popular culture may be failing to recognise the extent to which there is a widespread proto-political understanding of the malevolence of corporate capital generally and media capital specifically. This is not to say that symptomatic readings of strategic silences and repressions within texts are no longer valid (far from it) but it does suggest that a better balance is sometimes in order between such a decoding operation and acknowledging the possibility of radical or at least progressive cognitions and pleasures in popular culture.

PARANOIA AND THE MEDIA

There is a close relationship between a decoding strategy such as Jameson's, which homes in on textual fragments, and the repression model. The inverse relation between the small, perhaps rather marginal, signifying unit(s) Jameson seizes on and the vast socioeconomic relations of empire or multinational capitalism which those signs are read in relation to, inevitably suggests that the former is a symptom of the latter which remains largely unrepresented, perhaps unrepresentable. However, if we allow greater possibility for a text to represent the extensive social totality outside itself by its own figuring of an intensive (fictional) totality, then, without necessarily abandoning the question of any text's silences and repressions, we can accord greater weight to what it does actually represent.[35] The convergence of media and capitalism gives the paranoid totalities of films like *The Truman Show* and *Series 7: The Contenders*, a metonymic power, representing the larger whole of the system by the fact that the media is such a crucial component or part of it. Such films are postmodern insofar as they accord enormous significance and power to the media and cultural forms of control. They would, however, fall outside most definitions of the postmodern insofar as the paranoid sensibility recodes the fragmentary and apparently discrete signs of everyday life (a rainstorm or an advert say, in *The Truman Show*) into a frightening systemic totality of control and manipulation by remote Others.

For Jameson, representations of computer networks and information systems in conspiracy thrillers act as a 'distorted figuration' of the 'decentred global network' of advanced capital.[36] Again we have that distinctly Jamesonian integration of the postmodern with Marxism (decentred networks/capital). High-tech paranoia or conspiracy theories 'must be seen as a degraded attempt – through the figuration of advanced technology – to think the impossible totality of the contemporary world system'.[37] The tensions in combining postmodernism and Marxism are here evident: why is thinking the totality (a Marxist endeavour) impossible (a postmodern conclusion)? For Jameson, conspiracy is a means of 'fantasizing an economic system on the scale of the globe itself'.[38] In trying to expand our imaginative capacities to this scale, dominant film culture remains largely trapped within narrative structures that are still largely individualised. Jameson acknowledges this, indeed he says it is the 'fundamental form-problem of the new globalizing representations'.[39] But if this is so, it points to an uneven development that suggests that the postmodern is not culturally dominant. Nevertheless, if the formal architecture of classical realism remains intact, and with it, the centrality of individual causal agency, there are a number of smaller internal modifications and thematic trends which give a new social and collective resonance to individual actions. As Jameson notes of recent conspiracy films, there is 'no longer an individual victim, but everybody; no longer an individual villain, but an omnipresent network; no longer an individual detective with a specific brief, but rather someone who blunders into all of this just as anyone might have done'.[40] Alternatively, Jameson suggests that in *Videodrome* (David Cronenberg 1982 US), the rotation of the James Woods character through the narrative slots of villain, victim and detective, also displays a socialisation of the individual character, who is now no longer fixed in place by their own actions but shaped into roles by wider forces.[41] It is worth noting that in films like *The Truman Show* and *Series 7: The Contenders*, the conspiracy is not even secret but public and one in which everyone participates, another sign perhaps of a dawning awareness of collective responsibility and collusion.

It is less clear in what ways, for Jameson, such paranoid representations *are* distorted but we can identify a number of problems from a Marxist perspective. Paranoia within popular culture entwines with a range of political values, many of them barely disguised racist fears of Jews, or more recently, Muslims. Within America after the Second World War, paranoia often took the form of anti-communism. Richard Hofstadter famously diagnosed a paranoid 'style' in American politics.[42] We can designate such right-wing paranoia as governed by *displaced* fear because it shifts attention away from the fundamentally causal networks responsible for the determination of people's lives on to other, often quite marginal and in relative terms powerless or remote groups whose own determined position within the world system is then concealed. However, the paranoia which we are dealing with in the media-focused films, does inevitably finger genuine power complexes and could thus be termed an example of *diagnostic* paranoia. Yet even here the problem with paranoia is the excessive projection of control on to a small cabal or elite. This reflects of course that economic and political elites do have substantial power within capitalism and vastly expanded opportunities to manipulate institutional mechanisms to their advantage. These elites are so remote to us and so single-minded in their pursuit of profits and power, they can indeed seem to be almost anti-human or non-human, as in David Icke's paranoid fantasies which imagine the world run by lizard people from another planet. One response to such fantasies is to poke fun at them, as the journalist Jon Ronson does in his book *Them: Adventures with Extremists*. This is unsatisfactory for the simple reason that such paranoid fantasies are irrational responses to problems that it is eminently rational to be deeply concerned about. They mark a cultural scream in response to a news and informational media that is characterised by silence and complacency when confronted by a world of poverty, absurd misallocation of resources, war and ecological crisis.

Precisely because of these inevitable contradictions within capitalism, the elites are not in control in that smooth, seamless manner the paranoid sensibility implies. In our real world all these contradictions keep bursting and rippling through, providing massive challenges of ideological management for the media on a day-to-day basis.[43] The difficulty of such media management is repressed within the simulated worlds of *The Matrix*, *Pleasantville* and *The Truman Show*, where cultural control is virtually complete. These films also share an investment in the outsider(s), the small guerrilla band that enters the artificial media-constructed worlds and disrupts them. This too is typical of the paranoid sensibility which invests not only in a controlling elite but in a few elite individuals who somehow manage to escape the seamless functioning of the system and fight it. Between the elites at the top and those on the outside of the system, the vast majority in the middle are seen by the paranoid vision as passive and managed. The centrality then of the individual (despite the modifications and new collective resonances noted above) makes the paranoid vision eminently suited to the classical narrative forms which these films mostly adhere to (especially when buttressed by the star system), despite their postmodern thematics.

SERIES 7 AND THE LIMITS OF THE POSTMODERN

Films depicting paranoid media totalities are *about* postmodern tendencies but they are not enunciated from a postmodern position.

This is true not only because they are about totalities of control, but also because they are satires on the postmodern. Jameson, following the logic of his argument in the 1984 essay, famously argued that our capacity for parody and satire has been eroded and replaced by postmodern pastiche.

> Pastiche is, like parody, the imitation of a peculiar or unique, idiosyncratic style, the wearing of a linguistic mask, speech in a dead language. But it is a neutral practice of such mimicry, without any of parody's ulterior motives, amputated of the satiric impulse, devoid of laughter and of any conviction that alongside the abnormal tongue you have momentarily borrowed, some healthy linguistic normality still exists. Pastiche is thus blank parody.[44]

This is clearly not the case with these films, the most complex and radical of which is the relatively low-budget film (and one significantly without stars) *Series 7: The Contenders*. This film is evidently a satire, adopting the language and conventions of reality television shows but in order to expose their ethical vacuousness and their corrosive political consequences on the public sphere and culture. In the film, selected contestants try to kill each other in order to 'win'. The way the film performs its satirical critique, however, is different from films like *Pleasantville*, *The Truman Show* and *Ed TV*. There is no invisible metanarrative outside the conventions of the show being parodied offering us a position of knowledge from which the spectator can easily spot the good protagonists and the bad protagonists, or even rely on the unfolding of the narrative and story world as the truth of that world against which to make secure judgements and unproblematised identifications.

In *The Truman Show*, for example, we are offered a classical narrative position whereby we the spectator 'know' the truth of Truman's world and that a substantial part of the narrative is all about his partial or false knowledge of the situation converging with our fuller knowledge about his life. *Series 7* is more complex because we the spectator are locked into the discourse of the show, there is no 'outside' for us and therefore no narrator's discourse we can trust to show us the truth. The film begins *in media res* with a caption warning viewers of the violent nature of the television programme. Then we go straight into a review of star contender Dawn killing a fellow contestant in a grocery store before the series' title credits roll. At one level, locking us into a media discourse from which there is no escape sounds highly postmodern but, at the same time, the discourse is satirised and therefore this implies some normative judgements (Jameson's 'healthy linguistic normality') not recognised by the discourse being satirised. We are clearly meant to be alarmed at the nature of this society and critical of the gap between its self-presentation and explanations and what we would take to be socially desirable, while at the same time seeing this as a critique of certain trends within our present society. When the show proudly tells us that the contestants have been selected by government identification numbers and we see lottery-style balls being presided over by a smiling television compère, the links between media capital and the state are evidently supposed to be read as darkly worrying. Despite being locked into the discourse of the show (and it is significant of course that this is the seventh series of the show and we never get any *history* or back story as to its development) we perceive the satire emerging from the discrepancies and contradictions displayed by the contestants. For example, when Connie the religious nurse goes to confession, she admits to impatience, swearing, a couple of lies and impure thoughts about a certain television personality. She omits, however, the fact that she has already killed two people on the show. There are also discrepancies and contradictions within the discourse of the show as it constructs its narrative and constantly performs the necessary ideological management of events to justify and legitimise itself. When one of the contestants tries to escape, he is defined as a 'vicious coward' and when Dawn's newly born baby is taken away from her by the show's operatives, the narrator informs us that this is for the 'physical and emotional security' of mother and baby (despite Dawn's screams and protestations).

The major challenge to the discourse of the show, however, comes at the climax when Dawn and fellow contender Jeffrey (who were once teenage sweethearts) turn on their cameramen, shut the coverage down and make a bid for freedom. At this point the show reconstructs their movements using CCTV footage of various public spaces and eyewitness testimony from the viewers (who are unredeemably complicit in the series and its very public conspiracy). They end up in a cinema (interrupting another mass media spectacle, but not one with the real-time possibilities of television) and try to hold the cinemagoers hostage. This scene they record on one of the stolen cameras, but the footage of what happens next, we are told by the show, was lost due to a 'technical fault'. Thus the climax is replayed by dramatic reconstruction with actors, which include a heroic senior executive for the show negotiating with Dawn and Jeffrey. What 'really' happens then is not available to us. To the end the spectator remains locked into the media spectacle as constructed by the (unseen) series producers while at the same time a critique of the show, its contestants, audience and wider society, has been launched. In *The Truman Show* we watch Truman perform a Jamesonian decoding of the world he thought he knew around him in order to reveal the socially determining totality, but we the spectator are securely positioned with access to a narrator's discourse we trust. *Series 7* is more radical because we the spectator have to perform a Jamesonian decoding of the repressions, inconsistencies and contradictions of the contestants and their (mediated) universe in order to read the film as a satire. The film's reflexive use of reality television conventions, its awareness of the politics of perspective and the constructed nature of discourse, and its political and ethical critique place the film in the modernist tradition rather more than in either the postmodern or classical narrative traditions.

CONCLUSION

By making postmodernism *the* cultural logic of late capitalism, Jameson ascribes to it a dominance it is hard to actually see, certainly as regards popular film culture, still largely dominated by (albeit modified) 'classical' narrative notions of time, space, logic and causal agency as well as other classical paradigms such as method acting, or still able to produce films with significant modernist roots such as *Series 7*. The 'postmodernism' of many of the films discussed above exists largely at the level of theme or content, rather than at the level of form, where we would expect to find the more profound indications of perceptual and cultural revolution. Postmodernism is today one of the many cultural resources at play, but it is not, I think, a cultural *dominant*, as Jameson argues. The sense in which one might argue that postmodernism is culturally *significant* (not the same thing as dominant) is that it gives a peculiarly articulate expression to certain trends within advanced capitalism, namely the significance of media culture and the global/spatial reach of capital. Jameson argues that modernism was the cultural dominant for monopoly capitalism in the early decades of the twentieth century. We have seen that Jameson reads modernism as an oblique (repressed) gesture towards the international scale of capital in its industrialised imperial stage, a stage in which the national border is increasingly crossed by capital (as commodities, or investment).

Yet for the millions of people who flocked to Hollywood movies, who read daily newspapers and cheap paperback novels, modernism was not remotely *their* cultural dominant. It is Jameson's, however, because modernism, he argues, articulates something of the leading-edge tendencies within the system: namely its abstraction, which in geographical terms refers to the enlarged space in which capital seeks to circulate. And it is for this reason that the Great North Road and the train (in Forster's *Howard's End*) and the plane (in *Dog Day Afternoon*, *Heat* and *Donnie Darko*), are such potent emblems of capital as a global mobile abstract force. Popular culture tries to give some concrete representation to this global mobility and abstract power through the lens of paranoia. Here then is the link between planes, trains and automobiles and the media: as emblems of capital they mark a shift from vehicles of transport and communication through physical movement to mediums of communication through representations and information. And the latter are a sign of a more advanced, mature system with even greater reach and speed.

There is some overlap between paranoia and Jameson's decoding strategy, which decomposes the seamless unity of the text, breaking it down into fragments, some of which can then be connected to some larger set of invisible but impinging socioeconomic forces. Jameson is clear, however, that the Marxist conception of the social totality (which stresses contradiction) is not the same as the paranoid visions of popular culture or the functionalist visions of a 'total system' which have dominated the work of some social and cultural pessimists such as Max Weber, Michel Foucault or Jean Baudrillard.[45] Yet Jameson's emphasis on capital at its most abstract and remote to the practical exclusion of other social levels does tend to lead to certain conclusions in which contradictions and struggle are smoothed away and a pure 'logic' manifests itself. The notion of the method school of acting as an outdated paradigm, for example, suggests a linearity of cultural development that smoothes away the real combined and uneven development of the times. Judged against capital in its most global abstract modes, the individual as a model of subjectivity is clearly in trouble. But judged against other cultural and economic trends, the method school and the old monadic/autonomous subject shows remarkable cultural resilience. Indeed, the whole therapy business, which springs from the same cultural wellsprings as the method school (the 'I' as a discrete unit of emotional needs and demands), shows little sign of waning (unfortunately).

I have also suggested that one facet of Jameson's methodology, namely the lack of detailed mediation between different social levels such as cultural institutions and political contexts, does tend to lead to a certain pessimistic functionalism as he charts the mode of production's inexorable development. Perhaps for every generation, the latest extension of capital's powers of commodification seems to definitively spell the end of something. Back in the nineteenth century Marx wrote how such qualities as virtue, love, conviction, knowledge and conscience, were now up for sale. Jameson, in the 1984 essay, defines postmodernism as a culture 'where exchange value has been generalised to the point at which the very memory of use-value is effaced'.[46] This is powerful stuff and undeniably speaks to immense pressures, forces and dangers at work. But cast your ear a little closer to the ground, stray a little from such an abstract (although profoundly necessary) concept as mode of production, and you will hear the murmur of ordinary people speaking (when they are invited) on radio and television programmes for example, and for many of them, clearly, virtue, love, conviction, knowledge, conscience, battered and bruised as they are, still mean something, they are not simply commodities to be exchanged for something else (a career, in the case of most politicians for example). Herein too lies the danger of an over-reliance on symptomatic readings of the political unconscious, because clearly it privileges the specialised critic's role in hermeneutic discovery and downplays the extent to which popular culture can actually express (albeit always within certain limits and parameters) critical cognitions of the world. For the characters in *Series 7* the capacity to generate critical cognitions, or critical distance, is virtually eclipsed. For them, 'the massive Being of capital'[47] has indeed triumphed. But this is not the case for the watching audience. Perhaps postmodernism, like *Series 7*, is a warning. But we have not arrived there yet. There is still time to make sure we never do.

NOTES

1. Reprinted in Fredric Jameson, *Postmodernism: Or, The Cultural Logic of Late Capitalism* (London: Verso, 1993).
2. Perry Anderson, *The Origins of Postmodernity* (London: Verso, 2002), p. 57.
3. The *New Left Review* essay was a more developed version of an earlier essay, 'Postmodernism and the Consumer Society' published in *The Anti-Aesthetic*, edited by Hal Foster (Port Townsend: Bay Press, 1983).

4. Fredric Jameson, *The Cultural Turn: Selected Writings on the Postmodern, 1983–1998* (London: Verso, 1998), p. 110.
5. Theodor Adorno and Max Horkheimer, 'The Culture Industry: Enlightenment as Mass Deception', in J. Curran, M. Gurevitch and J. Woolacott (eds), *Mass Communication and Society* (London: Open University Press, 1977).
6. Colin McCabe, 'Realism and the Cinema: Notes on some Brechtian Theses', in Tony Bennett (ed.), *Popular Television and Film* (London: BFI/Open University, 1981), pp. 216–35.
7. Jameson, *Postmodernism: Or*, p. 4.
8. Fredric Jameson, *Modernism and Imperialism* (Derry: Field Day Theatre Company, 1988), pp. 11–12.
9. Jameson, *Modernism and Imperialism*, p. 15.
10. Jameson, *Modernism and Imperialism*, p. 17.
11. Jameson, *The Cultural Turn*, p. 108.
12. Fredric Jameson, *The Geopolitical Aesthetic: Cinema and Space in the World System* (London: Indiana University Press and BFI, 1992), p. 61.
13. Fredric Jameson, 'Class and Allegory in Contemporary Mass Culture: *Dog Day Afternoon* as a Political Film', in *Signatures of the Visible* (London: Routledge, 1992), p. 44.
14. Jameson, 'Class and Allegory in Contemporary Mass Culture', p. 46.
15. See his analysis of the figure of Quint as a representative of small, private and local business in *Jaws* (Steven Spielberg 1975 US) in 'Reification and Utopia in Mass Culture', *Signatures*, pp. 28–9. The tension between threatened or declining small business practices and large corporate concerns derives from the American political tradition of populism. It can be seen in *Klute* (Alan Pakula 1971 US), where the prostitute Bree Daniels has, as one of her clients, an old Jewish garment factory owner, Mr Goldfarb. His 'harmless' sexual desires, he just watches Bree (Jane Fonda) strip, are contrasted to the murderous, predatory, psychopathic sexuality of the corporate executive. Significantly, the film's denouement is located in the garment factory. The threat of corporations to small business practices continues in more recent films such as *You've Got Mail* (Nora Ephron 1998 US), although here big business is not conceived of as a threat, more like 'progress', and *Anti-trust* (Peter Howitt 2001 US), another example of paranoid media surveillance.
16. Fredric Jameson, *Marxism and Form* (Princeton: Princeton University Press, 1974), p. 104.
17. Jameson, 'Class and Allegory in Contemporary Mass Culture', p. 51.
18. Jameson, 'Class and Allegory in Contemporary Mass Culture', p. 42.
19. Jameson, 'Class and Allegory in Contemporary Mass Culture', p. 42.
20. Jameson, 'Class and Allegory in Contemporary Mass Culture', p. 48.
21. Jameson, *Postmodernism: Or*, p. 11.
22. Karl Marx and Friedrich Engels, *The Communist Manifesto* (Harmondsworth: Penguin Books, 1985), p. 83.
23. Marx and Engels, *The Communist Manifesto*, p. 85.
24. Jameson, *Postmodernism: Or*, p. 19.
25. Jameson, *The Cultural Turn*, p. 35.
26. Jameson, *Marxism and Form*, pp. 367–8.

27. See for example Michael Ryan and Douglas Kellner's *Camera Politica: The Politics and Ideology of Contemporary Hollywood Film* (Bloomington: Indiana University Press, 1988).

28. Diachronic analysis focuses on the detailed temporal development of whatever is being studied. This contrasts with synchronic analysis which freezes the object of study in order to focus on its internal structure and components in any one period. Jameson's mode of analysis is more synchronic than diachronic, although obviously there is no absolute division between them, more a matter of emphasis.

29. This for example is the gist of Jameson's argument in response to critics who have suggested he pay closer attention to the history of cultural institutions. See 'Marxism and Postmodernism' in *The Cultural Turn*, p. 45.

30. In Marxist theory the mode of production is sometimes referred to as the base, while the realms of politics, culture, education, religion, the media, the state, and so forth are understood as the superstructure supported by the base.

31. Jameson discusses Pakula's *Klute* (1971), *The Parallax View* (1974) and *All The President's Men* (1976) in *The Geopolitical Aesthetic*.

32. Sean Homer, *Fredric Jameson, Marxism, Hermeneutics, Postmodernism* (Cambridge/Oxford: Polity Press/Blackwell, 1998), p. 20.

33. Fredric Jameson, *The Political Unconscious: Narrative as a Socially Symbolic Act* (London: Methuen, 1981). Jameson writes that history 'is fundamentally non-narrative and nonrepresentational', p. 82. This means that any narrativisation and representation of historical material is ontologically an exercise in repression. This marks the influence of Althusser on Jameson. As with Althusser it also suggests an overly absolute division between narrative and representation, and the conceptual social and political sciences where knowledge of the world is, for Jameson, generated.

34. See Nick Heffernan's excellent reading of the film in his book *Capital, Class & Technology in Contemporary American Culture* (London: Pluto Press, 2000).

35. The distinction between the extensive social totality and the signifying work which a text performs to construct its own intensive social totality, comes from the great Hungarian literary Marxist, Georg Lukács. See *Writer and Critic* (London: Merlin Press, 1978), p. 38.

36. Jameson, *Postmodernism: Or*, p. 37.

37. Jameson, *Postmodernism: Or*, p. 38.

38. Jameson, *The Geopolitical Aesthetic*, p. 9.

39. Jameson, *The Geopolitical Aesthetic*, p. 33.

40. Jameson, *The Geopolitical Aesthetic*, p. 34.

41. Jameson, *The Geopolitical Aesthetic*, pp. 34–5.

42. Richard Hofstadter, *The Paranoid Style in American Politics and Other Essays* (London: Jonathan Cape, 1966). 'The distinguishing thing about the paranoid style is not that its exponents see conspiracies or plots here and there in history, but that they regard a "vast" or "gigantic" conspiracy as *the motive force* in historical events' p. 29.

43. Although arguably this is *less* true in America, where the media are more concentrated into powerful corporations interlocked with political elites than elsewhere in the democratic world. It has been widely noted just how unquestioning and actively supportive the American media were of President George Bush's pre-emptive war on Iraq.
44. Jameson, *Postmodernism: Or*, p. 17.
45. Jameson, *The Political Unconscious*, pp. 90–1.
46. Jameson, *Postmodernism: Or*, p. 18.
47. Jameson, *Postmodernism: Or*, p. 48.

5

'Making It': Reading *Boogie Nights* and *Blow* as Economies of Surplus and Sentiment

Anna Kornbluh

The concept of 'ideology' is the enabling obstacle of Marxist cultural criticism. As a formula of why people consent to the conditions of their own domination, it illustrates the politico-economic operation of 'culture', where culture comprises the practices of everyday life and the narratives that lend those practices the veneer of sense. But cultural critique based upon this formula is complicated by the fact that the charge of studying creative texts, be they folklore, poetry, or film, is to recognise the elements of imagination and elusion at play – meaning precisely that it is impossible to reduce a given text to its political-economic operation. Louis Althusser famously formulated ideology as a *symbolic* resolution of social antagonism, where 'symbolic' refers to strategies like narrative, myth and fantasy that fall short of radical social restructuring to alleviate class conflict.[1] Following the intervention of contemporary philosophers like Slavoj Žižek and Douglas Kellner, the Marxist interpretation of cultural texts must register the necessarily ambiguous quality of these symbolic resolutions, tackling a logical duality.[2] On the one hand, a given text participates in this process of symbolisation, integrating social relationships and antagonisms into some relatively coherent form or narrative. On the other, the text can interrupt the seamlessness of symbolisation, either by calling attention to itself as a creative text, or by creatively asserting a counter-symbolic critique. To take a well-known example, many Hollywood films revolve around an individual solution to a broad social problem, such as poverty, that is overcome through true love between individuals. Ambiguity arises from the fact that such stories might discourage political activism ('I don't need worker's rights, I just need a rich husband') but might just as easily unwittingly ignite a critical consciousness in the spectator who remains unconvinced by the limited symbolic answer offered within the narrative ('The story is so unrealistic, and that rich husband isn't even cute – and why is marriage her only chance to get out of the ghetto?'). The risk that either of these positions might be adopted is at the centre of ideology; the ideology-critique of a text rests not in exposing the false consciousness of the story from some impossible standpoint 'outside' ideology, but rather in exploring how the film's narrative and form manage this risk.

To explore some of these problems of representation and ideology the following discussion focuses on a cluster of films about the 1970s, a time of structural transition within American capitalism. I argue that these films construct a vocabulary of excess, illicit industries and insatiable mother figures to offer an ideological and personal resolution of class struggle, while simultaneously highlighting the aysmmetrical nature of material surplus (for some) and emotional reciprocity within capitalism. In making this argument, I will discuss developments in 1970s political economy crucial to contemporary capitalism, review the prototypical seventies film, *Saturday Night Fever*,[3] and turn to two millennial films that nostalgise the decade, *Boogie Nights*[4] and *Blow*.[5]

The ideology-critique of Hollywood film focuses on both technical conventions of editing, lighting and shot structure that achieve an illusory presence of reality,[6] and story, the way the events of the plot come together to form a narrative with delineated parameters of intelligibility, along with the incorporation of such stories into the narratives of everyday life. The stories in *Boogie Nights* and *Blow* present the excessive economies of the illicit field of pornography and the underworld of the narcotics trade, employing Oedipal conflict between mothers and sons to emotionalise economic difficulties. These representations recall the 1970s, a time of macro-structural transformation into an economy of surplus based upon ever-widening divisions between the haves and the have-nots, in terms that obscure the realities of their time. Moreover, in connecting their economies of excess to morality and psychological struggle, the films engage in a familiar ideological strategy, suggesting that the answer to social problems of excess is individual – we should simply adopt a moral code of conduct in which we refrain from indulgence and offer one another love. Keeping in mind, however, our formula of the necessarily conflicted content of ideology, I claim that these representations of excess exceed their own solutions. The manifestation of this conflict is the unhappy ending: while the films posit a personal solution to social problems, their unhappy endings belie the inadequacy of these solutions. Both of these films bear poignant elements of suffering, messages that evoke identifications lingering after the screen goes black. This melancholic hangover invites audiences to reflect on the link between public and private spheres, since the stories overtly tie this oedipal pain to social forces of excess (greed, insatiability, money, dehumanisation).

THE REGIME OF SURPLUS: 1970s POLITICAL ECONOMY

Writing this essay in the year 2003, I need only glance at the business page of today's newspaper to detect the dominance of 'symbolic' exchange in our economic era. Most of the companies traded in the Dow Jones Index traffic in information; stocks rise or fall not with respect to real profit or loss, but based on the difference between actual profit or loss and anticipated profit or loss (stocks can decrease in value for a company earning a profit if the profit happens to be less than was forecast the previous quarter); the wealthiest and most successful investors are not shareholders of high-performing stocks, but rather the clairvoyants speculating in advance on whether or not the shares, or the currency, will perform well; a rise in consumer spending is seen as a sign of a healthy economy regardless of whether the consumers pay real money or incur debt to make the purchases. Similarly, a cursory glance down the street offers a glimpse of extremes: overweight kids in the H2 military style SUV, which gets seven miles per gallon of gas, visit the McDonald's drive-thru to stock up on Super-Size saturated fats, the Styrofoam packaging never biodegrading. This age of speculation, debt and dematerialisation, coupled with waste, obesity and fatuousness, is what we are calling the regime of surplus.

Neither accident nor ancient history produced this age of surplus. The major economic and cultural policies that shape lives in the US today were enacted in the 1970s. And yet, the dominant image of the 1970s in film and popular culture portrays not economic restructuring, but big pants, brilliant lights, and bad hair. Consistent with the duality of representation that we are tracing, this fixation on aesthetic elements belies cultural memory as actually a kind of forgetting of the political and financial developments of the era. But at the same time, the emphasis on the largesse of leisure suits, Afros and platform shoes does unwittingly convey something historically accurate about the political reality of the 1970s: the intensification of capitalism's tension between excess (the accumulation of surplus value and the assemblage of mountains of waste) and social and economic stability. Watergate, Vietnam and the failure of the Equal Rights Amendment loom large in today's conception of the 1970s, but the decade also witnessed dismantling of the social welfare state, implementation of agreements to begin what we now call 'globalisation', dissolution of the Fordist contract, advent of money market funds, and popularisation of brokerage houses. Surplus accumulation became the structuring principle of the US economy; the over-indulgent disco inferno of sex, drugs and polyester testifies to this prominence of excess.

Under the leadership of Richard Nixon, the US had enacted a host of economic shifts by 1973. For labourers, the most obvious and instantaneous constriction was Fordism's dissolution. Named after its innovator Henry Ford, Fordism affirmed the interdependence of production and consumption, and calculated compensation for workers to allow them to afford to consume, at some point in time or in some quantity, the products they produce. Henry Ford recognised that 'mass production meant mass consumption, a new system of the reproduction of labor power, a new politics of labor control and management, a new aesthetics and psychology, in short, a new kind of rationalised, modernist, and populist democratic society'.[7] In other words, Fordism ensured a basic correlation between production and consumption. Fordism's tenets contributed to an economy that was favourable to both organised labour and corporate profits, and this balance was stable during the period from the post-Second World War boom through to 1973.[8]

In 1973, American corporations adopted a new set of economic theories and policies, enacting broad structural changes for how Americans worked and consumed. Reacting to mounting competition from the recovered Japanese and West European economies, American companies demanded greater 'flexibility' in their production strategies. The American government echoed this insistence with respect to social programmes and commitments. By 1972, President Nixon had

adopted wage and price controls to cool inflation, a series of tax cuts to stimulate the economy in time for the elections. He closed the gold window and allowed the dollar to float against other currencies, ending the Bretton Woods monetary system that had stabilized the international currency market since World War II.[9]

The resulting devaluation of the dollar and inflation in the economy, compounded by higher oil prices during the Arab-Israeli war, led the Nixon government to scrap Fordism.

The new regime of 'flexible accumulation' seeks to relieve the tension between the pillars of capitalism (growth, exploitation and technological dynamism) and the tendency of these elements to culminate in over-accumulation – essentially, the production of more than can be consumed, where production includes then factories that might lie idle, unemployment, excess products or inventories, all coupled with surplus money capital.[10] By breaking unions, streamlining communication, and decentralising production, corporations have become internationally mobile, which has translated into 'flexibility' through strategies like subcontracting to countries with lesser labour laws and lower wages and fewer benefits. The term most often used to describe this regime of flexibility and mobility is 'globalisation'.

The Great Inflation and the popularisation of credit cards dispatched the problem of how to produce growing rates of consumption among workers whose real earning potential was declining. As Bruce Schulman notes, 'with double-digit inflation, thriftiness became just plain dumb. Saving money meant paying for tomorrow's higher-priced goods with yesterday's diminished dollars. Borrowing, on the other hand, made sense.'[11] With serendipitous timing, in 1973 the Visa Corporation patented technology enabling the quick transfer of information through magnetic strips on the back of credit cards. These two dynamics together produced a tremendous expansion of consumer borrowing, reaching $315 billion per year by 1979.[12] The repayment of tens of billions of these borrowed funds was deferred, and thus was born a nation in which the average household credit card debt burden is now $9,000.[13]

Other policy changes contributed to a morphing regard for money. Beyond assuming debt, changes in banking laws in the 1970s encouraged consumers to instrumentalise their savings by investing in the stock market. These included the end of Regulation Q, a 1933 policy fixing the maximum rate of interest banks could pay to customers; the Fidelity Corporation's innovation of Money Market funds, essentially checking accounts in which the balance was invested in the stock market; and the deregulation of broker commissions at the New York Stock Exchange, giving rise to competition amongst brokers and incentivising the brokers to expand their client bases to include average Americans.[14] All these developments amounted to substantial shifts in the fundamental financial relationships in the American economy. Visa allowed consumers to buy things they couldn't afford; the failure of the Carter administration to combat inflation left Americans to take their financial livelihoods into their own hands, effectively segregating the state from the market in the minds and wallets of the average citizen; the increase in stock market investing encouraged average Americans to consider money not as a means to goods and services, but as a means to more money.

SURPLUS NOSTALGIA: POLITICAL ECONOMY IN THE MOVIES

The legacy of these shifts in both the structure of the US economy and the politico-cultural values of US citizens is the ascension of the regime of surplus. Crippling consumer debt, profit wrought from speculation and futures trading, and the desperate construction of ever-new arenas for consumption ushered in an era in which government works harder to fatten corporate coffers than to feed children. While the Marxist critique of narrative should not be reduced to a judgement on the historical truth value or realism of a creative text, the events of the 1970s were so radically formative of contemporary capitalism that they can be expected to surface in any retrospective representation of the time, like a kind of ambient sound or, better, like an unconscious.

Where, however, would 1970s nostalgia films be without John Badham's *Saturday Night Fever*, the paradigmatic seventies film actually made during the seventies? Interlocking themes of class mobility, ethnic identity and gendered social life, the film enjoys iconic cultural status and has inspired volumes of academic criticism. After a title sequence showcasing the industrial evacuation of suburban New Jersey, the diegetic presence of class constrictions is affected by the disapproving female figures of Tony Manero's mother and his dance partner. Ms Manero exerts suffocating pressure upon Tony to follow his brother's example and find a career that will make the family proud. A clerk in a hardware store, the prospect of advancement over thirty years makes Tony grimace. While Ms Manero angrily exhorts her son to make something of himself, Tony's dance partner Stefanie matter-of-factly delivers the prognosis: 'You got no class ... you're nowhere on your way to no place.' The exit from the road to nowhere is the glittering disco, where Tony receives much longed-for recognition for his talents.

Drawing a contrast between Stefanie's WASP aspirations and Tony's limited horizons, the story revolves around his quest for an outlet for expression and recognition. His need for personal expression has prompted many critics to view the film as a tale of the progressive expansion of the parameters of acceptable masculinity, in a time when racial and gender democratisation of the workforce seemed to challenge the conventional notions of masculine power and function.[15] At the same time as he may challenge gender norms by vocalising concern for his coiffure, Tony is forced to acknowledge the limits of the relief he finds in the world of disco. That sort of escape isn't what Stefanie has planned or executed for herself, as Tony realises when she brushes off questions like 'When are we gonna talk about how we feel when we're dancing?' Stefanie is motivated by the physical fitness and social superiority that the dance prize might bring to her, but she shows no interest in emotional exchange with Tony, and she has already begun to go somewhere, working as a secretary and living in Manhattan. Over the course of the film, Tony moves closer to Stefanie's plans, seeming to accept the inadequacy of disco as a solution to his social constriction and limited economic prospects. The great tragedy of the film comes not from the world of disco and too much indulgence, but from the confrontation with pervasive, indeterminate constraints on identity: pushing the limits of human balance out on the rafters of a bridge, Tony's friend Bobby aims for the freedom he feels slipping away as he prepares to marry his pregnant girlfriend and sign up for life in the struggling middle-class family. In a stirring implication that there's no real way out, Bobby's playful taste of freedom precipitates a fatal fall.

Saturday Night Fever ends on an indecisive note, unclear as to what Tony's professional, social and romantic prospects truly are. While dancing and the emotional expression it offers have proved a false solution to his social position, the metaphor of an individual being able to 'make something' of himself remains active. One solution has been dismantled; another retains the veneer of legitimacy. This give and take leads Douglas Kellner and Michael Ryan to identify *Saturday Night Fever* as a classic example of the dialectical character of an ideological text, since it 'presents the ideological metaphor as if it were absolute, but it also shows the indeterminacy within the apparently uncontestable revelation of absolute truth'.[16] The same metaphor reigns supreme in both *Boogie Nights* and *Blow*, the prominent 1970s nostalgia films from the millennium, but their modes of indeterminacy differ. In both of these films, 'making it' has not proved to be all that was desired. *Boogie Nights* and *Blow* revolve around the heroes' persistent unhappiness, both against a backdrop of acquired wealth.

Paul Thomas Anderson conceived *Boogie Nights* as a portrait of the dark side of 1970s excess, as if 'there had to be punishment for all that pursuit of pleasure'.[17] Anderson's critical edge manifests itself in the depiction of this underside, which is not so much immorality or perversion as the transition from industrial to corporate capitalism and the personal costs entailed therein.[18] With a modest background and a failed education, financial independence is an unreachable summit for Eddie Adams, our post-industrial hero. Unable to offer support or encouragement, his mother instead offers shame and pain. *Boogie Nights* expands upon *Saturday Night Fever*'s device of the disapproving mother as the form of appearance of economic constraints, adding an element of abuse to emphasise the dire personal importance of economic success. The narrative effect of this use of the mother figure is to circumscribe desperation: instead of an inevitable response to an increasingly unjust economy, it issues from an intimate space of unrequited love. Near the beginning of the film, a painful interaction between Eddie and his insatiable mother introduces the personal consequences of economic disenfranchisement: as Eddie returns home late after working one of his two jobs, his mother launches a broad attack on his life. 'Where were you? Did you see that little slut girl? Does it make you feel like a stud to see trash like that? ... What are you gonna do? You can't do anything. You're a loser. You can't even finish high school because you're too stupid! So what are you gonna do?' When Eddie tearfully responds that he's going to take his stuff and go away, his mother retorts 'That is not your stuff! Cause you didn't pay for it, Stupid! None of this is yours!' Eddie begs his mother not to destroy his beloved posters, not to destroy his fragile sense of worth. 'Please don't be mean to me! ... I have got good things and you don't know it. I wanna be something. I am something. Don't tell me I'm not!' Through a tear-cracked voice, Eddie insists upon his minimal humanity in the face of the dehumanising economy.

From this brutal scene of abuse, the camera cuts to the next room, where Eddie's father is tearfully tying his tie, helpless to intervene on his son's behalf. This shot conflates his familial impotence with his professional attire, evoking as much pity for his limited horizons as for his submission to his wife. Similarly, a slightly earlier scene subjects both Eddie and Mr Adams to the social and sexual wrath of the mother. Opening with a series of stylised jump cuts from sausage sizzling in a skillet to percolating coffee to popping toast, the scene evokes the trappings of the household economy as a context for the clash between maternal emotion and paternal productivity. Upon entering the kitchen for breakfast, Mr Adams tries to kiss his wife good morning. She snaps 'Ugh, shave if you're going to do that!', palpably repulsed by the prospect of affection. Rebuffed, Mr Adams tries his luck with affection on the other side of the table, asking Eddie how work is going. Before this exchange develops, Ms Adams angrily interjects: 'You work at a car wash and a bar! The idea of school never occurred to you?!' Crestfallen, Eddie and his father surrender their feeble connection and flee the unhappy home for their respective jobs, their ladders to some celestial happiness.

With the pathos of these sequences, the film articulates anxieties about class mobility and self-actualisation, but uses a vocabulary of abusive mothers and tyrannical wives. The pressure that Eddie feels to go somewhere, to do something, to be someone is simultaneously the cultural imperative of an economy allegedly based on individual success and a personal desperation to be recognised by his unloving mother. From the historically specific recession of the US economy in the 1970s, the film moves to the seemingly timeless problem of hateful mothers and impotent fathers. Convinced that 'everyone has one special thing', his being an enormous penis, Eddie seeks recognition in the world of pornography, an industry whose descent from material production and old technology (film) to the new 1980s technology of video is succinctly dramatised by the film. Once ensconced in the field, this recognition and the affection it occasions is clearly the source of Eddie's peace. Although he earns significant money, Eddie seems to derive more joy from the companionship and praise of his co-workers than from either his money or the potential promiscuity in his new world. His pleasures are largely innocent and childlike; he does not share his rise to stardom with a lover, finding rather deep fulfilment from his attachment to Amber Waves. Described early on as 'a wonderful mother – the mother to all of us', Amber is literally the matriarch of the film company. She refers to herself as 'mommy' and to Eddie as 'my baby boy'. In this film, the extremity of Ms Adams' cruelty is a figure for the rise of the regime of surplus, and the lack that persists in this state of surplus is a lack of affection. The film then offers a solution to this imbalance of surplus and lack, in the figure of the indulgent world of sexuality and drug use – in short, the solution to surplus-driven economic constriction, already coded as emotional pain, is *not* a move away from surplus, but rather *still further* economic excess, this time coded as emotional pleasure. The contrast between Eddie's relationship with his mother and with Amber explicates that Oedipal pleasure is attainable only within this alternative excessive economy. At the same time, Ms Adams' ravenous vexation haunts Eddie: he never reunites with her, and he extrapolates her demands into his own form of greed and dissatisfaction. Forsaking the precious boundaries of his new world, Eddie tries to subsist without his new family, winding up a street hustler brutalised by homophobes. Humbled and alone, he returns to Amber's world, and the film concludes with ambiguity as to his success and the first on-screen revelation of the famous penis, as if Eddie must resign himself to the fact that all he has is this 'one special thing'.

Several complex implications issue from this constellation. At the ideological level, intimate happiness and personal acceptance are incontrovertibly linked to economic success (the classic American Dream). Within the film, 'recognition' is the figure of success: getting compensated for something he possesses (a large penis) constitutes a kind of humanising moment for Eddie, in which society, and the forces of the economy, recognise him as a subject. (In a twist particularly amusing for Lacanians, in this story it is *literally* penile wholeness that induces the (mis)recognition of Eddie as a phallic whole.) At the same time, Eddie's unshakable unhappiness propels him through wealth and back into poverty. Neither money nor recognition can stem his desperation. By treating this desperation as the intimate fall out of Eddie's economic background, the film lays the ground for an understanding of the relationship between economic production and the production of social identity, personal emotions, and even unconscious longings.

Consistent with the emotional effects and theoretical suggestions of *Boogie Nights*, *Blow* chronicles the life and business adventures of the notorious California cocaine dealer George Jung, focusing much more on the relationship between mothers and sons than the political economy of the War on Drugs. In place of the world of porn, *Blow* showcases the illegal drug trade as its excessive economy of choice, charting the growth of the cocaine market in the US in the late 1970s and early 1980s. Parallel to both *Saturday Night Fever* and *Boogie Nights*, early events in the narrative of *Blow* situate the hero as the victim of an unloving mother greedy for a wealthier husband. To convey the formative influence of this relationship, *Blow* constructs two scenes that almost perfectly mirror each other, thirty years apart. In the first, a family dinner is soured by an explosion of anger from George's mother, perpetually dissatisfied with George's father for failing to earn 'enough' money despite working seven days a week. As George winces under the brunt of Mrs Jung's attack, Mr Jung, a gentle hero, begs her 'Not in front of the kid.' This minimal display of concern for George without seemingly heeding Mrs Jung's feelings prompts her to storm out of the house, an absence that lasts for months.

During that time, George accompanies his father to the bank to sign foreclosure papers. Ever the optimist, his father consoles himself with wisdom for George: 'Sometimes you're flush and sometimes you're bust. When you're up, you never notice it, and when you're down you never think you'll get back up. It doesn't really matter. It only seems like it does.' But the ongoing sting of Mrs Jung's abandonment betrays the futility of Mr Jung's philosophy, implying that happiness does not coexist with a modest, indifferent approach to money. Adoring of his father but unconvinced by his logic, George vows right then and there 'I didn't ever want to be poor.' Responding to his mother's use of money to express insatiable discontent, George in turn vows to use money to quench that kind of demand. Reliving the same scene thirty years later, George asks his own wife to spare him financial berating in the presence of his daughter, repeating the plea 'Not in front of the kid.' Unlike the scene in his own childhood, in which discontent springs from poverty, George has become relatively wealthy, and the cause of uxorial malaise is his decision to withdraw from the drug trade, his truncation of unlimited future growth. Pursuant to this difference, *no* amount of money will satisfy the insatiable, demanding, unloving mother.

George's tragic undoing finally ensues from his last desperate effort to earn enough money to win the love of a woman – this time, his daughter. After his perennially harsh mother turns him in to the police, George emerges from prison hoping to rebuild a relationship with his daughter. While no longer living glamorously, neither George nor his daughter is suffering dire poverty, but only the promise of a trip to California finally secures her affections. Meant to finance this adventure, George's final drug deal becomes the third strike against him when his partners turn out to be narcotics agents. The film ends with a poignant glimpse of George's loneliness in prison, a daydream of a reconciliatory visit from his daughter, and a voice-over in which he sagely accepts responsibility for his fate: 'In the end, my ambition far exceeded my talent.' These last words fade to a close-up of the real

George Jung, gazing at the spectator from the permanent confines of prison. George blames himself when the film takes pains to make clear that he was never violent, greedy, or stupid – he simply wanted the basic maternal/feminine recognition that he thought wealth guaranteed. Just as in *Boogie Nights*, the sympathy mobilised exceeds the conclusions of the story. The pathos of the film, while consistent with the project of emotionalising the economy, is characteristically ideologically ambivalent – it inspires audience dissatisfaction with the conditions of George's life.

SURPLUS SYMPATHY: PATHOS AND THE UNRAVELLING OF IDEOLOGY

At or near the opening scene of all three of these films, the main protagonists are confronted by their mothers, and excoriated for their failure to amount to anything. For all three of these men, the quest for some kind of recognition, affection and approbation from the mother forms an explicit backdrop of their future projects. What separates *Boogie Nights* and *Blow* from *Saturday Night Fever* is most crucially *Saturday*'s ambiguous conclusion in which Tony has found a potentially affectionate female companion without fundamentally altering his financial prospects. By contrast, both of the millennial films depict the hero's ascension to fortune and even feminine love as unambiguously haunted by a persistent unhappiness. Money changes everything, but not enough. The metaphor of self-betterment is upheld, while the pleasures attached to it are deflated.

It is tempting to locate the difference between an ambiguous ending and two unhappy endings in real time, to attribute it to the ability to appreciate, with hindsight, the gravity of shifts in the 1970s. However, *Saturday Night Fever* diverges from the thematisation of emotional excess in *Boogie Nights* and *Blow*. In Tony Manero's world, the relation of excess transpires between the social and economic world and Tony's personal feelings. He has too much passion to be confined in a blue-collar job, to be hemmed in by his parents' bourgeois aspirations, to find gratification in working-class New Jersey. For the outsiders looking in, like Tony's mother or his boss, the disco club appears indulgent and excessive, but this view serves to reinforce their constrictive function. The people on the inside of the club, in contrast, know the limitations of their ephemeral pleasures there, as evidenced by events like Tony's abdication of first prize in the dance contest.

By contrast, in both *Boogie Nights* and *Blow*, the relation of excess occurs between the characters' unhappiness and their successes. Despite loving husbands and sweet children, the mother figures exhibit perpetual dissatisfaction and cruelty; despite a certain excision of economic constraints and a certain feminine approval, unhappiness persists, culminating in misery for George and disillusion for the Eddie. Far from portraying the heroes as spoiled brats unable to appreciate their successes, both of these films use close-ups, direct gazing at the camera, and even first person narration, all while depicting desperation ensuing from the mothers' unloving conduct, to actively solicit audience identification with the heroes' pain. These strategies of identification structure the films' claim that insoluble pain endures beyond the ephemeral promise of bourgeois bliss.

Although their strategies vary somewhat, all these films intervene in the problem of surplus economies. The economic conditions appear as the insatiable mother figure and the ascension of the regime of surplus capital (where production and consumption are no longer socially integrated in the way they were under Fordism) is figured by the ascension of a regime of harmful excess (too much sex, too much drugs, too much fantasy-escapism). As ideological operations, the films posit a personal resolution to broad social problems. But, as the destabilising moment of this ideological gesture, these personal resolutions fail: the heroes remain unhappy and the audience retains a palpable sense of that sadness. Far from mere obfuscations of political reality, these lingering emotions derive from a connection between libido and economy. At the base of the metaphoric substitutions (the mother as the 'economy') and ideological distortions (personal success as a solution to economic and emotional lack) lies the representation of *libidinal economy*, an irrefutable structural connection between feelings and materiality. Within these films lurks a theoretical claim that economic context effectively informs personal development, aspirations and fantasies, hopes and grudges, and emotional baggage. Beyond Freud's notion that the libido exercises quantitative equilibrium 'like' an economy, is a more provocative Marxist position that the libido is at the centre of 'the' economy. Alongside this position persists the ideological effect that you can pull yourself up by your bootstraps, and that the source of social problems are unloving mothers, not relations of exploitation – illicit industries, not the legitimate capitalist system of domination. The films substitute pathos for critique, in a distorting gesture. But this substitution obtains through assuming a relationship between emotional activity and critical social change. And it is precisely this relationship between emotion and politics that must be productively harnessed to realise social alternatives.

The revelation of this connection between emotions and politics accomplishes the theoretical ground on which it is possible, and necessary, to claim a profound overlap between the private and public, the personal and political, the libido and the economy. For only through attention to this relationality at the core of both the economy and the subject can we circumvent vulgar deterministic claims (the politico-economic context dictates identity) while refuting the equally vulgar voluntarist claims (we choose who we are). Similarly, only through a formula of ideology as necessarily conflicted can we appraise the ambiguity of culture and work to extract a common vocabulary for affiliation from the distorting content of cultural narrative. Such subtleties are the charge of Marxist cultural criticism today.

NOTES

1. Louis Althusser, *Lenin and Philosophy, and Other Essays*, trans. Ben Brewster (New York: Monthly Review Press, 2001).
2. Althusser, *Lenin and Philosophy*, Douglas Kellner, *Media Culture* (New York: Routledge, 1994), Slavoj Zizek, *The Sublime Object of Ideology* (London: New York: Verso, 1989).
3. Norman Wexler, 'Saturday Night Fever', Director John Badham (Paramount, 1977).
4. Paul Thomas Anderson, 'Boogie Nights', Director Paul Thomas Anderson (New Line Cinema, 1997).
5. Nick Cassavetes, 'Blow', Director Ted Demme (New Line Cinema, 2001).
6. For an overview of such theories, please see 'The Classic Realist Text' in Robert Stam, *Film Theory: An Introduction* (Malden: Blackwell, 2000).
7. David Harvey, *The Condition of Postmodernity* (Oxford: Basil Blackwell, 1989), p. 139.
8. Harvey, *The Condition of Postmodernity*, p. 141.
9. Bruce Schulman, *The Seventies* (New York: The Free Press, 2001), p. 162.
10. Harvey, *The Condition of Postmodernity*, p. 181.
11. Schulman, *The Seventies*, p. 135.
12. Joseph Nocera, *A Piece of the Action* (New York: Simon and Schuster, 1994), p. 234.
13. <http://money.cnn.com/2003/03/13/pf/banking/creditcard_survey> (accessed August 2003).
14. Nocera, *A Piece of the Action*, p. 236.

15. Judi Addleston, 'Doing the Full Monty with Dirk and Jane: Using the Phallus to Validate Marginalized Masculinities', *The Journal of Men's Studies*, vol. 7, no. 3 (1999).
16. Michael Ryan and Douglas Kellner, *Camera Politica* (Bloomington: Indiana University Press, 1988), p. 116.
17. John Leland, 'Rake's Progress', *Newsweek*, 10 November 1997, pp. 72–3.
18. For an insightful discussion of *Boogie Nights*, which refutes the claim by reviewers that it indicts 1970s morality, arguing instead that it critiques the rise of the corporation, please see Robert C. Sickels, '1970's Disco Daze: Paul Thomas Anderson's *Boogie Nights* and the Last Golden Age of Irresponsibility', *Journal of Popular Culture*, vol. 35, no. 4 (2002).

6

The Critics Who Knew Too Little: Hitchcock and the Absent Class Paradigm[1]

Colin McArthur

Gay Keane (Ann Todd): I remember the first time you called on me, with two tickets for the Shaw play. Do you remember? And you had forgotten to dress. The look on mother's face as we left the house! It took you five years to forgive that look.

Anthony Keane (Gregory Peck): It took her fifty years to perfect that look!

The Paradine Case

INTRODUCTION: WHY HITCHCOCK?

Recently designing a course on Hitchcock, I was obliged to address the question of what might constitute an appropriate critical discourse at this historical moment. I had noted the marked turn towards British film history in academic film studies in the UK and beyond and wished to connect with that movement: and, not least, I had become increasingly uneasy about the unseemly haste with which the category of *class* had been evacuated from political and cultural discourse in general and film studies in particular. To mount a course on a named director might seem rather old-fashioned, but the film studies cat can be skinned in any number of ways and I retain an enormous personal investment in the pleasure to be derived from certain directorial signatures, not least Hitchcock's. That said, the trajectory of film theory over the last three decades makes it problematic simply to erect a descriptive/celebratory course on any filmmaker. Greatly influenced by Robert E. Kapsis' book,[2] my syllabus took the form of examining the successive critical paradigms which had been brought to bear on Hitchcock's films – the early 'master of suspense' paradigm; the auteurist (in its French, British and North American variants and its structuralist and narratological inflections); the feminist/psychoanalytic; and, most recently, the gay/lesbian/queer. Needless to say, they do not succeed each other in any neat, hermetically sealed way, but are heavily interpenetrated. There are some stirrings towards Hitchcock among reader reception critics but not yet a paradigm. The most curious absences from this list – although they flash briefly from time to time in the above orientations – are *race* and *class*, the missing paradigms which became an additional topic of the course and, in the case of *class*, the central focus of this essay.

The increasing attention to British cinema is one of the more encouraging aspects of academic film studies (although the price already being paid is an excess of unwarrantable critical claims and fact-grubbing on behalf of particular filmmakers, a price, it should be said, my own generation paid in its auteurist enthusiasm for Hollywood). Alan Lovell, in a pleasing rhetorical manoeuvre, entitled a recent essay 'British Cinema: The Known Cinema', a reference to his own earlier paper 'British Cinema: The Unknown Cinema'.[3] The profusion of recent writing on British cinema confirms the validity of Lovell's later title. However, a crucial question immediately arises. Within what critical paradigms is this reappropriation of British cinema to be accomplished? If we take a long perspective, it can be seen that Hitchcock has to some extent already figured in the turn to British cinema. Tom Ryall's pathbreaking *Alfred Hitchcock and the British Cinema*[4] has not yet (Charles Barr's *English Hitchcock*[5] excepted) been seriously followed up, but its politique is exemplary – to reinsert Hitchcock into the British film cultural and industrial milieu. Given its orientation, it is much more concerned with institutional rather than textual questions, but Ryall points to an earlier dimension of the reappropriation which is highly textual, that associated with a collection of essays, edited by Charles Barr, *All Our Yesterdays*[6] which is 'broadly anti-realist and pro-a cinema of fantasy'. Ryall quotes Barr on Hitchcock's British films:

These films … are rich in precisely those elements which make Hitchcock important to a new and productive school of structuralist and psychoanalytic criticism. The same elements that have drawn Laura Mulvey and Raymond Bellour into detailed analyses of, for instance, *Notorious* and *North By Northwest* … are strikingly present in the British films … Some of the silent films are, already, powerful Oedipal stories with sophisticated narrative structures . . . Increasingly, Hitchcock makes a point of showing us characters asleep or otherwise unconscious ... as if to convey all the more strongly the oneiric, subjective logic of the action.[7]

This 'anti-realist' bent is most succinctly discernible in Julian Petley's concept of 'the lost continent',[8] a domain of British cinema seething with libidinal energy – all the more demented for being constrained within English reserve – encompassing figures such as Hitchcock and Powell and Pressburger and British genres such as Gainsborough melodramas and Hammer horror films.

While recognising the critical sophistication of this rereading, I would wish to pause on the decided flight from realism and note, particularly in the above quotation from Barr, a certain imperialism associated with the (feminist/)psychoanalytic paradigm and its tendency to homogenise critical discourse round questions of gender and sexuality. This essay will attempt to engage with that paradigm on its own terrain, so to speak, that of looking and being looked at, but to reinsert the category of *class* into the process. Above all, it is the wish to retain this category, so cursorily jettisoned in recent discourse, which fuels this project.

CLASS: THE VANISHING CATEGORY

Indicating the frightening ease with which class has been pushed off the academic agenda, David James reports that, at the 1989 gathering of the major American organisation of film and television scholars, the Task Force on Race and Class voted to dissolve and reconstitute itself as the Task Force on Race.[9] James's invaluable account of how this particular evacuation of class relates to the politics of American higher education, the lacunae in classical Marxist theorisations of class and the imperialism of psychoanalytic feminism in American film studies, needs to be supplemented by a more detailed socio-historical explanation such as is offered by Patrick Joyce.[10] Joyce speaks of the paradox involved in class being abandoned as an explanatory category precisely when economic life is in its greatest period of turmoil since the 1930s; the shift from production to consumption; the perplexing simultaneity of the rise of globalism and localism; the 'dispersive' effect of the new technologies; sharpened redefinitions of the concept of the self; and the rise of 'identity' politics. As Joyce tartly observes, however, the only identity not registered in the latter is that of *class*. It might be added that the demise of the Soviet Union and the perception that the Western democracies have 'won' the Cold War has been the final nail in the coffin of class as an explanatory concept. While it is entirely understandable that, for instance, feminism might wish to dislodge class in favour of gender, it is particularly galling that class should be evacuated from its own heartland, Marxism. Characteristically, this does not take the form of an outright abandonment of class, rather a drift towards other determinations (though that concept is likely to be abandoned as well), usually gender.[11] In addition to these complexly interwoven extra-filmic factors, there were (and are) specific filmic elements inhibiting the development of a class-based Hitchcockian critical paradigm. The most substantial pre-auteurist British critical engagements with Hitchcock – those of John Grierson in the 1930s and Lindsay Anderson in the 1940s – were mounted from a social-democratic rather than a Marxist perspective and (though this is to crudify their positions somewhat) from a concern with 'content' rather than 'form' to use terms which are not wholly adequate. Thus, Grierson, writing in 1930:

Hitchcock is the only English director who can put the English poor on the screen with any verisimilitude ... Will Hitchcock take counsel from Arnold Bennett, and give us a film of the Potteries or of Manchester, or of Middlesborough – with the personals in their proper places and the life of a community instead of a benighted lady at stake?[12]

And Anderson, writing in 1949 about a group of Hitchcock's British films, described them as gaining

a particular excitement from their concern with ordinary people (or ordinary-looking people) who are plunged into extraordinary happenings.[13]

Grierson and Anderson shared a profound distrust of cinematic artifice, a consequent suspicion of Hollywood, and a commitment to a social realist aesthetic (modified by their own distinctive senses of 'poetry') which would put the lives of 'ordinary people' on screen. Grierson's advice to Hitchcock elicits Julian Petley's derision as 'the most off-beam prescription in the history of film criticism',[14] understandably so from his 'lost continent' perspective. I have to agree with Petley that had Hitchcock taken Grierson's advice we might have been denied the excellence of his American films. But, once again, I would wish to pause and concur with Grierson and Anderson that the exclusion, marginalisation or stereotypical representation of particular groups is an important issue. The earliest 'master of suspense' critical paradigm was, as the name suggests, concerned with the mechanics of Hitchcock's films (albeit non-analytically). The French auteurists, as evidenced by, for instance, the Rohmer–Chabrol book,[15] chose to stress religion rather than class and, even if Robin Wood's book[16] had not been part of the British auteurist sub-paradigm virtually founded on a distaste for British cinema,[17] it was precisely the question of class which most repelled Wood when he contemplated Hitchcock's British films, as he was to confess when, in the revised 1989 edition of his original book, he was to recant his earlier dismissal of the British period.

As Tom Ryall has pointed out, Hitchcock's career might have developed in different directions – towards European 'art cinema', or even towards a version of documentary in which the (petty-) bourgeoisie rather than the proletariat might have been the subject. At one point Hitchcock even seemed willing to adopt the mantle of the cine-laureate of the middle classes.[18] Anderson had been appreciative of Hitchcock's capacity to render the middle classes on screen but, like Grierson, what he really hankered after was a more nuanced delineation of the proletariat. Whichever class Grierson and Anderson wished to see represented on screen, their remarks on Hitchcock's films are posed primarily at the level of film 'content'. Erecting a class paradigm in relation to Hitchcock's films must also involve a consideration of their formal elements. A prior step, however, is to probe more fully than previous critics have felt necessary Hitchcock's own class formation.

HITCHCOCK AND THE ENGLISH PETTY BOURGEOISIE

Donald Spoto's biography of Hitchcock[19] is not sensitive to the nuances of the British class system, sometimes describing the Hitchcocks as Cockney, and therefore working class, at other times suggesting they were middle class. Ryall is more sure-footed on Hitchcock's class origins, but since his project is to reinsert Hitchcock into British culture, he is more interested in the wider filmic context of interwar Britain. By the time Alfred was born in 1899 his father owned a greengrocer's shop and was therefore, in more accurate sociological terms than Spoto offers, a *petty bourgeois*. In 1899 the middle classes in general, and the petty bourgeoisie in particular, were under threat, squeezed between the traditional power of the *haute bourgeoisie* and the increasingly enfranchised proletariat.[20] Since, by the time of his death in 1914, William Hitchcock's business interests had extended to a fishery in Limehouse, he belonged precisely to the class fraction most threatened by new legislation such as the Workmen's Compensation Act (1897), which made employers responsible for injuries sustained in the workplace, and the Trades Disputes Act (1906), which gave trade unions immunity from legal action by employers for damage incurred as a result of industrial action, and by the generally redistributive tax policies of the Liberal government of 1906–14. This perceived onslaught on middle-class interests led, in 1906, to the formation of the Middle Class Defence League comprising businessmen, self-employed workers and shopkeepers and some sympathetic Conservative and Liberal MPs. The same sense of middle-class oppression gave rise to the Anti-Socialist Alliance and the United Kingdom Property Owners Association. Spoto does not tell us whether William Hitchcock was a member of any of these organisations, whether he was a typical or atypical petty bourgeois, or whether the prevailing sense of his class being under siege significantly affected the young Alfred's psychic formation. The earliest photograph of Alfred included in Spoto's biography evinces no comment from him, despite its curious features. Taken about 1907, it shows William Hitchcock in the uniform of what appears to be a Territorial Army regiment and Alfred, about eight years old and astride a pony, in an identical miniature version of his father's uniform. Although it was not uncommon throughout Europe at this time to dress children in military (more usually naval) uniform, taken as a whole the photograph suggests that William was an orthodox enough patriot to have joined the TA and to have inculcated some of the same values in his son, values likely to have been typical of the Edwardian petty bourgeoisie.

The British petty bourgeoisie is relatively unstudied in comparison with those of some other European countries, so it is not easy to draw a psychological profile of that class fraction in this period. Nevertheless, some work has been done on a sub-fraction of the petty bourgeoisie, white-collar clerks, the fastest growing occupational group in British society in the period 1850–1910. Since our concern here is with the typical psychic make-up of the class fraction within which Hitchcock was born and raised, Ian Bradley's remarks on white-collar clerks (the group, incidentally, within which Hitchcock found his first employment) may be pertinent:

The first handbook for clerks published in 1878 listed the qualities they required as 'patience, perseverance, cheerfulness, and perhaps more than any other quality, a humble distrust of self and a deferential respect for the judgment of others'. It went on to add that the model clerk should be 'quiet and unassuming' in his clothing.[21]

This latter point brings to mind Spoto's account of Hitchcock's wardrobe:

> six identical dark suits ... six identical pairs of shoes, ten identical ties, and fifteen identical shirts and pairs of socks.[22]

Without wishing to canvass an exclusively class theory of psychic determination, I note Spoto's account of how Hitchcock's 'natural quietness and youthful eagerness'[23] commended themselves to his employers in his first clerking job, and also Spoto's account of his energetic application in his first full-time job in the film industry.[24]

There are several teleologies at play in Spoto's biography, several predetermined narratives to which Hitchcock is made to conform. One of these is that the characteristics of the mature man should be discernible in his early life (a trope of the bourgeois biography more generally). Predicated as the biography is on the teleology which culminates in the great works of Hitchcock's later Hollywood years, its author is at a loss to explain his young subject's diligence in lowly work apart from, he implies, Hitchcock's fully formed artistic ambitions. From the point of view of the class-based explanation I am offering here, however, Hitchcock could be read in Spoto's account as a kind of Uriah Heep figure, humble and eager to please, the very embodiment of the injunctions to white-collar clerks quoted by Bradley. Clearly Hitchcock was a figure of immense artistic potential, but that is not at all incompatible with his inhabiting the primary identity of a petty bourgeois clerk at this early stage of his life.

The central teleology in Spoto's biography is the Freudian one. As a consequence, he has gone out of his way to research accounts of Hitchcock's mother and Alfred's relationship with her (as opposed to his relative indifference to the father). It is easy to see how the following passage might be readable into Hitchcock's films:

> Each evening ... Alfred was made to answer her detailed questions about the business of the day ... 'I always remember the evening confession,' he

recalled fifty years later ... It tells us something about the degree of their psychological intimacy, although there seems something overwhelming about it, something too intimate, a devotion exacted by a mother whose interest in her son's life imprisons rather than frees, investigates rather than encourages – and inculcates guilt of a scrupulous and neurotic kind.[25]

Beyond the data of his lineage, his occupation and his poor health, Hitchcock's father is shadowy in Spoto. Virtually the only other comment on him is to relay the notorious locking in the cell story with the observation that, if it is true, it reveals in William Hitchcock 'an oddly cruel streak'.[26] This gloss by Spoto reinforces the Oedipal trajectory of his narrative. Contrary to his spare treatment of the father, Spoto has sought out an eyewitness account of Hitchcock's mother:

According to a cousin, Emma Hitchcock was a smartly dressed woman, very quietly spoken and with an aristocratic manner. She was very meticulous when preparing a meal, at which she was very good. She would not venture out of her room unless neatly, perfectly dressed, and she quietly conducted her affairs in a dignified manner.[27]

Spoto does not comment on the specifics of this description. Rather, he uses it to put some measure of flesh and blood round his contiguous references to her 'doting affection' and her insistence that Alfred 'satisfy her whims'. That is to say, Spoto locates his description of Emma Hitchcock within his own teleological narrative which will come to a horrifying climax in *Psycho*. Without wholly discounting this reading, I would wish to situate the above description of Emma within the framework of English petty bourgeois life in the early post-Victorian period and suggest that, shorn of Spoto's Oedipal glosses, what the description yields is typicality rather than monstrous otherness. Unless, therefore, the Hitchcocks were markedly untypical of the English petty bourgeoisie of the time, they are likely to have inculcated in young Alfred the qualities of respectability, restraint, diligence, deference to social superiors, coolness to inferiors, and a certain sense of their class being under threat. This does not seem wildly out of kilter with what we know about Hitchcock. There is one other feature of the petty bourgeoisie of the time – its capacity for (and dread of) getting things wrong socially, succinctly captured in the following poem by Hilaire Belloc:

> The Rich arrived in pairs
> And also in Rolls Royces.
> They talked of their affairs
> In loud and strident voices.
> The Poor arrived in Fords
> Whose features they resembled;
> They laughed to see so many Lords
> And Ladies all assembled.
> The People in Between
> Looked underdone and harassed
> And out of place and mean
> And horribly embarrassed.[28]

The petty bourgeois response to constantly being 'on edge' is summarised by François Bédarida:

> Their reaction ... was a wide adoption of various kinds of conformity: political – hence their unfailing support for the Conservative Party between the wars; social – the cult of respectability was a fetish; moral – adherence to a puritanical strictness of behaviour; religious – assiduous attendance at an Anglican church or Nonconformist chapel. Even more than in 1914 they made desperate and absurd efforts to ape their betters, in their houses, furnishings, dress, reading habits and general way of life, *and to be recognised by them*, without ever succeeding. [italics added][29]

With the obvious substitution of Catholicism for Anglicanism or Nonconformism, it seems not unreasonable to assume that this is close to the kind of world into which the young Alfred was interpellated. However, this in itself offers little insight into how Hitchcock's films work as a result of this class determination. My criticism of Grierson's and Anderson's remarks on Hitchcock was that they took no account of the formal features of his films, of the possibility that the question of class might be pursued in relation to style as well as representation. The feminist/psychoanalytic paradigm's project of seeking to reveal the trans-individual, familial, societal structures of patriarchy made manifest in the *mise en scène* of Hitchcock's films is intriguing. The key question posed by this essay is whether there is another transindividual structure at play in Hitchcock's *mise en scène*, but this time generated by *class* rather than gender.

PETTY BOURGEOIS SCOPOPHOBIA AND H.M. BATEMAN

The key concept in the feminist/psychoanalytic paradigm is *scopophilia* – the fascination of looking. Given the terms of the petty bourgeois identity outlined above, the key concept in any attempt to find such an identity at play in cinematic *mise en scène* would be rather *scopophobia* – a fear of looking or, to reverse that, of being looked at. Such a mechanism is discernible in the work of some British artists, including Hitchcock. However, in order to demonstrate that it is not peculiar to Hitchcock, but is a product of his class formation, I will trace the recurrence of scopophobia in the work of H.M. Bateman, the cartoonist and illustrator. Allowing for certain differences between them – Bateman was born in 1888, Hitchcock in 1899; Bateman, born in Australia, returned to England as an infant while Hitchcock spent his entire early years in a London suburb; Bateman was a keen sportsman, Hitchcock gargantuanly inert; Bateman was abstemious, Hitchcock a glutton; and while Bateman's family seemed to have no religious affiliations, the Hitchcocks were Catholic – there is a marked correlation in important aspects of their lives. Like Hitchcock, Bateman was brought up in a petty bourgeois milieu (his father was a small businessman) in a London suburb. Bateman's official biography[30] was written in 1982 by a family member (Anthony Anderson) and is, therefore, more reticent and 'innocent' than Spoto's. In particular, it does not have an explicitly Oedipal narrative. It is all the more interesting, then, that Anderson's account of Bateman's mother, shorn of Spoto's Freudian innuendoes, should so closely parallel the latter's account of Emma Hitchcock. Bateman's mother emerges as a distant and forbidding woman who eventually moved in with her son and his wife and, according to Anderson, 'bent her son's will to her own'.[31] Anderson's description of Bateman as shy, introspective and hypochondriac applies also to Hitchcock, as does Bateman's customary stance to the world – 'slightly on the edge of things – the observer'.[32]

Both Hitchcock and Bateman passed from petty bourgeois meagreness to considerable wealth, becoming extremely retentive of their assets in the process. Spoto and Anderson cite startling examples of their stinginess. And both men were sexually inexperienced when they married and their relationships with their spouses became increasingly tense as they grew older. Like Hitchcock, Bateman often put an image of himself into his drawings and it seems clear that their particular expressions of petty bourgeois angst sometimes translated into similar images. Spoto links the locking in the cell story to the theme of guilt in Hitchcock's films. Bateman's cartoons *The Man Who Filled His Fountain Pen With the Hotel Ink* (1916) and *The False Income Tax Return and Its Rectification* (1917) are interesting both for their theme of guilt and for their proto-cinematic style being, in essence, cinematic storyboards. Spoto gives innumerable examples of a macabre streak in Hitchcock. This too was present in Bateman. Anderson tells of his using his own blood, spilled while participating in the bouts of sparring he so much enjoyed, to draw pictures.[33] His Hitchcockian tendency to appear in his own cartoons sometimes took a macabre turn, as in *The Man Who Will Not Share the Fire* (1921) in which a demented Bateman takes an axe to the vexatious title figure. Spoto and many other critics have drawn attention to the Hitchcockian theme of monstrous horror lurking just under the surface of 'normal' life and 'ordinary' people. This feature is particularly evident in two Bateman cartoons of the First World War, *The Recruit Who Took To It Kindly* and *It's the Same Man* (both 1917). To cap the Bateman–Hitchcock correlation, both men in their later years put considerable effort into constructing themselves not simply as popular entertainers but as 'serious artists'.[34] However, the main evidence for associating Bateman with petty bourgeois scopophobia is the long series of cartoons and advertisements, mainly from the 1920s and the 1930s, the title of each one beginning *The Man Who ...* (a pleasing homology with Hitchcock's *The Man Who Knew Too Much*). As described by Anderson[35] each piece revolves round a figure who has become the centre of unwelcome attention through a social gaffe. The deployment of the concept of scopophilia within the feminist/ psychoanalytic paradigm ushered in a repertoire of terms associated with vision, notably *look*, *gaze* and *glance*. To deploy the concept of scopophobia requires a somewhat different vocabulary in which the key term would be *stare* (and its structural opposites, a haughty aversion of the eyes from the offender and the latter's covering his face with his hands in guilt or humiliation). Both mechanisms are at play in *The Man Who Threw a Snowball at St Moritz* (1926), *The Man Who Coughed at the Bridge Tournament* (1931), *The Man Who Arrived at the Country Club With a Mixed Bag* (1934) and *The Woman Who Said She Had Never Heard of the New World Gas Cooker* (1939). Taken together, they represent the forays of the wretchedly aspiring petty bourgeois into the world of the upper middle class and the dreadful pay-off when he/she is unmasked. Seldom has the viciousness of the British class system been represented with such ferocity.

THE MAN WHO WILL NOT SHARE THE FIRE.

1. The Man Who Will Not Share the Fire (H.M Bateman/*Punch*, reproduced by permission)

IT'S THE SAME MAN.

2. It's the Same Man (H.M Bateman/*Punch*, reproduced by permission)

3. The Man Who Coughed at the Bridge Tournament (H.M Bateman/*Punch*, reproduced by permission)

THE MAN WHO ARRIVED AT THE COUNTRY CLUB WITH A MIXED BAG

Don't make an unforgivable faux pas—match up with

4. The Man Who Arrived at the Country Club With a Mixed Bag (H.M Bateman/*Punch*, reproduced by permission)

PETTY BOURGEOIS SCOPOPHOBIA AND HITCHCOCK

The feminist/psychoanalytic paradigm has so thoroughly appropriated Hitchcock's films (often delivering dazzling critical insights) that it may have inhibited questions about the extent to which it has homogenised processes of looking solely round gender and sexuality. Such gender-based looking is undoubtedly there, both within the films themselves in the looking of the males and the being-looked-at of the females and in the relationship between spectators and screen. My suggestion is, however, that not all looks in Hitchcock's films relate to gender and sexuality: several relate primarily to class (needless to say, often articulated with the gendered look) and insisting on this helps reinsert Hitchcock into British culture. To recall the extent to which Hitchcock was marked by his petty bourgeois interpellation may not change devastatingly the way we read his films. It should, however, remind us that his British films in particular come out of a highly class-structured and class-conscious social formation, albeit one in process of change, and are likely to bear the traces of this, if only in their interstices. For example, Hitchcock's much-noted obsession with blonde, fair-skinned heroines predates his translation to Hollywood and may have class (not to mention racial) implications; certain films resonate with class tensions (particularly *Rebecca* (1940), *The Paradine Case* (1947), *Under Capricorn* (1949) and *Frenzy* (1972)); and Scotty's (re)transformation of Judy into Madeleine in *Vertigo* (1958) has a class as well as a sexual dimension.[36] If we accept the idea of the continuing resonance of Hitchcock's having been interpellated as a petty bourgeois, it is tempting to read the auction room scene in *North By Northwest* (1959) – in which Thornhill (Cary Grant) makes a mockery of the proceedings in order to have the police summoned – as a comic catharsis of the petty bourgeois terror of 'making an exhibition of oneself'. Certain Hitchcock sequences strongly recall the Bateman cartoons, notably the entry of Flusky (Joseph Cotton) to the Governor's ball in *Under Capricorn*, his shaming of his wife Hetty (Ingrid Bergman) and her mortified dash from the ballroom under the Batemanesque stares of the aristocratic guests, and the emergence of Father Logan (Montgomery Clift) from the courtroom into the withering stares of the public in the 1953 film *I Confess* (a displacement, perhaps, of Hitchcock's sense of outraged convention on to a scene more usually talked about in terms of his Catholicism). Thinking about class should send us back to the scene in *The Paradine Case* in which the accused killer, Mrs Paradine (Alida Valli) is brought into court. The looks exchanged between her and the spectators carry both class and ethnic charges, she being both a false *haute bourgeois* and a foreigner. And there are further Batemanesque displacements, as in the malevolent staring at Manny Balestrero (Henry Fonda) at the insurance office in *The Wrong Man* (1956). Such a displacement may be at play in a justly famous scene which has tended to be read, in the 'master of suspense' paradigm, as an exemplary 'Hitchcock touch' and, in the auteurist paradigm, as a 'dry run' for the scene in *Marnie* (1964) in which Strutt (Martin Gabel) enters the Rutland home and recognises Marnie (Tippi Hedren). The scene is, of course, the mobile crane shot towards the end of *Young and Innocent* (1937), which ends as a close-up on the face of the murderous 'blinking man'. If, rather than raiding Hitchcock's British films for what they can tell us about his 'mature' Hollywood pictures, we attempt to situate them in British culture, another reading of the scene might be suggested. Stephen Shafer[37] provides statistical evidence of significant class interaction in British films between 1929 and 1939. For example, in 1934 over 20 per cent included the theme of class consciousness or elitism. An intriguing aspect of this was the number of films in which characters pretend to belong to another class. The *Young and Innocent* scene is constructed partly round this phenomenon. The runaway middle-class hero has earlier pretended to be working class and in the 'blinking man' scene, the tramp who can recognise him as the murderer changes his rags for a posh outfit which will permit his entry to an upmarket hotel. The drama in the scene arises from the psychic collapse of the 'blinking man' – disguised as the drummer in a blackface band – as his being recognised becomes inevitable. It is the idea of being looked at which induces his collapse during which – like other Hitchcockian scopophobes – he attempts to conceal his face with his hand.

No one should write about this scene without mentioning that other great lacuna in Hitchcock criticism – *race*. The fact that the band is blackface is one of the few moments in Hitchcock's work when the repressed issue of race is glimpsed. The manner of Hitchcock's representation of the band suggests that he was entirely complicit with the attitude to race dominant in British (popular) culture at this time.[38] Anyone seeking to explore issues of race with regard to Hitchcock's work will have to plough the hard furrow of 'reading for absences'.[39]

Reading Hitchcock's films with class questions in mind may also bring back into focus some of his films which other critical paradigms have passed over in virtual silence. *Mr and Mrs Smith* (1941), although in many respects a classic romantic comedy of remarriage, centrally concerned with '(re)creating the couple', nevertheless is structured at certain moments in unambiguously class terms within a scopophobic *mise en scène*. The Smiths, having returned to a restaurant with romantic associations for them, are dismayed to find it has gone downmarket. Their response to a group of gawking urchins looks and sounds like a Bateman cartoon as they turn their icy class stare on the children and Mr Smith (Robert Montgomery) says 'Just outstare them. That'll make them embarrassed.' However, there is another instance of scopophobia which, even though in a comedy, is almost as unsettling as the scene from *Young and Innocent*. Smith, hoping to make his estranged wife jealous, arranges to meet an acquaintance and his two women friends in a posh nightclub he knows his wife will be attending. To his horror, the two women turn out to be 'floozies' and he has to endure his wife's searching stare as he sits with them. Like the blinking man, his scopophobia causes him to cover his face. Just as the rescrutiny of *Young and Innocent* reveals the repressed issue of race, so does the re-examination of *Mr and Mrs Smith* reveal a barely concealed homoerotic subtext.

Some critical paradigms regard the break between Hitchcock's British and American films as significant (as it palpably is in institutional terms), often raiding the former for the light they throw on the latter. It would be an oversimplification to suggest that class issues are paramount in the British films and cease to matter in the American ones. Just as Freudo-Lacanians would claim that Hitchcock's Oedipal formation resonates in both, so too does it seem not unreasonable to suggest that his class formation might similarly resonate. Class issues are readily understandable by American audiences. Anyone who doubts that a subtle ensemble of class distinctions exists in America – despite myths to the contrary – should read Paul Fussell's *Class: Style and Status in America*.[40] Fussell notes that it was in America that what is perhaps the best-known modern guide to social behaviour, Emily Post's *Etiquette*[41] was published.

Above all, the retrieval of *class* as a critical category might modify the tendency of some (particularly American) critics to read Hitchcock's British films not as complex texts emerging from a particular society at a particular historical moment, but teleologically as already programmed chrysalises out of which the resplendent butterflies of the late Hollywood films will eventually flutter. William Rothman's *Hitchcock: The Murderous Gaze*[42] is heavily weighted towards British Hitchcock, but very much in these terms. Recent criticism, partly in reaction against the tyranny of 'spectatorialism' – seeing the text as constructing the spectator – has become interested once more in what real, historically situated audiences do *with* films as opposed to what is ostensibly done to them *by* films. One of the most sophisticated examples of this 'historical reading strategies' approach is Janet Staiger's *Interpreting Films: Studies in the Historical Reception of American Cinema*,[43] which, at one point, traverses readings of *Rear Window* on the way to outlining what a 'historical materialist reception study' might look like. Staiger suggests that the first stage would be to consider what reading strategies would be likely to have been available to 1950s audiences. She demonstrates that the (albeit limited) range of reviews she considers appealed to four major discourses: psychoanalysis, authorship, the generic conventions of Hollywood cinema and current social issues. Concretely, the first tended to refer to the 'Peeping Tom' elements of the film and how these structure the narrative; the second to Hitchcock's 'technique'; the third tended to assign the film to one or another genre (e.g. 'melodrama', 'detective'); and the fourth to refer to the contemporary situation of city dwellers. An obvious absence from contemporary reading strategies was feminism, which did not (re)emerge until the 1960s. However, there was another reading strategy prevalent in the 1950s which tended to divide cinemagoers into levels of aesthetic preference ('highbrow', 'middlebrow', 'lowbrow') and which may have affected audience responses. Staiger is able to demonstrate that, in one case, the reviewer's sense of himself as 'highbrow' and his gender caused him to respond in contradictory terms to *Rear Window*. On the one hand, writing for a 'highbrow' publication, he dismissed the film but, on the other hand, as a 'normal' male he found the only tolerable thing to be Grace Kelly. Strictly speaking, since he wrote for an upper-class readership and presumably belonged to that class, he should have welcomed the film for its 'sympathetic' representation of that class by way of the Grace Kelly character, but this was not so, indicating that contradictions may abound in the response of individual spectators, tending to throw neat categories like 'dominant ideology' – relatively easy to demonstrate at a textual level – into disarray. Staiger talks briefly about the class differences between the Stewart and Kelly characters being repressed to reappear as personality differences.

It is possible to extrapolate from Staiger's discussion of the complexity of 'historical reception studies' some general thoughts on class as it relates to the 'reading' rather than the 'writing' of Hitchcock's films. A clue is offered by the observations of a Scottish cinema owner writing in 1937 and referred to by Tom Ryall. It seems at this time that British film exhibitors regarded British films as suitable for the middle-class elements in their audiences, especially on the south coast of England, but that they posed problems for the working-class elements. To quote Ryall:

> A Scottish cinema operator suggested that 'British films' was a misnomer as the domestic industry, in fact, produced 'English films in a particularly parochial sense' and that these were 'more foreign to his audience than the products of Hollywood, over 6000 miles away'.[44]

This observation, which, in terms of Staiger's classification, may involve both class and ethnic subjectivities, accords exactly with my own experience of viewing British films as a working-class Scot upwards of sixty years ago.

CONCLUSION

The point of this essay is not to dislodge the feminist/psychoanalytic paradigm from its well-earned hegemonic place in relation to Hitchcock. It is, rather, to bolster the complexity that paradigm aspires to by suggesting another form of psychic structuration, based on class, which intertwines with the Oedipal. Even psychoanalysis's most ardent proponents have admitted its tendency to essentialism, its impulse not only to homogenise the interpellations of, say, a mid-nineteenth-century Viennese of the *haute bourgeoisie*, a turn of the century petty bourgeois Londoner, and a blue-collar New Yorker born during the Second World War, but to regard these interpellations as all but complete in early infancy. The addition of the class determination outlined here would, indeed, help deliver a genuinely non-unified subject, would help reinsert Hitchcock back into British culture and, not least, would restore the category of *class* to the film studies lexicon.

NOTES

1. This essay first appeared in the journal *Film Studies*, vol. 1, no. 2 (Spring 2000).
2. Robert E. Kapsis, *Hitchcock: The Making of a Reputation* (Chicago: University of Chicago Press, 1992).

3. Alan Lovell, 'British Cinema: The Unknown Cinema' (British Film Institute Education Department seminar paper, 1967) and 'British Cinema: The Known Cinema', in Robert Murphy (ed.), *The British Cinema Book* (London: British Film Institute, 1997).
4. Tom Ryall, *Alfred Hitchcock and the British Cinema* (London: Athlone Press, 1996).
5. Charles Barr, *English Hitchcock* (London: Cameron and Tayleur, 1999).
6. Charles Barr (ed.), *All Our Yesterdays: 90 Years of British Cinema* (London: British Film Institute, 1986).
7. Charles Barr, 'Introduction: Amnesia and Schizophrenia', in *All Our Yesterdays*, p. 20.
8. Julian Petley, 'The Lost Continent', in *All Our Yesterdays*, pp. 98ff.
9. David E. James and Rick Berg (eds), *The Hidden Foundation: Cinema and the Question of Class* (Minneapolis: University of Minnesota Press, 1996).
10. Patrick Joyce (ed.), *Class* (Oxford: Oxford University Press, 1995), p. 4.
11. See, for example, David Morley, *Family Television: Cultural Power and Domestic Leisure* (London: Comedia, 1986).
12. Cited in Forsyth Hardy (ed.), *Grierson on the Movies* (London: Faber & Faber, 1981), p. 110.
13. Lindsay Anderson, 'Alfred Hitchcock', *Sequence*, no. 9, 1949, pp. 113–24.
14. Petley, 'The Lost Continent', p. 105.
15. Eric Rohmer and Claude Chabrol, *Hitchcock: The First Forty-Four Films*, trans. Stanley Hochman (London: Roundhouse Publishing, 1992).
16. Robin Wood, *Hitchcock's Films Revisited* (New York: Columbia University Press, 1989). (First published 1965.)
17. See, for example, V.F. Perkins, 'The British Cinema', *Movie*, June 1962, pp. 2–7.
18. Ryall, *Alfred Hitchcock*, p. 177.
19. Donald Spoto, *The Dark Side of Genius: The Life of Alfred Hitchcock* (London: Frederick Muller, 1983).
20. Ian Bradley, *The English Middle Classes are Alive and Kicking* (Glasgow: William Collins, 1982), p. 95.
21. Bradley, *The English Middle Classes*, p. 97.
22. Spoto, *The Dark Side of Genius*, p. 477.
23. Spoto, *The Dark Side of Genius*, p. 37.
24. Spoto, *The Dark Side of Genius*, p. 55.
25. Spoto, *The Dark Side of Genius*, p. 18.
26. Spoto, *The Dark Side of Genius*, p. 16.
27. Spoto, *The Dark Side of Genius*, p. 17.
28. Cited in Bradley, *The English Middle Classes*, p. 111.
29. François Bédarida, *A Social History of England: 1851–1990*, trans. A.S. Forester (London: Routledge, 1990), p. 208.
30. Anthony Anderson, *The Man Who Was H. M. Bateman* (Exeter: Webb and Bower, 1982).
31. Anderson, *The Man Who Was* ... , p. 122.
32. Anderson, *The Man Who Was* ... , p. 43.
33. Anderson, *The Man Who Was* ... , p. 13.
34. Both Kapsis and Anderson describe this in detail.
35. Anderson, *The Man Who Was* ... , p. 157.

36. Virginia Wright Wexman, 'The Critic as Consumer: Film Study in the University, *Vertigo* and the Film Canon', *Film Quarterly*, vol. 39, no. 2 (Spring 1986), pp. 32–41.

37. Stephen Shafer, *British Popular Films, 1929–1939: The Cinema of Reassurance* (London: Routledge, 1997), pp. 142–6.

38. John M. McKenzie, *Imperialism and Popular Culture* (Manchester: Manchester University Press, 1986).

39. Edward Said, *Culture and Imperialism* (London: Chatto and Windus, 1993).

40. Paul Fussell, *Class: Style and Status in America* (New York: Arrow Books, 1983).

41. Emily Post, *Etiquette* (New York: Funk and Wagnall, 1955).

42. William Rothman, *Hitchcock: The Murderous Gaze* (Cambridge, MA: Harvard University Press, 1982).

43. Janet Staiger, *Interpreting Films: Studies in the Historical Reception of American Cinema* (Princeton: Princeton University Press, 1992).

44. Ryall, *Alfred Hitchcock*, p. 171.

7
Economic and Institutional Analysis: Hollywood as Monopoly Capitalism

Douglas Gomery

Karl Marx wrote as a political economist and, while neoclassical-based theories have come to dominate the world, we ought not forget the history, debates and critical tools which Marxism offers, particularly in relation to Hollywood as a textbook example of monopoly capitalism. I am not downplaying Marxism's important component in the history of cultural criticism, but simply going back to the basics of economics. The motion picture industry in capitalism is just that: a collection of businesses seeking profit and power. I shall not simply reformulate Marxist economics, but seek to position Marxist economics at the centre of a debate in film studies. Hollywood defines for our world images and sounds of ideology, class, race and gender – from the basis of corporations. And has done so for most of the twentieth century.

THE CORPORATION

Many still believe that the studios are controlled by banks and Wall Street. This 'financial control' is no longer an appropriate framework for understanding the history of the US film industry. V.I. Lenin's *Imperialism: The Highest Stage of Capitalism*, first published in 1916, is well known; less familiar is Lenin's source for his idea of financial control, Rudolph Hilferding's *Das Finanzkapital*, published in Vienna in 1910. It was the Soviet's success in 1917 which popularised and gave substantial credence to the concept of financial control. Indeed Lenin had placed financial control as one of the five pillars of modern capitalism.[1]

Marxist economist Paul Sweezy, for one, argues that in the US the dominance of financiers ended with the Great Depression, replaced by corporate hegemony. Sweezy agrees that financial control did exist between 1890 and 1930, as bankers helped to form new companies, and then moved to occupy a position on boards of directors. Financial capital became a component of a new power complex rather than simply the directing hand. The corporation with many options for raising money could operate without banks, and thus became the centre of capitalist economy. Thus Sweezy asserts, since the 1930s, bankers occupied secondary, not primary, roles in the US economy. Sweezy argues that the primary unit for economic analysis should be the corporation.[2]

Thus we need to concentrate on the ownership, management, and operation of the large Hollywood corporations which have dominated the US studio system since 1930. We can see this change as early as the coming of sound. The major studio corporations were able to stand up to the most powerful corporation in the US at the time – the American Telephone and Telegraph (AT&T) – because through their trade association, the Motion Picture Producers and Distributors Association (MPPDA), they colluded and collectively opposed all attempts by AT&T to raise prices and seize a greater share of the sound movie profits. In fact the studio corporations gained a measure of power they had given up under the original licence agreements of 1928. Specifically, the film monopolists by 1936 paid lower (not higher) prices for sound equipment and service from AT&T.[3]

STATE SUPPORT

Once the dominant corporations came to be as a result of the coming of sound, the state supported them. Through the National Industrial Recovery Act (NIRA) of 16 June 1933, the federal government sanctioned and supported the monopolistic behaviour of the large motion picture corporations at the expense of the small exhibitors and producers. Title I of the Act established a National Recovery Administration (NRA) to institute and supervise codes for 'fair competition' to promote cooperation and hopefully push the US out of the Great Depression. The administration of Franklin Roosevelt assumed that the dominant trade association of each industry would author the code. In exchange for a government-approved code, each industry became exempt from prosecution under all anti-trust laws. The law (and the administration's attitudes) clearly favoured the preservation of the monopolistic status quo.[4] The Motion Picture Producers and Distributors Association, more common known as the Hays' Office, became Hollywood's organ for self-regulation.

The Hollywood corporate oligopolists quickly embraced the NRA. They rightly saw it as an opportunity to obtain a legal sanction for their monopoly power. Ten days before the US Congress even passed the legislation, the Hays' Office offered its first proposal: pool all production and distribution under a single governmental commissioner. The government passed. Thus two weeks later the Hays' Office proposed a second plan: reinstate the monopolistic practices utilised in 1929–30, the peak period of industry earnings. Since they would be hurt by such behaviour, the small, unaffiliated exhibitors, through their trade association, the Allied States Association of Motion Picture Exhibitors (Allied States) set forth their own plan. In brief, Allied States recommended that all current and proposed monopolistic behaviour be outlawed. There was little doubt the Hays' group's code would be accepted; the only question was could Allied States exact any concessions. The struggle began in July 1933 and ended in November when President Roosevelt signed the motion picture code. The Hays' group conceded only on the issue of the ability of labour to organise. The corporations were so confident of their power they felt that labour organising would prove little hindrance to their power and profits. They were right.[5]

In sum, the US federal government, through the National Industrial Recovery Act of 1933, openly sanctioned the monopolistic behaviour of the large firms in the motion picture industry. Instead of the informal collusion which had existed throughout the 1920s, open and explicit collusion and exploitation took place, free from any threat of anti-trust action. Thus it was strong action by the state which increased the profits of the movie monopolists and guaranteed strict barriers to entry, at a point of the most severe economic downturn of the twentieth century. Moreover this analysis of the NRA hardly scratches the surface of state–film industry interaction. We know little, for example, about the tax laws, or special tariffs imposed by the state.

OWNERSHIP AND MANAGEMENT

The studio corporations have always been hard to manage. They are always profitable in the long run, but running them scientifically has proven a failure. Consider the case of RKO in the 1930s. Throughout the 1930s in a condition of receivership, RKO remained a major studio. RKO as a corporate enterprise had a reputation for a rocky financial history and failed to attain through most of its corporate life any kind of financial solvency. With the entry of Floyd B. Odlum into the corporation as a stockholder in 1936, RKO was to see what is generally considered its most profitable period – which ended when Odlum sold his interests to Howard Hughes.

To do a case study of RKO in the 1930s, the historian needs to focus upon market relations under monopoly capitalism – looking for tendencies towards maximising profits, accumulating capital and systematically avoiding risks. Changes inside RKO should follow major structural changes in monopoly capitalism: the emergence of the corporate man (as outlined by Baran and Sweezy), an elaboration of a complex authority, hierarchy and bureaucracy, the proliferation of competition in new directions – internally – as a result of a non-price competitive system, namely cost reduction and innovation.

During the mid-1930s, the chief way that RKO in particular and the studios in general found to accumulate capital, maximise profits and avoid risks was through a sophisticated oligopoly in which they agreed on the rules to keep out competition, and yet tried to out-gross each other so as to maximise profits – but with minimum risk. One of the more obvious corporate internal structural changes occurs in management. Control of the corporation no longer rests in outside individuals or interests but, as Baran and Sweezy suggest, real power is held by insiders whose careers are tied up with the corporation. Perhaps Henry Ford himself best summed up this new era of capitalistic management that from 1930 on characterised the studio system:

> Modern corporation or joint-venture capitalism has replaced tycoon capitalism. The one man band owner-manager is fast being replaced by a new class of professional managers, dedicated more to an advancement of the company than to the enrichment of a few owners.[6]

Since the 1930s the corporations known as Hollywood have had a series of new owners/managers – who replaced the entrepreneurs who built the new enterprises (exemplified by Adolph Zukor, Marcus Loew and William Fox), and their successors in the 1930s like Odlum who tried to operate corporations like business scientists. Odlum took RKO, which was almost out of business, and remade it as a major company. Odlum was a self-made utilities lawyer whose major instrument to success was Atlas Corporation. Odlum bought up depressed companies like RKO, turned them around, and then sold out for his profits. Odlum managed, as a result, to make the impressive figure of $100 million in the middle of the Depression. By 1935, his statisticians were studying RKO.[7]

In 1936, Odlum bought a large chunk of RKO's depressed stock. Between 1936 and 1943 he relied on a hierarchy of intermediaries who operated RKO. Odlum spearheaded the reorganisation of RKO. His statisticians found RKO was a mass of separate units – mostly theatres – independently working organisations who seemed hardly to take notice of each other. RKO had always been an uneasy amalgam of corporate bosses (RCA, NBC, Westinghouse Electric, its theatre circuit) whose shifting managements had resulted in very shifting policies. The result was a vast over-duplication of jobs, executives and responsibilities. Odlum's central aim in reorganisation was to wipe out this duplication, simplify through centralisation and hierarchise the corporate structure. For example, in 1936 RKO had approximately 80 active subsidiaries and affiliated companies. Odlum truly for the first time merged them.[8]

Odlum selected a Chicago corporate reorganisation lawyer Leo Spitz – who would stay until the reorganisation had been completed. Spitz's replacement was Peter Rathvon, an Atlas executive, Odlum's chief assistant. He then hired industry veterans Ned Depinet and Charles Kroener. Both had experience in distribution and sales, where the money entered the system – as was happening at Warners, Paramount and Loew's.[9]

This centralisation and bureaucratisation of authority worked well, and RKO thrived. Like others before and after, the one area Odlum would fail to add some business science to was production. While the chain of hierarchy and bureaucracy could be established in the distribution and exhibition areas, the production department at RKO – as was the case through the corporate history of Hollywood – basically could not be routinised. Odlum then simply found a buyer, Howard Hughes, and cashed in. He also proved that while the studio system could be run like a factory, it was not a factory but a flexible system, and needed someone to innovate the system to solve this vexing production problem.[10]

LEW WASSERMAN: THE CREATOR OF MODERN HOLLYWOOD

As Hollywood adapted to the TV era, Lew Wasserman of Universal led the way. Beginning as an agent, Wasserman moved into independent television and film production and took over a whole studio, Universal, in 1962. During the following two decades, Wasserman showed the film industry how to use a flexible system of production and distribution, deal with television, and in the process reinvent itself. Five achievements rank Wasserman as the leading executive of his age.

First, Wasserman initiated independent production, based in Hollywood. As an agent he 'sold' his clients as corporate properties, and turned MCA (parent company of the Universal studio) into the leading independent producer of radio, television and film. James Stewart and Alfred Hitchcock were allied with Universal as 'independents', able to package their own projects, yet always dependent on the studio for distribution and release.

Second, Wasserman accumulated a library of film titles to then sell to broadcast TV, pay TV, and then exploit again as the home video era commenced. He even bought a film library from Paramount, and so initiated a new era in which studios prospered by milking long-term value from their libraries of older films (and TV shows).

Third, Wasserman pioneered movies made for television even as Universal produced and syndicated half-hour and hour-long broadcast television shows. With TV movies Universal became the largest network supplier of network broadcast television programming, reaching a crest in 1977 by providing *Roots*, the most popular TV show of its era.

Fourth, with his broadcast TV base providing the dependable profit streams, Wasserman returned to the feature film and pioneered the blockbuster motion picture, dominating an era from the pioneering exploitation of *Jaws* (Steven Spielberg 1975) through to the then record-setting *E.T.: the Extra-Terrestrial* (Steven Spielberg 1982).

Fifth, Wasserman's final innovation in business practice would through the late 1970s fundamentally redefine feature filmmaking. He coupled mass saturated advertising of the film on prime-time television with simultaneous bookings in new shopping mall cineplexes across the United States with the release of *Jaws* in 1975. The film created a sensation and with it Universal initiated the era of blockbuster feature film, and forever altered the Hollywood filmmaking and distribution landscape. Advertising on television became the key to turning a feature film into a blockbuster, enabling the studio distributor to milk millions and millions of dollars from 'ancillary rights'.

Jaws was not the first film sold by and through broadcast television, but its million dollar success proved that strategy was the one that would redefine Hollywood. The Wasserman-led Universal money-making machine reached its climax and closure with *E.T.* in 1982, bringing the company that was languishing two decades earlier revenues that needed to be measured in the billions of dollars. Lew Wasserman showed the Hollywood oligopoly how to reinvent itself during the 1960s and 1970s.[11]

LATE TWENTIETH-CENTURY HOLLYWOOD

Twentieth-century cinema ended on 19 May 1999 with the premiere of George Lucas's much awaited *Star Wars: Episode I – The Phantom Menace*, a tribute to Wasserman's innovations. Two weeks before the premiere, fans were purchasing tickets – 22 years after Lucas's original *Star Wars* had opened. For his $115 million cost, producer and director George Lucas took 90 per cent of the money Twentieth Century Fox collected from box office revenues – after a distribution fee. Toymaker Hasbro paid Lucas a quarter of a billion dollars in licensing fees plus stock options; PepsiCo agreed to spend $2 billion to promote *Episode I – The Phantom Menace* and two future sequels along with its soft drinks. Pepsi guaranteed at 3,000 screens across the US to sell toys and other merchandise in the lobby. (Indeed even before the movie premiered retailers reported selling out of the new toys and action figures.) Collectors stood for hours so they could get figurines of one of the movie's villains, Darth Maul, and Wall Street bid up the prices of toy stocks. This motion picture defined popular entertainment for the early summer of 1999, as no event could. Such was the power of Hollywood motion pictures.[12]

Star Wars: Episode I – The Phantom Menace opened to a record $28.5 million worth of tickets sold the first day, as buyers filed in front of theatres, and overwhelmed the telephone, and internet, circuits. That it set such a record was hardly news; the only question was how long would the revenue keep flowing in? The answer?: well into the twenty-first century. The latest edition of *Star Wars* represented the economic power of Hollywood. With its distribution by one of the Big Six studios, there was no way – even with its $115 million cost, that *Star Wars: Episode I – The Phantom Menace* would not make vast profits. Theatre owners signed to play it for months; pay TV longed for its video release; home video retailers knew that it should make them profits later in the year 2000. Twentieth Century Fox, a core member of Hollywood's six dominant firms, had turned out another myth-making product shaping class, race, gender and ideology.[13]

While heralded a rich and powerful man, George Lucas alone could not distribute his epic; he needed Twentieth Century Fox. He also needed pay TV networks, and home video retailers to exploit the expected multiple streams of revenues. Prior to 1950, movie theatres were the lone source of revenues. Then came additional revenues from reshowings on broadcast television, then Hollywood added multiple venues on cable TV, and finally got a significant boost from home video rental and sales. Indeed, by the mid-1990s domestic box office takings in the US and Canada ranked only the equivalent of domestic and foreign home video sales and rentals. Domestic and foreign pay TV ranked next, with domestic broadcast and basic cable coming further behind.

But with all this additional money pouring into the system, still only six major studios gathered the bulk of it. Whatever the venue – theatrical, cable TV, or home video – the locus of the production and distribution of most of the films most people saw as the twentieth century ended continued to be Hollywood in general, six major studios in particular. In a profile of a former, powerful Hollywood agent, Michael Ovitz, Lynn Hirschberg of *The New York Times* put it best:

> Hollywood is a small community – there are only six big movie studios, four big TV networks, and three big talent agencies. [The people who own and run these organisations] talk to one another every day. They confide, they feud, they forgive, they do business together, they vacation together.[14]

As the twenty-first century commenced, the Hollywood film industry remained a closed oligopoly of the Big Six – (in alphabetical order) Disney (owned by The Walt Disney Corporation), Paramount Pictures (owned by Viacom), Sony Pictures (owned by Sony), Twentieth Century Fox (owned by News Corporation), Universal Pictures (owned by Seagram/Vivendi), and Warner Bros. (owned by Time Warner). All competed to produce and release the top hits, but all cooperated to make sure the game remained only among themselves. Who was on top which year varied, but only the Big Six premiered possible blockbuster hits in multiplex theatres during the 1990s – and well into the twenty-first century.

A TITANIC EXAMPLE

1998 saw a record year for going to the movies as the Hollywood industry reaped the benefits of *Titanic* (James Cameron), which was released late in 1997. By the end of 1998 *Titanic* had grossed some $600 million in the US from patrons in theatres alone. So popular was

Titanic that it was still collecting theatrical revenues even as the film spectacular was being released in its video versions. The $7 billion collected in theatres in the US and Canada set a record, some 9 per cent greater than the year before. Attendance also jumped more than 5 per cent, to nearly 1.5 billion tickets sold.[15]

The Big Six profess to bet millions of dollars each summer (and Christmas) and this leads to intense competition between them across production, distribution and presentation. The blockbuster system also guarantees larger than normal profits for the members of the Big Six oligopoly as long as they are able to keep new companies from entering into this prescribed game of blockbuster making. They alone could exploit the system of movie making and viewing.

Indeed, the defining moment of the past decade came when Twentieth Century Fox and Paramount delivered the much-delayed, much-maligned *Titanic*. Costing between $220 million and $240 million, *Titanic* was considered too long, too expensive, and too accident-prone. But by year's end it already had grossed $134 million, on its way to a worldwide record. The very executives who had earlier scaled back their spending and their expectations were now even more perplexed. As we know now, all the delay and a story often-told made no difference. The film grossed more than any in history.[16]

In the end, the Big Six remain firmly in place, and even as new releases were being hammered into place, there always existed an optimism based on the fact they and they alone were members of an exclusive club – one where long-term failure was almost impossible. Summer would lead to autumn when (like spring following the Christmas season) Big Six executives could launch their more artistically ambitious projects. But they knew summer, like Christmas, meant go-for-broke, when the big movie-going audiences were out there, wallets in hand. Summer was blockbuster time. Most of the movies that would be released in summer had been in the works for years – a glimmer in a filmmaker's eye. All desired to make the next *Titanic*.

THE BIG SIX AND MERGER MANIA

Indeed, a new Warners commenced with the new decade of the 1990s with the $15 billion consolidation of Time and Warner, bringing this Hollywood studio into the centre of the largest media company in the world. In 1993 Viacom acquired the Paramount studios, Rupert Murdoch's Twentieth Century Fox studio expanded from his original

1986 takeover, and a newcomer – Sony – took Columbia Pictures and reorganised it as Sony Entertainment. In 1995 Canadian liquor giant Seagram bought the massive entertainment colossus MCA, and renamed the entertainment giant after its centrepiece – the Universal studio. Seagram would at the beginning of the next century sell out to France's Vivendi. The vast profits that are available from owning a member of the Big Six have driven this merger mania. New owners wanted in.

However, Vivendi's attempts to buy into Hollywood via Universal have ended in failure. Despite their size and the exclusivity of the club, its members can be vulnerable as Vivendi have now found and Matsushita before them. Thus it surprised no one that in June 2003, Edgar Bronfman Jr, head of Seagrams, former owner of Universal, was seeking to line-up a team of investors in his quest to regain the assets Vivendi had acquired in 2000. As Vivendi subsequently plunged into turmoil and its share price collapsed, that deal came to be seen by many as a major blunder by Bronfman. He could – in the summer of 2003 – redeem his family's name by buying about 70 per cent of the Vivendi entertainment assets, leaving Vivendi a small stake so it could avoid heavy taxes in the deal. The entertainment assets include the Universal Music Group; Vivendi Universal Entertainment, which owns the cable networks USA and Sci-Fi Channel; the Universal Pictures movie studio; a TV production business; and a stake in the theme park business. Selling those properties would leave Vivendi, based in Paris, with holdings that include the European wireless company Cegetel and the French pay television company Canal Plus. The Vivendi story shows that despite the size and exclusivity of the club, members can be vulnerable – especially companies from other countries.

Yet with all these takeovers and changes the structure of the industry has changed little. These six Hollywood operations – Warner, Paramount, Twentieth Century Fox, Sony, Disney and Universal – still define the world's dominant motion picture makers and distributors. Although many fans look back to the 1930s and 1940s as the golden age of the movie business, in fact the end of the twentieth century was the era when the Big Six achieved its greatest power and profitability. Pretenders, as analysed below, try to enter; none have succeeded, although the DreamWorks SKG experiment continues. Dozens have tried and failed, so the odds against DreamWorks SKG are long indeed. Indeed, through the 1980s and 1990s MGM had virtually dropped out, unable to match the power of the Big Six.

THE MPAA

Business strategies came and went. The oligopoly remained. During the 1990s this six-member oligopoly retained tight and firm control. The movie business oligopoly in Hollywood was one of the tightest in the media business. Two scholars looked at the position in 1994 and concluded that 'An examination of concentration ratios indicates that high levels of concentration exist in most of the [media] industry segments' and were surely correct for motion pictures, and so this industry deserves our close attention.[17]

We can most easily see oligopoly power in the activities of the Big Six's trade association – the Motion Picture Association of America (hereafter the MPAA) – where the six deal with common concerns from rating films to smoothing the way for international distribution and protecting their valuable copyrights around the world. While critics of the film industry usually focus only on the MPAA's ratings system, its long-time head, Jack Valenti, earns his $1 million a year salary by helping the Big Six expand revenues from around the world. Indeed Valenti can more often be found abroad, far from his home office in Washington, DC, two blocks from the White House. While Valenti's total Association budget ($60 million per annum it is estimated) would make and market a single modest blockbuster, the Big Six know it is money well spent – protecting their turf and expanding their markets.[18]

They collude. The studios joined together to cooperate, even to the point of co-producing expensive feature films, Twentieth Century Fox and Paramount's co-financing of *Titanic* being the key example. In the end the game is profit maximisation. Since these are the only six players in town, the worries are not about losing money in the long run, but about maximising profits. So the studios spend enormous efforts to craft hits in their theatrical runs so that the revenues will be as high as possible, all the while trying to keep costs as low as possible. Such has been the case since Universal's Lew Wasserman pioneered the blockbuster strategy with the release of *Jaws*.

Through the MPAA, the Big Six cooperated on common issues, which then freed them – and them alone – to pursue the blockbuster like *Titanic*, which could set in motion such a vast array of profit-making deals. The revenue flows seemed to never cease. For example, because of its fabulously successful theatrical re-release in February and March 1997, Fox's *Star Wars* trilogy regained its crown as the top-grossing set of films. Add in the moneys from foreign revenues, pay TV, home video, and broadcast TV, as well as merchandising tie-ins, and *Star Wars* stands as a multi-billion property, fully amortised, with millions more expected in the future from further re-releases.

CONCLUSION

Thus through the last two decades of the twentieth century the Big Six took on new owners, or management teams, and still remained the 'majors'. Year in, year out they controlled between 80 and 90 per cent of the expanding movie business in the US and a bit less in the rest of the world. Every few years a couple of bold pretenders – during the 1980s Orion Pictures and New World – emerged to challenge the Big Six, but none ever survived after creating only a modest hit or two. No challenger has survived in the long haul, although as the 1990s were ending DreamWorks SKG was mounting a serious challenge. In the real Hollywood industry, the dozens of independent producers have no choice but to distribute their films through one of the six major studios if they wish to maximise their return on investment, and if they want the largest possible audience to see their work.

Thus in its almost ten-year history DreamWorks SKG founders Steven Spielberg, former Disney executive Jeffrey Katzenberg and billionaire David Geffen could not join the exclusive Hollywood oligopoly. Despite occasional hits like *Saving Private Ryan* (Steven Spielberg 1998), the company could never build its own studio lot and had to rent space at Universal City. DreamWorks might distribute its films in the US, but for world distribution, it depended upon its patron Universal.[19]

DreamWorks was to have been a fully integrated studio, with a full slate of movies, television, music and multimedia. But with the exception of the hit ABC comedy *Spin City* and an also-ran record division, the company is almost entirely dependent on new-release movies, many of which are co-produced with other studios. In 2000, DreamWorks had a total box office haul of $670 million for ten features, but the public was distracted by its Oscar winner, *Gladiator* (Ridley Scott). A more costly blockbuster – *A.I.*, a Steven Spielberg epic – failed. Dreamworks lacked other dependable revenue streams such as TV advertising or a film library. For DreamWorks, 'it's crucial to keep the lights on', says an executive with close ties to the studio.[20]

DreamWorks shows that a studio cannot be dependent just on making films. It must have power in distribution and presentation – theatrical and television and video – as well. In 2001 – with little fanfare, Steven Spielberg, partner for DreamWorks announced that they have renewed their distribution agreement with Universal Studios. Spielberg stated 'This alliance is particularly gratifying for me because Universal has been an important part of my life for 32 years.' While Jeffrey Katzenberg stated 'Dreamworks and Universal have a five-year history that has seen both companies grow a great deal.'[21] DreamWorks was best understood as a subsidiary of Univeral, not as a new member of the exclusive studio system club.

NOTES

1. V.I. Lenin, *Imperialism: The Highest Stage of Capitalism* (Peking: Foreign Languages Press, 1975 [1916]); Rudolf Hilferding, *Das Finanzkapital* (Berlin: Dietz Verlag, 1947 [1910]).
2. Paul M. Sweezy, *The Theory of Capitalist Development* (New York: Monthly Review Press, 1970), pp. 239–53 and Paul A. Baran and Paul M. Sweezy, *Monopoly Capital* (New York: Monthly Review Press, 1966), pp. 1–78.
3. J. Douglas Gomery, 'The Coming of Sound to the American Cinema: A History of the Transformation of an Industry', Unpublished Ph.D. dissertation, University of Wisconsin-Madison, 1975, pp. 406–29.
4. Bernard Bellush, *The Failure of the NRA* (New York: W.W. Norton & Company, 1975), pp. 52–5; Ellis W. Hawley, *The New Deal and the Problem of Monopoly* (Princeton: Princeton University Press, 1966), pp. 53–72.
5. *Variety*, 6 June 1933, p. 7; *Variety*, 13 June 1933, p. 5; *Variety*, 20 June 1933, p. 5; *Variety*, 27 June 1933, p. 4; A.B. Moment, *The Hays Office and the NRA* (Shawnee, OK: Shawnee Printing Company, 1935), pp. 1–35; Michael Conant, *Anti-trust in the Motion Picture Industry* (Berkeley: University of California Press, 1960), p. 85; Will H. Hays, *The Memoirs of Will H. Hays* (Garden City, NY: Doubleday, 1955), p. 448.
6. Baran and Sweezy, *Monopoly Capital*, p. 17; see also p. 30.
7. *Saturday Evening Post*, 11 June 1937, p. 34.
8. *Variety*, 25 November 1936, p. 7; *Variety*, 22 November 1941, p. 5.
9. *New York Times*, 19 June 1942, p. 27; *New York Times*, 20 June 1942, p. 8; *Variety*, 4 March 1942, p. 2.
10. *Variety*, 4 March 1942, p. 2; *Variety*, 22 December 1943, p. 33; *Fortune*, May 1953, p. 212.
11. See Douglas Gomery, 'Hollywood Corporate Business Practice and Periodizing Film History', in Steve Neale and Murray Smith (eds), *Contemporary Hollywood Cinema* (London: Routledge, 1998), pp. 47–57.
12. Joseph Periera, 'Star Wars Merchandise Launch Draws Thousands of Shoppers on the First Day', *Wall Street Journal*, 4 May 1999, p. B13; Ron Grover, 'The Force Is Back', *Business Week*, 26 April 1999, pp. 74–8; Bruce Orwall and John Lippman, 'From Creator of "Star Wars", a New Legal Force', *Wall Street Journal*, 10 March 1999, pp. B1, B6.
13. 'As "Star Wars" Opens, Many Gauge Payoff', *Wall Street Journal*, 20 May 1999, p. B2; Bruce Orwall and John Lippman, 'Return of the Franchise', *Wall Street Journal*, 14 May 1999, pp. B1, B6; Thomas E. Weber and

Stephanie N. Mehta, 'Web, Telephone Prove No Match for "Star Wars"', *Wall Street Journal*, 13 May 1999, p. B1.

14. Lynn Hirschberg, 'Michael Ovitz Is On the Line', *New York Times Magazine*, 9 May 1999, p. 49.

15. See the latest edition of the *International Motion Picture Almanac* (New York: Quigley Publishing Company) for a concise review of the year for the Hollywood major studios.

16. Leonard Klady, 'H'wood's B. O. Blast', *Variety*, 5–11 January 1998, pp. 1, 96.

17. See Alan B. Albarran and John Dimmick, 'Concentration and Economics of Multiformity in the Communication Industries', *The Journal of Media Economics*, vol. 9, no. 4 (1996), pp. 41–50.

18. Dyan Machan, 'Mr. Valenti Goes to Washington', *Forbes*, 1 December 1997, pp. 66, 68, 69–70; Paul Karon, 'MPAA's 75th Year Under Fire', *Variety*, 22–28 September 1997, pp. 11, 16; web site <www.mpaa.org> (last accessed 15 May 2003).

19. 'DreamWorks SKG', in Tracy Stevens (ed.), *2001 International Motion Picture Almanac* (La Jolla, CA: Quigley Publishing, 2001), p. 639.

20. Mark Lacter, 'Mr. Nice Guy', *Forbes*, 16 April 2001, p. 56.

21. *DVD News*, 23 April 2001, vol. 5, no. 15, p. 1.

8

Hollywood, Cultural Policy Citadel

Toby Miller

We are conventionally told today that two models govern the economics of cinema. The first is *laissez-faire*, represented by Bollywood, Hong Kong and, *primus inter pares*, Hollywood. The second is *dirigisme*, represented by Western Europe and other parts of the South. Let's look at the binary oppositions that supposedly sustain this distinction:

LAISSEZ-FAIRE FILM INDUSTRY	*DIRIGISTE* FILM INDUSTRY
No state investment in training, production, distribution or exhibition	Major state subvention of training and production, minimal or no support for distribution and exhibition
No governmental censorship, or governmental censorship	Governmental censorship
Copyright protection	Copyright protection
Monopoly restrictions	Monopoly restrictions
Export orientation	Import substitution
Market model	Mixed-economy model
Ideology of pleasure before nation	Ideology of nation before pleasure
Governmental anxiety over the impact of film sex and violence on the population	Governmental anxiety over the impact of imported film on the population

On the left-hand side we have a set of ideal-types generated from the discourse of neoclassical economics. Their equivalents on the right derive from the discourse of cultural policy. While they have some items in common, such as the role of the state in policing property, their fundamental missions seem incompatible. But we shall observe them overlap in this chapter, across the terrain of cultural policy, screen subjectivity, and the role of the state in Hollywood. Then we'll revisit the binary to redraw it.

CULTURAL POLICY

Dirigisme is a necessary part of making the state appealing to its population. In Marx's words: 'it is impossible to create a moral power by paragraphs of law'. There must also be '*organic* laws supplementing the Constitution' – i.e., cultural policy.[1] These organic laws and their textual efflorescence come to represent what Althusser called each 'epoch's consciousness of itself'.[2] Gramsci theorised this supplement as an 'equilibrium' between constitutional law ('political society' or a 'dictatorship or some other coercive apparatus used to control the masses in conformity with a given type of production and economy') and organic law ('civil society' or the 'hegemony of a social group over the entire nation exercised through so-called private organisations such as the church, the unions, the schools, etc.').[3]

Jacques Donzelot operationalises these ideas in his concept of policing, which describes 'methods for developing the quality of the population and the strength of the nation'.[4] As well as materially improving urban life, middle-class reformers in nineteenth-century Western Europe thought that teaching the working class to value the nation was a good bet for avoiding industrial strife and class struggle.[5] Bio-power emerged as a system for endowing the population with abilities, both in terms of belonging and as a set of practical, industrial skills. Since that time, cultural policy has oscillated between training for citizenship and training for employment, especially since the First World de-industrialised in the latter part of the twentieth century. What began as an investment in content to encourage loyalty has become an investment in cultural production to encourage employment.

This history should not imply a happily functionalist world without conflict. Cultural policy raises difficulties for ideologues on behalf of the supposedly non-paternalistic state that simply allows its citizens the opportunity to determine their own screen desires. If cultural-capitalist societies identify themselves as sources of free expression, as evidenced in the absence of a state that seeks to direct the work of cinema, what should their governments' stance be on film? Should they adopt one at all? Western cultural-capitalist countries are wont to take two rhetorical positions here. The first offers the market as a system for identifying and allocating public preferences for cinema, denying the state a role other than as a police officer patrolling the precincts of property – deciding who owns what and how objects should be exchanged. The second identifies certain filmic tendencies as transcendentally laden with value, but vulnerable to the public's inability to remain transcendental in its tastes. This latter position encourages a *dirigiste* role for the state, one that appears to coerce the public into aestheticisation and is routinely accused by certain critics of 'cultural magistracy'. Nevertheless, it would be misleading to argue that the market and the state never work in tandem. In some cases, cultural-capitalist and *dirigiste* roles operate together, as the market is declared the proper venue for the popular sector of the film industry, while heritage, documentary, and the avant-garde are assumed as state responsibilities. Across the First and Third Worlds, there is also public investment in film, in search of economic development as much as cultural fealty. Cultural industrialisation schemes involve training programmes, capitalist enterprises, state assistance, and international financial institutional investments by agencies such as the European Union. The latter, for example, increasingly directs its screen assistance to building an industry rather than sustaining or creating a culture.

But as a rough guide, a useful heuristic distinction can be drawn between economic and uplift approaches to funding culture. The economic approach suggests that culture circulates satisfactorily through the mechanics of price. The uplift approach suggests that cultural improvement of the population is necessary, because market processes favour pleasure over sophistication. Markets fail to encourage and sustain art's function of defining and developing universal human values and forms of expression, because popular taste is ephemeral. Of course, conventional capitalist logic is opposed to the deployment of public funds in the service of an ethically derived set of preferences – the contested presumption that 'it is more worthwhile to look at a Titian on a wall than watch a football game on television'.[6] As most people supposedly prefer the latter – a preference that can be quantified through preparedness to pay for the right – it is deemed paternalistic to force them to subsidise the former as part of their generic tax burden on the grounds that timeless art can in fact only survive if the *polloi* are required to admire it. Film may, however, be reconceived within the economic wing of this Manichean divide, as a public good that makes a collective contribution to the aesthetico-intellectual functioning of a community, via the mutual impact of popular and high culture. On this view, cinema can be subsidised so long as it contributes to the community and becomes a resource.[7] Both art-house and popular movies contribute – one to intellection, and the other to fun. The idea is to allow the market to gauge popular fashion, and the state to ensure the continuation of elite taste and heritage appreciation – a method of keeping unpopular culture alive. This notion of film as fun (via the market) and serious (via the state) is central to much cultural policy. Implied spectators lie at the heart of each discourse. The spectators of the market must learn to control their passions. The spectators of uplift must learn to cultivate their cultural knowledge.

SCREEN SPECTATORSHIP

Two basic discourses underpin these differences. Each is an effects model, for they both assume the audiovisual *does* things *to* people, to citizen/consumers as audience members. The first model derives from the social sciences and is applied without consideration of place. I call this the *domestic* effects model, or DEM. It is universalist and psychological. The DEM concerns itself with such crucial citizenship questions as education and civic order. It views the screen as a machine that either perverts or directs the citizen. Entering young minds osmotically, it can enable or imperil the learning process. And it may also drive the citizen to violence, through aggressive and misogynistic words, images and narratives. The DEM assumes, then, two kinds of audiovisual impact on citizenship. On the one hand, it may promote 'good' conduct:

- learning and self-control
- training and the superego; and
- professional preparation and personal responsibility

On the other hand, it may induce the diametric opposite of each 'positive' effect, respectively:

- ignorance and self-indulgence
- guesswork and the id; and
- lassitude and selfishness

The DEM is found in a variety of sites, including laboratories, clinics, prisons, schools, newspapers, psychology journals, music companies, TV networks, film-studio research and publicity departments, everyday talk, programme classification regulations, conference papers, parliamentary debates, and state-of-our-youth or state-of-our-civil-society moral panics . It generates cultural-policy interventions in education and censorship. In the case of Hollywood, the DEM finds expression in self-regulatory industry codes, hand-wringing state inquiries, and subsidised academic psychologism.

The second way of thinking about audiovisual citizenship is a *global* effects model, or GEM. The GEM is specific and political rather than universalist and psychological. It is at the heart of both 'mainstream' concerns with productivity and decline and 'minority' demands to eradicate national, gender, ability or racial stereotypes, on the premise that they provoke discrimination and even violence, and that the dissemination of positive images will improve society. Whereas the DEM focuses on the cognition and emotion of individual human subjects via replicable experimentation, the GEM looks to the knowledge of custom and patriotic feeling exhibited by collective human subjects, the grout of national culture. In place of psychology, it is concerned with politics. The audiovisual does not make you a well- or ill-educated person, a wild or self-controlled one. Rather, it makes you a knowledgeable and loyal national subject, or a duped viewer who lacks an appreciation of local culture and history. Belonging is the touchstone of the global effects model. Instead of measuring responses electronically or behaviourally, as its domestic counterpart does, the GEM looks to the national origin of texts and the themes and styles they embody, with particular attention to the screen genres of drama, news, sport and current affairs. GEM adherents hold that local citizens should control local broadcast networks because they alone can be relied upon to be loyal reporters in the event of war, while reflectionist claims for the role of fiction are thought to mean that only locally sensitised producers make narratives that are true to history and custom. This model is found in the discourse of cultural imperialism, everyday talk, record industry and telecommunications policy, international organisations, newspapers, cultural diplomacy, post-industrial service-sector planning, and national-cinema discourse. In the case of *dirigisme*, the GEM finds expression in national industry themes, cultural-commercial state evaluations, and subsidised academic critique.

Both of these models are deeply flawed analytically and politically. The DEM suffers from all the disadvantages of ideal-typical psychological reasoning. Each massively costly laboratory test of media effects, based on, as the refrain goes, 'a large university in the mid-West', is countered by a similar experiment, with conflicting results. As politicians, grant-givers, and jeremiad-wielding pundits call for more and more research to prove that the audiovisual makes you stupid, violent and apathetic – or the opposite – academics line up at the trough to indulge their hatred of popular culture and ordinary life and their rent-seeking urge for public money. Meanwhile, issues of class, race and especially masculinity in US society are erased from view. As for the GEM, its concentration on national culture:

- denies the potentially liberatory side-effect of pleasure in imports
- forgets the internal differentiation of audiences
- valorises frequently oppressive local *bourgeoisies* in the name of developing and maintaining national culture; and
- ignores the demographic realities of its 'own' terrain

The DEM sustains psychological reductionism, the GEM textual reductionism.

THE STATE AND HOLLYWOOD

Just as the DEM and the GEM are ironically close to one another, the *laissez-faire* side of my original table is in fact characterised by massive state intervention and the *dirigiste* side by massive business-leechery. Everyone knows that national cinemas supposedly sustained by governments in the name of reflecting the public back to itself on screen are frequently sheltered workshops for indolent *bourgeoisies* rather than serious grapplings with the complex world of national demography. You don't see too many lesbian *Sámi* in Norwegian film or North African immigrants in French cinema. But most of us probably *do* accept the US myth about Hollywood as free enterprise. My goal is to reveal that assumption as fundamentally flawed, both historically and today.

The US claims that its success is a function of satisfying the needs of audiences, not a consequence of policy. The film industry is supposed to be a pure market of private enterprise and consumption, so it seems sensible to evaluate *laissez-faire* as an account of Hollywood cinema, to question whether this is a free market based purely on consumer demand. Here are four tests:[8]

1. Freedom of entry to new starters?

Neoclassical economics says that the degree of real competitiveness in an industry can be gauged by the openness of its markets to new entrants. Given that US domestic anti-trust policing has been a joke since the 1980s, and the close ties of television to film following deregulation by the Federal Communications Commission, continued governmental limits of 25 per cent foreign ownership of US radio and television stations permit limited external participation and encourage domestic oligopoly.[9] There have been foreign owners of major Hollywood studios in the recent past, such as Australia's Channel Seven and News Corporation, Canada's Seagrams, France's Canal Plus/Vivendi, and Japan's Sony, plus a new domestic venture in DreamWorks, but control of studio output remains in California and New York. What matters spatially is not the company's headquarters, or its major shareholders' residence, but where its actual product development and management are domiciled – who controls it. On the distribution front, the US government endorses trust-like behaviour by film companies overseas, while prohibiting it domestically.

2. No state subsidies?

Neoclassical ideologues claim that state subsidies in other countries undertaken in the name of cultural sovereignty impede the free market and disadvantage other nations because, allegedly *ipso facto*, such intervention stifles innovation, thereby aiding US dominance.[10] But this woefully misreads the constitutive nature of US governmental assistance to Hollywood. The US state has a long history of direct participation in production, and the local film industry has been aided through decades of tax-credit schemes, State and Commerce Department representation, the Informational Media Guaranty Program's currency assistance,[11] and oligopolistic domestic buying and overseas selling practices that keep the primary market essentially closed to imports on the grounds of popular taste (without much good evidence for doing so). In 2000, the US had:

- 205 state, regional and city film commissions, offering luxury hotels, private-plane travel, location scouts, and other hidden subsidies to the film industry via reduced local taxes, free police services, blocked public wayfares, purpose-driven crop cultivation, re-routed rivers, and municipal bond issues
- Small Business Administration financing through loans and support of independents
- State and Commerce Department briefings and plenipotentiary representation; and
- the Californian State Government's 'Film California First Program'

International negotiations on so-called video piracy have resulted in PRC offenders being threatened with beheading, even as the

US claims to be watching Chinese human rights as part of most-favoured nation treatment, while protests by Indonesian filmmakers against Hollywood that drew the support of their government saw Washington threaten industrial sanctions, and the US pressured South Korea to drop its screen quotas as part of 1998–99 negotiations on a Bilateral Investment Treaty.[12]

With large conglomerates owning studios and networks, and Wall Street demanding routine success of industries used to routine failure, there is an increasing tendency for films to be made with foreign investment.[13] Nearly 20 per cent of the US$15 billion expended on Hollywood production in 2000 was, for example, German, and derived from tax subsidies.[14] Control of these funds remains firmly in Yankee hands, just as it did during unsuccessful purchases of studios by others over the previous decade – and it is dependent on utilising state financing, albeit from another country.[15] No wonder that *Canadian Business* magazine – archly, and with a deeply endearing hypocrisy – refers to 'Hollywood's Welfare Bums'.[16] Lastly, with the Republican Party owned by minerals and manufacturing and mistrustful of film's putative liberalism, the service industries have their bidding done by purchasing Democrat lobbyists. In return for campaign funds, the Democratic Party obeys the will of the studios via protectionist legislation such as the Consumer Broadband and Digital Television Promotion Act and various anti-counterfeiting amendments to attack file-sharing and the use of multiple platforms for watching films.

3. A relationship between the cost of production and consumption?

Unlike most forms of manufacturing, the production of film drama is dominated by a small number of large companies with limited, individually differentiated outputs. Most investments fail, a cost that can only be borne by big firms. Although the means of production are standardised, economies of scale are rare when each project is costly and unlikely to succeed. The absolute significance of story over price for audiences – who are accustomed to paying the same amount for all releases – goes against neoclassical economics' standard assumptions about the role of price in balancing supply and demand. Instead, films are transformed from services to products and then services again, as they move between theatrical, video, televisual and internet forms of life.[17] Costs are not reflected in ticket prices or cable fees, but are amortised through a huge array of venues, so reusable is each full copy of each text, unlike a car or painting. There is a clear correlation between GDP, public-sector broadcasting, and the purchase of US screen output in both Asia and Europe – the richer the nation and the stronger its public media, the less need it has for Hollywood material.[18] This indicates that economic power exploits poor countries, not that prices are determined by consumer desire.

4. Textual diversity?

Open markets supposedly make for diverse products, permitting extensive freedom of choice for customers. Do we have this on US screens? In the 1960s, imports accounted for 10 per cent of the US film market. In 1986, that figure was 7 per cent. Today, it is 0.75 per cent. Foreign films are essentially excluded from the US, as never before. Neoclassical reactionaries attribute this to US audiences, who are said to be 'unusually insular and intolerant of foreign programming or films, because historically they are exposed to very little'.[19] As a country with huge everyday use of non-English languages and a thriving Spanish-language cultural market, this account of the US is as laughably off the mark as we have come to expect from these ideologues. Minimal screen diversity is due to the corporatisation of cinema exhibition, in combination with increases in promotional and real-estate costs for independent distributors and exhibitors and higher demands from the original producers, who have had to put more and more money 'on the screen' to compete with the Hollywood 'look'. This has reached the point where subtitling and dubbing have become insupportable – the average Hollywood film had US$21 million budgeted for advertising in 1999, an unthinkable figure for European rights-holders, and overall average film costs have doubled in less than a decade, increasing by 6.5 per cent between 1999 and 2000, to US$54.8 million. As for propaganda, the state and the film industry have often worked together. In the embarrassingly macho language of US political science, the media represent 'soft power' to match the 'hard power' of the military and the economy.[20] During the First World War, films from the Central Powers were banned across the US. In the 1920s and 1930s, Hollywood lobbyists regarded the US Departments of State and Commerce as its 'message boys'. The former shaped messages, undertook market research, and shared business intelligence. The latter pressured other countries to permit cinema free access and favourable terms of trade. During the invasion of Europe in 1944 and 1945, the military closed Axis films, shuttered their industry, and insisted on the release of US movies.[21] After the Second World War, ideological and monetary gains could be made from a closer alignment with anti-Marxism, and the Motion Picture Export Association came to refer to itself as 'the little State Department', so isomorphic were its methods and contents with Federal policy and ideology. Today, the Department of Commerce produces materials on media globalisation that focus on both economic development and ideological influence, problematising claims that Hollywood is pure free enterprise and that Washington is uninterested in blending trade with cultural change.[22] Meanwhile, the Justice Department is authorised to classify all imported films, and has prohibited Canadian documentaries on acid rain and nuclear war as 'political propaganda',[23] and the new hybrid of SiliWood blends Northern Californian technology, Hollywood methods and military funding, clearly evident in the way the film industry sprang into militaristic action in concert with Pentagon preferences after September 11 2001 and even became a consultant on possible attacks. So with NASA struggling to renovate its image, who better to invite to a lunch than Hollywood producers, so they would script new texts featuring the Agency as a benign, exciting entity? And why not form a 'White House-Hollywood Committee' while you're at it, to ensure coordination between the nations we bomb and the messages we export?[24]

In summary, the neoclassical vision of Hollywood asserts that the supposedly neutral mechanism of market competition exchanges materials at costs that ensure the most efficient people are producing, and their customers are content. This model may occasionally describe life in some fruit and vegetable markets today. But as an historical account, it is of no value: the rhythms of supply and demand, operating unfettered by states, religions, unions, superstition and fashion, do not exist as such. Or rather, those rhythms exist as enormously potent prescriptive signs in the rhetoric of international financial organisations, bureaucrats, journalists and lobbyists. Little old rent-seekers they.

BACK TO BINARIES

The binary table with which we began needs serious revision:

HOLLYWOOD FILM INDUSTRY	NATIONAL FILM INDUSTRY
Massive state investment in training via film schools and production commissions, major diplomatic negotiations over distribution and exhibition arrangements	Major state subvention of training and production, minimal or no support for distribution and exhibition
Governmental censorship	Governmental censorship
Copyright protection as a key service to capital along with anti-piracy deals	Copyright protection
Monopoly restrictions minimised to permit cross-ownership and unprecedented concentration domestically and oligopolies internationally	Monopoly restrictions
Export orientation aided by plenipotentiaries, equal reliance on local audience	Import substitution, some export to cognate language groups
Market model, mixed-economy practice	Mixed-economy model
Ideology of pleasure, nation, and export of Américanité	Ideology of nation, pleasure, and job creation
Governmental anxiety over the impact of film sex and violence on the population, as alibi for no cultural policy discourse	Governmental anxiety over the impact of imported film on the population, as alibi for bourgeois subvention

The craven lies that Washington and Hollywood purvey in the pages of the press, the corridors of trade, and the ideology of everyday rhetoric can stand no longer. Hollywood is a citadel of cultural policy, and the nation's hypocrisies over this heavy hand of government should be revealed for what they are.

NOTES

1. Karl Marx, *The Eighteenth Brumaire of Louis Bonaparte* (Peking: Foreign Language Press, 1978), pp. 27, 35.
2. Louis Althusser, *For Marx*, trans. Ben Brewster (Harmondsworth: Penguin, 1969), p. 108.
3. Antonio Gramsci, *Selections from the Prison Notebooks*, ed. and trans. Quintin Hoare and Geoffrey Nowell-Smith (New York: International Publishers, 1978), p. 204.
4. Jacques Donzelot, *The Policing of Families*, trans. Robert Hurley (New York: Pantheon, 1979), pp. 6–7.
5. David Lloyd and Paul Thomas, *Culture and the State* (New York: Routledge, 1998), p. 18.
6. Ronald Dworkin, *A Matter of Principle* (Cambridge, MA: Harvard University Press, 1985), p. 225.

7. George Yúdice, *El recurso de la cultura: Usos de la cultura en la era global* (Barcelona: Editorial Gedisa, 2002).
8. Some of this material draws on Toby Miller, Nitin Govil, John McMurria and Richard Maxwell, *Global Hollywood* (London: British Film Institute, 2001).
9. Bruce Stokes, 'Lights! Camera! More Inaction', *National Journal*, July 1999, p. 2106.
10. A. Marvasti, 'Motion Pictures Industry: Economics of Scale and Trade', *International Journal of the Economics of Business*, vol. 7, no.1 (2000), pp. 99–115.
11. See for example John Izod, *Hollywood and the Box Office 1895–1986* (New York: Columbia University Press, 1998), pp. 61–3, 82, 118.
12. See Aida Hozic, *Hollywood: Space, Power, and Fantasy in the American Economy* (Ithaca: Cornell University Press, 2001), pp. 87–8, 117 and Carolyn Hyun-Kyung Kim, 'Building the Korean Film Industry's Competitiveness', *Pacific Rim Law and Policy Journal*, no. 9 (2000), pp. 353–77.
13. Don Groves and Anthony D'Alessandro, 'H'W'D' frets over Foreign Aid', *Variety*, 12–18 February 2001, p. 77.
14. Steve Zwick, 'Top Marks for Hollywood: German Film Production Companies are Pouring into Big U.S. Movies – with Mixed Results', *Time International*, 16 October 2000, p. 58.
15. Thomas H. Guback, 'Government Support to the Film Industry in the United States', in Bruce A. Austin (ed.), *Current Research in Film: Audiences, Economics and Law*, vol. 3 (Norwood: Ablex, 1987), pp. 92–3, 98–9.
16. Joe Chidley, 'Hollywood's Welfare Bums', *Canadian Business*, 13 April 2000, pp. 11–12.
17. Barry R. Litman, *The Motion Picture Mega-Industry* (Boston: Allyn and Bacon, 1998), p. 25.
18. Michel Dupagne and David Waterman, 'Determinants of U.S. Television Fiction Imports in Western Europe', *Journal of Broadcasting and Electronic Media*, vol. 42, no. 2 (1998), pp. 208–20.
19. Colin Hoskins, Stuart McFadyen and Adam Finn, *Global Television and Film: An Introduction to the Economics of the Business* (Oxford: Clarendon Press, 1997), p. 45.
20. Joseph S. Nye Jr., 'Limits of American Power', *Political Science Quarterly*, 117, no. 4, 2002–03, pp. 545–9.
21. John Trumpbour, *Selling Hollywood to the World: U.S. and European Struggles for Mastery of the Global Film Industry, 1920–1950* (Cambridge: Cambridge University Press, 2002), pp. 3–4, 62, 63, 98.
22. Marjorie Ferguson, 'The Mythology about Globalization', *European Journal of Communication*, vol. 7, no. 1 (1992), pp. 83–4.
23. Richard A. Parker, 'The Guise of the Propagandist: Governmental Classification of Foreign Political Films', in Bruce A. Austin (ed.), *Current Research in Film: Audiences, Economics and Law*, vol. 5 (Norwood: Ablex, 1991), pp. 135, 137.
24. David Chambers, 'Will Hollywood go to War?', *Transnational Broadcasting Studies*, no. 8 (2002).

9

State Cinema and Passive Revolution in North Korea[1]

Hyangjin Lee

INTRODUCTION: 'IF THE PARTY DECIDES TO, SO DO WE'[2]

In the preface to his book, *On the Art of Cinema* (1973), the present North Korean leader, Kim Jong Il asserted that *Juche* (self-reliance) oriented art and literature are 'communist art and literature that meet the requirements of the new age and the aspirations of the popular masses'.[3] What does this conveniently elastic cliché mean for filmmakers? How does film realise such political imperatives in a form of popular entertainment? What is the degree of cultural autonomy in North Korean film practices? This chapter will pursue these questions, in order to explore the ways in which film materialises the political revolution led by the state in North Korea.

Juche literature and art theory is the theoretical backbone for contemporary North Korean filmmaking. In a 1955 speech,[4] Kim Il Sung defined *Juche* as the state ideology of North Korea, a theory which rejects the universality of mass-initiated class revolution. Instead, it proposes the ideas of the Great Leader who stressed the significance of a specific national culture, and its 'unique' colonial and post-colonial history in materialising revolution. The ideas of the Great Leader on revolution qualify the *Juche* theory as a 'creative adaptation of Marxist-Leninism to the Korean situation for revolutionary purposes'.[5] Based on this nationalistic application of Marxism, North Korea insists that the anti-Japanese revolutionary literature led by Kim Il Sung initiated the Korean proletarian art movements under the Japanese colonial rule (1910–45).[6] In other words, it was 'Kimilsungism' prior to Marxism that awoke the colonial intellectuals from the feudalistic worldview and bourgeois class limitation.

Blending Marxism with the Confucian political ideology is the foremost strategy adopted in representing the 'uniquely Korean' style of revolution by North Korean cinema.[7] First, the deification of the Great Leader places him as the decisive agent in instigating and continuing revolution. Articulation of the personality cult of the Great Leader, therefore, is the ultimate form of nationalism expressed by North Korean cinema. 'The Great Leader is the father of the nation ... Heaven sent him to save us from national class enemies.'[8] This is a typical line delivered in North Korean literature in an attempt to mystify his aura as the founder of the liberated nation. For example, in the film *Souls Protest* (2000) similar lines are repeated: 'The General is from heaven. He is the saviour of our white clothed nation.[9] Let's go back home soon to welcome him.' The people are travelling home after long years of forced labour at Japanese military internment camps, but are killed by a bomb planted by the Japanese. As in this film, the journey home symbolises the reunion between the father-nation/the Great Leader and his children/the masses, suggesting the past-recurrent attributes or 'revivalist movements'[10] of the nationalistic revolution depicted by North Korean cinema. Also, the unfinished journey home implies that the nation state begins to traverse the second path of revolutionary struggle: 'the war of position'.[11] Instead of actual national struggles, the state seeks to build the political-ideological programme against the dominant power of colonial forces.[12]

Second, the selection process of 'new organic intellectuals'[13] assists in the creation of the Great Leader foundation myth: they are the organisers of social hegemony and state domination. The realisation of a model worker is one of the most important theses in *Juche* cinema art theory.[14] What distinguishes the chosen ones (the model workers) from the masses are their ideological correctness, sense of responsibility and broad-mindedness in educating the masses. As the main actors of the revolution, the chosen ones speak for the Party, representing the revolutionary state. This type of stereotypical characterisation of the eldest son-like leaders signifies the birth of 'new organic intellectuals' who will lead the masses to revolution. Through this repetitive identification process, the authority of the Great Leader is transferred to the revolutionary state. In the process, the familial hierarchy between leader and led is transformed into a command system between the Party and the masses. The Party is the real agent of revolution, deciding the form and content of popular social movements in North Korea.

The revolution depicted by North Korean cinema can be understood as an example of 'passive revolution' found in a socialist country.[15] Chatterjee's counter-argument to Gramsci's remarks on the historical formation of capital through passive revolution focuses on Western vs. non-Western cultural contexts. Here, I will argue that the focus should not be on Western vs. non-Western contexts, but that passive revolution is a general form of social change led by the dominant social group in any society regardless of whether it is capitalist or not. For example, the 'passive revolution' in North Korea is carried out by the oppressive socialist regime at the apex of which is the Great Leader, which insists on the necessity and continuity of class revolution. The cinematic elaboration of the political revolution led by the state displaces the spontaneity of the masses, who are looking forward to the new social orders.[16] It encourages the political passivity of the audience, implying the division between leader and led as the ideal command system for advancing revolution. Furthermore, the traditional relationship based on affection and familial ideals appears to weaken the radicalism of rejecting the hierarchical human relationships and cultural norms of the old class society.

Noting this 'nationalistic' application of Marxism to film theories and practices in North Korea, my discussion here will focus on the following three aspects. First, I will outline the origin and evolution of the 'socialist' filmmaking tradition in Korea, as a way to examine the centrality of the theoretical orientations adopted in contemporary North Korean cinema from a historical perspective. The transformation of socialist realism, informed by Marxist-Leninism, into *Juche* theory, based on Great Leader Literature, will be the focus of the first part of my discussion. The second phase of my discussion will be on the main features of contemporary North Korean film. My aim here is to highlight its nature as a state enterprise for the socio-politicisation of the masses. I will examine the production process of the multi-part saga that is the *Nation and Destiny* series (1992–). This series can be said to be most representative of contemporary North Korean cinema. The historical saga presents the vicissitudes of individuals who belong to various social strata and different classes, such as the anti-Japanese fighters, colonial intellectuals, Korean War veterans, South Korean spies and defectors, Koreans abroad, comfort women, returnee Korean-Japanese, naturalised Japanese wives, Party members and working-class heroes. Each episode is loosely based on real historical figures. This will be followed by the third part of the discussion, a textual analysis of the representation of the relationships between and among the Great Leader, the new organic intellectuals and the masses, portrayed by the nine episodes of *KAPF Writers* (1996–97) from the *Nation and Destiny* series. KAPF is an acronym of Korean Proletariat Art Federation in Esperanto (Korea Artista Proleta

Federation). Intertwining history and fiction, the nine episodes of *KAPF Writers* provide the contemporary audience with a full account of the origins of *Juche* theory as the state ideology from the vantage point of the 1990s. Based on the discussion of these three aspects of North Korean film, I will conclude that North Korean cinema serves to justify the passive revolution led by the dominant social group in a 'classless society'.[17]

FROM SOCIALIST REALISM TO THE *JUCHE* ART AND LITERATURE THEORY

In the wake of the colonialism and imperialism that blighted the history of the Korean peninsula particularly from the early twentieth century following Japan's annexation in 1910, Marxism had become the central literary canon among colonised Korean intellectuals by the 1920s. In this milieu, where political indifference and passivity characterised the general features of literary work, Marxism provided a new vision for a group of progressive intellectuals. Opposing the apolitical lyric romanticism, i.e. 'pure literature', a group of colonial intellectuals were convinced of the pedagogical effects of socially committed art and literature for galvanising the masses. The March First National Independence Movement in 1919 and the burgeoning labour movements were the social forces that drove this new literature to advocate the proletariat art movement for the purpose of the national class revolution.

KAPF was established in 1925, by merging two socialist-oriented literature circles, Yomgunsa and Pascula. Gim Gijin, Bak Yeongheui, Cho'e Seohae, Jo Myeongheui and Im Hwa were some of the leading figures. KAPF explored the notion of 'class literature' to communicate the oppressive life conditions of the underprivileged classes in opposition to the 'pure literature' written for and by the bourgeoisie classes and urban intellectuals. Through a series of debates on 'Content and Form', KAPF rejected the idea that content is bound to aesthetic quality. The nationalistic stances of KAPF in engaging the proletariat art movement clearly echoed Gramsci's ideas on content and form: 'Content is actually fighting for a specific national culture, a specific conception of the world, in opposition to other cultures and world views.'[18]

Within a couple of years, KAPF was transformed into a radical political body, declaring the 'art movement as a weapon for political struggles'. It concentrated on organisation, political agitation and ideological uniformity with the party line. In order to achieve the national-popular class revolution, KAPF was not merely engaged in art movements. It sent its members to factories and to the countryside to agitate and support labour strikes. At the same time, it led political demonstrations against the Japanese colonial rule in the name of the exploited Korean working masses, stressing that national liberation and class revolution could not be separated from each other. KAPF also promoted cooperation with international proletariat movements and Bolshevik-style popular art movements. This populism and internationalism of KAPF would, as shall be seen, evaporate with the personality cult and isolationism expressed by contemporary North Korean film.[19]

Despite criticism by the mainstream in the existing literature circles of the unsophisticated manners and strong ideological inclination which the new tendency writers adopted,[20] KAPF initiated socialist film movements in Korea. KAPF writers conceived film as the most effective educational tool for the largely illiterate masses. Between 1928 and 1931, KAPF members, such as Im Hwa, Gim Yuyeong and Gang Ho produced five 'tendency' films including *Wandering* (1928), *Imbecile Street* (1929) and *The Underground Village* (1931). In order to fund the filmmaking, KAPF established a foreign film distribution agency, the Dongyang Film Stoke Company, in 1927. In the following year, it founded a new film company, Seoul Kino, with the aim of making film along the lines of socialist realism. Most of their works, however, were left unfinished owing to the censorship of the colonial government combined with lack of finances. More importantly, the strong motivation to promote mass socio-politicisation appeared to leave the audience as the passive addressees of the one-sided communication.

In 1935, KAPF was finally dispersed after a series of arrests of its members. After the forced liquidation, the former KAPF members chose different paths: some of them quit filmmaking and returned to underground Korean Communist party activity, and some of them started making 'pure' or pro-Japanese films. Gang Ho and Yun Gijeong represent the first group, Gang making *The Dark Road* (1928) and *The Underground Village* (1931). The KAPF critic, Seo Gwangje, made the first pro-Japanese military film, *Troop Train* (1938). An Seokyeong, a co-writer of *The Underground Village*, also made a pro-Japanese military film entitled *The Volunteer Soldier* (1941). Gim Yuyeong, who made three out of five KAPF resistance films, was among those who turned to making non-political, literary films. 'What was gained is ideology and what was lost is art',[21] the statement of Pak Yeongheui, one of the early leading figures of KAPF, succinctly expresses the desolate conditions which the majority of colonised intellectuals confronted. The historical discontinuity of socialist filmmaking in Korea was not caused by the apostasy of individuals but it sheds light on the limited accountability of cultural struggles without a popular base.

The 1945 national division of the peninsula by the Allies made the majority of former KAPF members turn to the communist North under the Soviet military administrative rule. Before they crossed to the North, the former KAPF members sought to politicise in the South first. They condemned the national division by the occupation forces, and insisted on radical reforms for the newly liberated Korea. America's priority in the post-war settlement on the Korean peninsula was the creation of an anti-Communist regime and implantation of a capitalist market economy.[22] In this situation, the resumption of the socialist-oriented filmmaking tradition could be one of the most dangerous political activities against America's intentions. For socialist filmmakers, the cultural policy of the American military government was not very different from that of the Japanese colonial rule.

Since the occupation period (1945–48), the South has maintained anti-Communism as the state ideology and it was only in the mid-1980s that the South finally witnessed the revival of the KAPF tradition in the shape of popular democratisation movements. *Minjok Yeonghwa Undong*, the National Film Movement, was initiated by university students and radical intellectuals during this period. They established an organisation called Changsankkonmae.[23] Opposing the political passivity of commercial film practices, they made a series of films for factory workers, the urban poor, farmers and other underprivileged people and showed their films at factories, university campuses or other non-commercial venues. The South Korean independent film movements during the 1980s can be understood as part of the democratisation of society. *Oh, the Land of Dream* (1989) and *The Night before the Strike* (1990) are the most representative works of contemporary South Korean socialist-oriented films, endorsing pro-labour, anti-government and anti-Americanism. In a sense, the National Film Movement attempted to revive the revolutionary stances of KAPF, rejecting the capitalist social orders and ideological norms imposed on popular film practices.[24]

In the North, from 1948, the newly emerged 'socialist' regime gave new life to the former KAPF filmmakers. Under the patronage of the state, their frustrated dreams of filmmaking for socialist revolution seemed to be realised. However, the changing power politics within the Party limited their creative imagination and eventually removed them from the sites of cultural struggles for revolution. During the late 1950s and 1960s, most of the former KAPF members were purged through a series of anti-sectionalist struggles. Dogmatism influenced by foreign ideas, federal flunkeyism (worship of the powerful), bourgeois nihilism and reactionary tendencies were phrases used by Kim Jong Il to criticise the former KAPF members and their work.[25] The harsh criticism of KAPF by the Party continued until the early 1990s.[26]

In stricter terms, the historically weak position of the revolutionary state is responsible for the changing views on KAPF. The establishment of the socialist regime in the North was not the fruit of Korean communists' spontaneous movements or class struggles by the masses. The Democratic People's Republic of Korea emerged in 1948 after a three-year occupation period, with the assistance of the Soviet Union and China. Kim Il Sung took the headship of the revolutionary state, his symbolic link to the Soviet Union worn on his shoulders: he came back to Korea in a Soviet military uniform after the liberation. To win the ideological hegemony of the newly liberated society, he desperately needed to find his Korean identity and establish his own guerrilla activities as 'the tradition of Korean revolution'.[27] Although Kim counted on his old partisans, his domination over the indigenous Korean communists in the early period was possible by embracing all the different elements, including former KAPF members. In order to win popularity, collaboration with the former KAPF members seemed to be crucial, and they were mobilised to teach foreign ideas and implant political systems in the minds of the masses through film and literature.

The power struggles within the Party were left dormant until the Korean War (1950–53). The war gave an opportunity to Kim Il Sung to attack his South Korean rivals within the Party and the 1960s Sino-Soviet Dispute helped Kim to get rid of other factions. First, he purged Pak Heonyeong, the leader of the South Korean Communist party, and his followers including Im Hwa, formerly the leader of KAPF. Pak and Im were charged with spying for America during the war. However, the majority of Party members, who were also strongly supported by the Soviet Union and China, survived to contest the leadership of Kim Il Sung and his power struggles until the late 1960s. The North Korean revolutionary state won ideological hegemony through power struggles not class struggles. In this sense, Kim Jong

Il's current regime inherits the weak ideological position of a society where the mass-initiated revolution still remains as a theory.

The 'hegemonic alliance'[28] between the power elite and the indigenous communists, who survived the first stage of the elimination process during the Korean War, accounts for why the revolutionary state adapted KAPF socialist realism as the ideological foundation for the cultural construction of the people's lives in the early period. KAPF socialist realism represented the ideological hegemony of the power elite, which was extended from class domination to the securing of active consent in the form of a 'national-popular collective will'.[29] Marxist-Leninism provided the theoretical basis of the state ideology without strategic discrimination of different ideological orientations between the power elite. This opaque ideological position of the revolutionary state allowed for the dynamics of North Korean film culture until the late 1960s.

The ideological confrontations within the power block ended with the 1967 Gapsan Anti-sectionalist Struggle. The victory of Kim Il Sung's faction over pro-Soviet and pro-Chinese factions within the Party became the turning point in the theoretical orientation of North Korean art and literature from KAPF socialist realism to anti-Japanese literature led by Kim Il Sung.[30] The Party proclaimed the *Juche* theory as the official state ideology[31] and Marxist-Leninism disappeared in the 1972 Socialist Constitution of the Democratic People's Republic of Korea. Great Leader Literature became the pool from which *Juche* art and literature theory was elaborated. Leading the power struggles and cultural changes, Kim Jong Il prepared for his power succession to his father for the next three decades. His succession to power was realised with Kim Il Sung's death in 1996.

The exploitation of KAPF social realism and the process of eliminating the leading figures in the cultural and political history of North Korea clearly illustrate that the state is 'hegemony armoured by coercion'.[32] KAPF tradition served as the engine of the revolutionary state in adapting Marxism in the film theory and practice in the early years. The practitioners provided moral support and theoretical grounds to utilise film as the primary ideological tool for the socialist revolution. The *Juche* film theory is a contemporary rendition of KAPF socialist realism, even though the current ideologically hegemonic groups seek to keep KAPF in the past and rewrite history in the interests of the present time.

NATION AND DESTINY: WHO IS THE AGENT OF HISTORY?

The Dear Leader, General Kim Jong Il developed a great plan: to make a series of films on 'Choson Minjok Jeiljueui Jeongsin' (literally, 'the Spirit of the Greatest Korean People'), based on the themes of the song, 'My Country is the Best.' General Kim named the title of the series as Nation and Destiny himself, and led the whole process of production.[33]

The production diary of Nation and Destiny provides a panoramic view of contemporary North Korean film policy and practices. Film in North Korea is a state-planned industry and social institution. The entire production and reception process of Nation and Destiny encapsulates the role of North Korean film in the most definite terms: filmmaking is a national enterprise for mass education and film viewing is a compulsory social activity for ordinary citizens. Since Kim Jong Il's orders to make the series in 1991, 62 episodes of the Nation and Destiny series have been produced by 2003 and the scenarios of the following 38 films have already been written to complete the hundred episodes in the near future, as scheduled. In 2001, the North Korean Central Broadcasting organisation claimed that the Nation and Destiny series is 'the biggest hit in world film history, shown over one million times per year for more than several hundred million people during the last ten years'.[34]

The self-claimed success of Nation and Destiny is not merely about audience sizes, screening numbers or even about producing the world record for the longest series of films with the biggest budget in North Korean film history. Rather, Nation and Destiny is praised as a masterpiece of Juche art, satisfying the high standards of both ideological education and popular entertainment. It is also noted that the series 'faultlessly' observes the three principles of filmmaking given by Kim Jong Il. The principles are the theories of seed (to choose the 'right' subjects for mass education), modelling (to depict the representative images of a model worker), and the speed campaign (to produce films quickly, as the need arises). Furthermore, Kim Jong Il acclaims Nation and Destiny as a prototype of collective work, it having been produced under the direct supervision of the Party from the initial stage of choosing the themes to the final editing and printing process. In short, the series serves as the role model for state cinema in North Korea.

The Nation and Destiny series unquestionably marks the subordination of film to politics, disclosing the ways in which the personalised state, i.e. Kim Jong Il, uses film to infuse the ideas of the state-led revolution into the masses' minds. Kim gave orders for the National Preparation Committee for *Nation and Destiny* to be organised, in the first year of the production period. Kim located various organisations, factories and cooperatives that would supply the materials and human resources to the film production teams. In a speech the following year, Kim told art and literature workers that '*Nation and Destiny* was zealously applauded by our people at home and abroad. The foreign audiences were also deeply impressed and praised the series to be a world classic, which only Koreans can produce.'[35] The head of state decides all aspects of filmmaking, financing and viewing in North Korea. He even delivers the foreign audiences' responses and comments to the masses although, in reality, the series was never released abroad and the people are completely isolated from the outside world. The filmmakers are expected to serve as mediators between the Party and the audience, delivering what the head of state wants to address to the masses. Thus, the *Nation and Destiny* series shows to what extent the state's intervention shapes the film industry and how the unilateral communication process eliminates the possibility of different points of view and diverse tastes between the individuals in both filmmaking and film viewing.

The extraordinary devotion of Kim to propaganda afforded the political and ideological bases for his power succession to his father, Kim Il Sung, which was officially announced at the 1982 People's Central Committee.[36] The political career of Kim Jong Il started with his involvement in filmmaking, when he was appointed as the director of the Propaganda and Agitation Bureau in the Party in 1967. The younger Kim attained the confidence of his father and other Party members in his ability as a political agitator with the series of films he supervised during the late 1960s and 1970s. Most of them are about his father's anti-Japanese revolutionary struggles, including eight films which won the People's Prize Winner, such as *The Sea of Blood* (1969), *The Fate of a Self-defence Corps Man* (1970) and *The Flower Girl* (1972). These three films are the representative works of Great Leader Literature, which contemporary North Korean literature insists are based on stories written by Kim Il Sung in the 1930s.[37] Since the mid-1980s, Kim Jong Il has also made a series of films idolising his family blood. According to North Korean literature, Kim Jong Il and his parents, Kim Il Sung and Kim Jong Sook, are the three 'greatest people' whom Heaven sent.[38] Also, including his grandparents, Kim Hyeong Jik and Kang Ban Suk, and his late uncles, his whole family are depicted as the revolutionary fighters in these family-cult films. The purpose of making family cult films is to reinforce the idea that his power succession is predestined, granting him full powers as the head of a theocratic state. The mass production of personality and family cult films based on Great Leader Literature divides the North Korean film history before and after the 1967 Anti-sectionalist Struggle. In addition, the new development of North Korean film during the period highlights how the populism and party-tendency of KAPF socialist realism was substituted with popular heroism – hidden heroes – and the Party loyalty elaborated by the *Juche* theory.

Under the younger Kim's direct supervision, the film industry has also rapidly expanded since the 1970s, leading the majority of North Korean art and literature. Currently, approximately 130 films have been produced per year including 30–40 feature films. This annual figure has not been interrupted by the deteriorating economic conditions combined with the natural disasters in recent years. Most of the films are shown at various places including the state-owned cinemas, cooperative factories and other working places all over the country. On average, an individual will watch nine films per year. Including the Choson Art Film Studio, there are three film studios consisting of several production teams. The Choson Art Film Studio, established in 1947, is the first and biggest film studio in North Korea, and makes *Nation and Destiny* along with the Choson 4.25 Art Film Studio, which belongs to the North Korean army and mainly produces the military films; it has five film production teams consisting of around 50 directors. Since the 1980s, after the collapse of the Communist bloc, foreign films were hardly shown to local audiences except a small number of old films imported from the USSR, China or Eastern Europe. In recent years, the Pyongyang Film Festival of Non-aligned and Other Developing Countries has become the main channel through which to show foreign films to a limited audience.

Despite the industrial expansion and privileged position as a state cinema, North Korean film, however, has suffered from a decline in its propaganda effectiveness since the late 1980s. The radical alteration of the early Marxist-Leninist socialist realism into *Juche* theory led to conventionality and uniformity. Repetitive themes and stories, stereotypical characterisation, or old theatrical acting and slow editing styles, even suggest the backwardness of North Korean cinema that contradicts Kim Jong Il's *On the Art of Cinema*. The rigidity in applying the state ideology to the representation of history and society stifles the creativity of filmmaking. Debates and discussions remain as a formality to support Party decisions.

The politically imposed film practices in North Korea are conducive to the nationalistic adaptation of socialism: *Urisik Sahoejueui* (Our Style Socialism). Our Style Socialism aims to keep a distance from the outside world, which has already witnessed the decline of Marxist-Leninism, the collapse of socialist regimes in the USSR and Eastern Europe, and China's open policy. In the late 1980s, North Korea started making more films dealing with stories of Koreans abroad or in the South. Regardless of the variation of individual stories, the theme is identical: to maintain the 'purity' and 'revolutionary spirits' of the Korean working class, North Korea should keep a distance from the outside world.[39]

Isolationism is the psychological mechanism of North Korea, in defence of the immense pressures to open the closed society in recent years. The rapidity of globalisation in world film culture seems to be the more direct concern behind the isolationistic representation of the outside world. The *Nation and Destiny* series echoes this isolationistic policy of the state both at social and cultural levels. The isolationism expressed by North Korean film, however, evinces the dictatorial voices of the state depriving filmmakers of freedom of expression, in dealing with the rapidly changing society and the undeniable impacts from the outside world. As a result, despite the forceful intervention of the state, the audience is becoming indifferent to or critical of the intended messages and is showing more interest in the outside world reconstructed on the screen.[40] This is the complexity and multiplicity in relations among culture, ideology and politics. Film provides the audience with the possibility of new perspectives on the social reality represented on screen. In this sense, film in North Korea is an open space in a closed society, proving that cultural autonomy cannot be easily dictated by politics.

KAPF WRITERS: THE STAR SYSTEM[41] AND THE BIRTH OF NEW ORGANIC INTELLECTUALS

The *Juche*-oriented art and literature theory dictates that 'art and literature should glorify the prominence of the Great Leader and the revolutionary history, and create a prototype of truthful communist who is faithful to the Great Leader'.[42] *KAPF Writers* subscribes to this guideline, presenting an ideal relationship between the Great Leader, the new organic intellectuals and the masses. The nine episodes of *KAPF Writers* dramatise the different paths of individual KAPF members, contrasting those who led the self-destructive struggles without the guidance of the Great Leader and those who chose the 'right way'.

The conversion in *KAPF Writers* of the protagonist, Ri Chan, from an ingenious Marxist to the clergy of Kimilsungism encapsulates the birth of a new organic intellectual in the classless society. Chan used to be a typical colonial intellectual – coming from a rich family and studying abroad. The Tokyo Imperial University student and lyricist joined KAPF to confirm the hopeless future of Korean socialist art movements in the face of powerful colonial forces. When he learned about the anti-Japanese struggles led by Kim Il Sung and his literary works for the exploited Korean working masses, he finally realises who he must follow for the national class revolution.

KAPF Writers reconstructs a Star System to discriminate leader from the masses. The Star System depicted by the series is the selection process of model workers who teach the masses about the Great Leader's ideas on revolution. Through a series of trials, including the sacrifice of his sweetheart, Gim Gyeongran, a resistance poet, the protagonist proves his readiness to work as a messenger of the Great Leader and an avant-garde of the Party. The nomination of model workers through the Star System insists that the authority of the Party comes from the Great Leader and the Party does not rule the masses. The 'correctness' of the Great Leader in choosing a model worker from the masses justifies the division between leader and the led in advancing the revolution. The selection process of model workers signifies the birth of new organic intellectuals. Also, the series emphasises that their birth is materialised in the form of a collective will: the popular consent to the decisions of the Great Leader.

The Star System is visible in all North Korean films, stressing the transferred authority of new intellectuals from the Great Leader. In the series, the protagonist and his friends were once fascinated with foreign ideas (i.e. Marxist-Leninism) but were *reborn* as loyal guards of *Juche* ideas. The dramatisation of this selection process suggests that the new division between the dominant groups and the masses is purely technical and functional.[43] The new social division is supposed to be fundamentally different from class division, because the organic intellectuals serve the masses, instead of ruling the masses. Based on this interpretation, *KAPF Writers* reiterates the Party's guideline for filmmaking: every film should create the images of an ideal model worker armed with *Juche* ideology. At the same time, the films highlight how the role of the new organic intellectuals is institutionalised into the command power of the Party.

The stereotypical storylines and characterisations in *KAPF Writers* are devised to define the contemporary meanings of the political revolution led by the state. The films address Kim Jong Il's messages on ongoing revolution in present-day North Korea. The national class revolution must continue from generation to generation because his power inheritance is approved by his own father so that he can finish the war that his father started. Compared to his father, the younger Kim does not have the historical ground to claim his revolutionary career, such as anti-Japanese struggles or commanding the national liberation war against America. Therefore, Kim Jong Il needs his late father's legacy more than ever. The anti-Japanese revolutionary literature led by Kim Il Sung and the Great Leader Literature, which the younger Kim used to relegate KAPF to the past, especially needed to be reintroduced to address his capability as the Supreme Commander to lead the national liberation war against the Americans and old class enemies in the South. This 'nationalistic' application of Marxism by North Korean film supports the hypothesis that 'passive revolution' can occur in a socialist country, as Gramsci suggested in his remarks on the West.

In reinforcing the legitimacy of his reign, the articulation of filial piety of the protagonist to the late Great Leader continues to develop the foundation myth to the Kim Jong Il power succession.[44] Ri Chan is the only intellectual who fully understands the revolutionary thoughts of Kim Il Sung, well-informed of his anti-Japanese struggles. In the films, Kim Il Sung and his wife Kim Jong Sook treat Ri as a real son, providing an ideal environment for him to work as a new organic intellectual for the liberated nation. Ri is a self-reflective figure of Kim Jong Il, who is the only authoritative translator who fully understands the *Juche* theory that was created by the late Great Leader. As the protagonist proves his leadership to the masses with the loyalty and filial piety to the Great Leader in the films, Kim Jong Il also seeks to convince the masses of his rightful power succession with his extreme loyalty and filial piety to his late father. *KAPF Writers* reveals Kim Jong Il's attempts to justify the power succession by blending Confucian familial ideals with the ideas of political revolution led by the personalised state.

From a historical perspective, *KAPF Writers* represents the 1990s official view of the Party on KAPF and 'pure' literary works during the Japanese colonial period. First, it attempts to restore the contribution of KAPF to the history of North Korean art and literature to a limited extent. Through this, the films seek to justify the rule of Kim Jong Il who promotes *Gwangpok Jeongchi* (the Politics of Benevolence and Broadness), attempting to distinguish his ruling style from his father's. The series introduces virtuous images of the state, emphasising its greatness in forgiving the undesirable elements of the past and giving them another chance to work for the nation. However, the majority of main characters depicted in a positive light were dead before the liberation, and the protagonist, Chan, was not a leading figure of KAPF and his story is fictitious. Second, the episodes re-evaluate certain contributions of pure literature traditions led by lyric poets and writers, such as Yi Gwangsu, Gim Soweol and Yeom Sangseop. Through dramatisation of the revised art and literature history, Kim Jong Il stresses the sense of oneness to the masses after decades of a process of elimination and discrimination.

As in *KAPF Writers*, the manifestation of nationalism characterises the thematic features of North Korean film since the 1990s, overriding the themes of class domination and Party loyalty. The cinematic representations of the colonial history and post-colonial experiences of the people aim to suggest that the revolution is not completed yet and the state is still at war with national enemies, i.e. Americans. From a North Korean point of view, the past exists only for the present: history, which cannot justify the present needs of the Party, is radically altered or completely destroyed. One of the significant roles of film in North Korea is to promote the Party's new interpretations of history. The dramatisation of Korean proletarian art movements by *KAPF Writers* clearly reflects the present perspective of the Party's interpretation of revolutionary history.

MARXISM AND NORTH KOREAN STATE CINEMA

In discussing the origin and evolution of North Korean film, Marxism offers a useful conceptual framework for the analysis of the contradictory relationship between film and state. The application of the Marxist notion of class revolution to the nationalistic form is one of the most crucial themes in constructing cinematic discourses on nation and history. Although the Korean state acknowledges the contribution of Marxism to contemporary film practices to a certain extent, the mass-politicisation for class revolution by the past elite is the essence of North Korean film policy. The North Korean application of Marxism attempts to justify the ideological ground for the state's intervention in the cultural lives of the masses.

On the other hand, the Marxist notion of mass-initiated revolution also offers a critical insight into the subordination of film to politics in North Korea. As I discussed above, the autonomy of culture cannot be completely removed by political necessity. Culture is a site of struggle for the masses to challenge the ideological hegemony of the dominant social group. North Korean cinema is not an exception. The complexity and multiplicity of meanings expressed by a cultural text tend to disclose the oppressive apparatus of the state, which is an attempt to marginalise the masses as the passive addressees of the communication process. The contradictory relationship between film and politics in North Korea indicates that Marxist criticism of film practices in capitalist countries in the West is also very useful to the study of the origins and historical evolution of North Korean cinema as a means for 'passive revolution'.

Acknowledgement

The research for this chapter was supported by the 2003 Korean Foundation Fellowship for Field Research.

NOTES

1. In this chapter, I generally adopted the modified McCune-Reischauer system to transcribe Korean words. The personal names are given in the Korean order, i.e. family name first. Although family names are often written differently according to personal preference, I transcribed them consistently, following the system: Pak, So or Cho'e instead of Park, Suh or Cho. Finally, I adopted the spellings of places' or persons' names if they are already available in English texts, such as Pyongyang or Kim Il Sung.

2. It is a slogan in the background of factory scenes in the *Working Class* series: *Nation and Destiny 22–33, 43 and 44* (Cho Kyeongsun and others, 1991–).

3. Kim Jong Il, *On the Art of Cinema* (Pyongyang: Foreign Language Publishing House, 1994), p. 2.

4. Kim Il Sung, 'On Eliminating Dogmatism and Formalism and Establishing *Juche* in Ideological Work: Speech to Party Propaganda and Agitation Workers', in *Kim Il Sung Work 9: July 1954 to December 1955* (Pyongyang: Foreign Language Publishing House, 1982), pp. 395–417.

5. Kim Jong Il, 'Marx-Leninjueui-wa Juche Sasang-eui Gichi-reul Nopi Deulgo Nagaja' (Let us move forward with Marxist-Leninism and *Juche* Idea), in *Kim Jong Il Jeojakseon* (Selected Works of Kim Jong Il) (Seoul: Gyeongnam University Far-East Research Institute, 1991), p. 166.

6. Gim Jaeyong, *Bukhan Munhak-eui Ihae* (Understanding of North Korean Literature) (Seoul: Munhak-kwa Jiseongsa, 1994), pp. 203–13.
7. Lee Hyangjin, *Contemporary Korean Cinema: Identity, Culture and Politics* (Manchester: Manchester University Press, 2000).
8. *Wolmi Island* (Cho Kyeongsun, 1982).
9. *Paekeui Minjok*, 'white clothed nation' signifies the purity and diligence of the people who traditionally wore white cotton.
10. Partha Chatterjee, *Nationalist Thought and the Colonial World* (Minneapolis: University of Minnesota Press, 1986), p. 2.
11. Antonio Gramsci, *Selections from the Prison Notebooks*, ed. and trans. Quintin Hoare and Geoffrey Nowell-Smith (London: Lawrence & Wishart, 1971), pp. 180–5.
12. Partha Chatterjee, *The Nation and Its Fragments: Colonial and Post-colonial Histories* (Princeton: Princeton University Press, 1993), pp. 211–14.
13. Gramsci, *Selections from the Prison Notebooks*, pp. 5–13.
14. Kim Jong Il, *The Character and the Actor* (Pyongyang: Foreign Language Publishing House, 1987).
15. Chatterjee argued that 'passive revolution' is 'the *general* form of the transition from colonial to post-colonial national state in the 20th century'. Chatterjee, *Nationalist Thought and the Colonial World*, p. 50.
16. Gramsci used the spontaneity of the masses to limited extent, stressing the leadership of the party to educate them. See, Antonio Gramsci, *Selections from Cultural Readings*, ed. and trans. Quintin Hoare and Geoffrey Nowell-Smith (London: Lawrence & Wishart, 1971).
17. Disproving their claim, North Korea has a strict social stratification system. The Party classifies the population at three societal levels: the core, the basic and the unstable. These three strata are subdivided into 51 categories according to family origins and social backgrounds. For details see, Lee, *Contemporary Korean Cinema*, pp. 145–7; Seo Jaejin, *Bukhan Sahoe-eui Gyegupkaldeung Yeongu* (A Study of Class Conflict in North Korea) (Seoul: National Unification Institute, 1996).
18. Gramsci, *Selections from Cultural Readings*, p. 203.
19. The Study Group for History of Literature, *KAPF Munhak Undong Yeongu* (A Study of KAPF Literature Movement) (Seoul: Yeoksabipyeonsa, 1989), pp. 57–63 and 241–5.
20. Until the 1990s, the dominant/official South Korean views on the historical significance of KAPF were extremely sceptical. For example, most school textbooks introduced the 'pure literature' as the prevailing trend under the Japanese colonial rule but did not discuss the KAPF socialist movements in depth. The most popular 'pure literature' writers included Yeom Sangseop, Yi Gwangsu, Na Dohyang and Gim Dongin. The so-called 'pure literature' writers opposed the political engagement and class literature theory of the new tendency writers, advocating freedom of art from politics. See Yun Pyongro, *Minjok Munhak-eui Mosaek* (Searching for a National Literature) (Seoul: Peomusa, 1991), pp. 227–9.
21. Yun, *Minjok Munhak-eui Mosaek*, p. 262.
22. Jang Jip Choi, 'Political Cleavages in South Korea', in Hagen Koo (ed.), *State and Society in Contemporary Korea* (Ithaca and London: Cornell University Press, 1993), p. 19.

23. Changsankkonmae is the name of legendary peoples said to have lived in Changsankkot in North Korea. Changsankkot is well known in Korean literature on the origin of the popular social movements in old Korea. Therefore, Changsankkonmae symbolises the will and rightfulness of the spirits in protecting the people in their resistance to foreign oppression and class exploitation.

24. Byeon Jaeran, '1930 Nyeondae Jeonhu KAPF Yeonghwa Hwaldong Yeongu' (A Study of the KAPF Film Movement in the Late 1920s and the Early 1930s), in National Film Research Institute (ed.), *Minjok Yeonghwa 2* (National Film 2) (Seoul: Chingu, 1990), p. 219.

25. Kim Jong Il, 'Bandang, Banhyeongmyeong Bunjadeul-eui Sasang Yeodok-eul Ppurippaego Dang-eui *Yuil* Sasang Chegye-reul Seulde Daehayeo' (Concerning the Eradication of the Poisonous Thoughts of the Anti-party, Anti-revolutionary Elements and the Establishment of *Yuil* Thought) (25 June 1967), in *Kim Jong Il Jeojakseonjip* (Pyongyang: Korean Workers' Party Publishing House, 1992), pp. 230–1.

26. *Ryeoksa Sajeon II* (Dictionary of History II) (Pyongyang: Social Science Publishing House), p. 828.

27. Dae-Sook Suh, *Kim Il Sung: The North Korean Leader* (New York: Columbia University Press, 1988), p. 143.

28. Gramsci, *Selections from Cultural Readings*, p. 196.

29. Gramcsi, *Selections from the Prison Notebooks*, pp. 130–3 and 421.

30. Gim, *Bukhan Munhak-eui Ihae*, p. 14.

31. Although Kim proposed *Juche* on the state ideology of North Korea in 1955, it was only after 1967 that *Juche* theory was able to claim its full authority over Marxism-Leninism as the supreme state ideology.

32. Gramsci, *Selections from the Prison Notebooks*, p. 263.

33. Ri Hyeonsun and Eom Yeongil, *Dabujak* Minjok-kwa Unyeong-*e Daehan Yeongu* (A Study of the Multi-part Art Film *Nation and Destiny* 1(Pyongyang: Social Science Publishing House, 2000), p. 4.

34. *2002 Bukhan Yeongam* (2002 North Korea Yearbook) (Seoul: Yeonhap News, 2001), p. 765.

35. Kim Jong Il, 'Dabujak Yesul Yonghwa *Minjok-kwa Unmyeong*-eui Changjak Seonggwa-e Todaehayeo Munhak Yesul Keonseol-eseo Saeroun Jeonhwan-eul Ileukija' (Let's Reach a New Turning Point in the Construction of Literature and Art, Based on the Creative Result of the Multi-volume Art Film, *Nation and Destiny*) (23 May 1992), in *Choson Jungang Nyeongam 1993* (Choson Year Book 1993) (Pyongyang: Choson Jungang Tongsinsa, 1993), p. 50.

36. Takashi Sakai, 'The Power Base of Kim Jong Il: Focusing on Its Formation Process', in Park Han S. (ed.), *North Korea: Ideology, Politics, Economy* (Englewood Cliffs: Prentice Hall, 1996), pp. 105–22.

37. Gim, *Bukhan Munhak-eui Ihae*, pp. 217–19.

38. '3 Dae Wiin-i Naerin Seongsan' (Sacred Mountains to Which the Three Greatest People Came Down), *Choson Munhak* (Choson Literature), June 1994, pp. 21–3.

39. Kim Jong Il, *Juche Munhakron* (The Theory of *Juche* Literature) (Pyongyang: Munye Publishing House, 1992), p. 2.

40. From interviews with North Korean defectors in Yi Uyeong, *Nambukhan Munhwa Jeongchaek Bigyo Yeongu* (A Comparative Study of North and South Korean Culture Policies) (Seoul: the Research Institute for National Unification, 1994).

41. North Korea has an official recognition system for the exemplary worker in every sector of society. The Party appoints an individual as a national hero of endeavour, as recognition of her/his record-breaking achievement to renew the working target given by the Party or innovate the old working method with earnest working spirit. The late 1950s and 1960s *Chollima Undong* (literally a galloping horse movement) was a representative and most historical case. An individual who is appointed as the national hero of endeavour by the Party is given social prestige and various benefits as the cream of the society. The story of Jin Eungsan, the protagonist of *Working Class* parts in *Nation and Destiny* is loosely based on the life story of the historical figure, the first *Chollima* hero. In the film industry, there are some chosen film artists too. They are classified in two categories, as either 'the people's' or 'honour's' actors, director or artists. Most of those officially recognised North Korean film artists appeared in the *Nation and Destiny* series.

42. Kim Jong Il, *On the Art of Cinema*, pp. 13–14.

43. Gramsci, *Selections from Cultural Readings*; Anne Showstack Sasson, *Gramsci's Politics*, 2nd edn (London: Hutchinson Education, 1987), p. 139.

44. Yun Gideok, *Suryeong Hyeonsang Munhak* (Great Leader Literature) (Pyongyang: Munye Publishing, 1991).

10
Narrative, Culture and Legitimacy: Repetition and Singularity in Zhang Yimou's *The Story of Qiu Ju*

Xudong Zhang

MODERNISM AND ITS AFTERLIFE

Since the late 1980s, Zhang Yimou has established himself as the most recognised filmmaker from the People's Republic and a celebrated name brand in world cinema. After a rapid rise to fame, his works now invite an approach rarely afforded to PRC film artists (except perhaps in the case of Xie Jin), namely to have their entire corpus studied as a singular visual world bearing the signature of its *auteur*. Such recognition, to be sure, represents the pinnacle of an inherently aesthetic hierarchy that is nominally but not substantively repudiated by today's literary criticism, film and cultural studies. It comes with a tacit acceptance of the film authors' insistence that they be read within the parameters of the world of their own creation, and with the foremost resistance to any attempt to collapse the visual and the aesthetic into the immediate socio-political.[1]

Rather than reject from the outset such auteurist mythology, which today no longer seems to be a challenging intellectual task, I would like to use the residual values of such notions as autonomy, freedom and creativity, to trace and reconstruct the procedures of codifying in film texts the economic, social, and cultural-ideological world while establishing a critical distance between a necessarily politicised world of life and its necessarily aestheticised representation. Such a distance, while determined by the nature of artistic production, is above all made mandatory by the logic of historical analysis. One simply cannot tackle the historical overdetermination and political complexity of the 'content' of Zhang Yimou's recent films – understood here as something pertaining to the more general questions of the continuity and reinvention of tradition, the legacy of Chinese socialism, and the political nature of contemporary China – without a radical detour to or mediation in the realm of 'form', in this case the minute cinematic operations in both visual and narrative terms.

It is intriguing to note that, although the modernist aesthetic (notions of symbolism, aesthetic intensity, stylistic innovation and self-consciousness, formal autonomy or self-referentiality, etc.) remains crucial in Zhang's competitive edge vis-à-vis other contenders at international film festivals, its centrality can no longer be limited to a photographical ontology aimed at capturing the 'physical reality' of a historical moment of post-Mao Chinese reforms, as was the case during the 1980s. Rather, in his work in the 1990s, the ontological dimension is mingled seamlessly with the political, the latter understood not so much in terms of government policies and political doctrines, but the everyday world of Chinese society framed by its massive transition into the market system guided by an authoritarian party-state. This has required a shift away from the sculptural monumentality of the early Fifth Generation filmmakers (demonstrated in *Yellow Earth* (Chen Kaige 1983), *Red Sorghum* (Zhang Yimou 1988), or *To Live* (Zhang Yimou 1994) to a more subtle and supple narrative form, one which suggests a new collective sensibility embedded in Chinese everyday life conditioned by the so-called 'socialist market economy'. The formal, stylistic articulation of this new collective sensibility not only concerns the aesthetic and philosophical innovativeness of contemporary Chinese literature and culture, but indeed can provide a way by which to rethink intellectual and political issues related to the larger context of the nation state versus global imperial order, community and culture versus the prevailing rhetoric of the universal, historical continuity and discontinuity, and the singularity of the sovereign versus the generality of the abstract and the exchangeable. It is with these questions in mind that I turn to a close analysis of a film text, Zhang Yimou's award-winning 1994 film, *The Story of Qiu Ju*.

CULTURAL POLITICS OF DAILY LIFE

The Story of Qiu Ju is based on a story written by a neo-realist (*xin xieshi*) Chinese writer, Chen Yuanbin, entitled 'The Wan Family's Law Suit', which was published in 1992.[2] In the title of the literary version, the character 'wan' is both a common family name (therefore my above translation of 'The Wan Family's Law Suit') and the number 'ten thousand'. The resulting meaning, tinged with homophonic playfulness, is 'a myriad of lawsuits', which is never lost in the uniquely sensitive background of Zhang Yimou's deceptively relaxed filmic version.

Zhang Yimou, who has a record of butchering the literary text to suit his own cinematic vision, proves to be quite loyal to the story of the Wan family lawsuit, whose simple thematic and narrative structure is centred on stubbornness, repetition, contradiction, and the dialectic between multiplicity and singularity, which also constitute the formal and moral substance of his film adaptation. The story is about a peasant woman, Qiu Ju, who is determined to see justice done after her husband is kicked between the legs by the village chief as a result of a minor dispute. The dramatic substance of the film comes almost entirely from Qiu Ju's repeated – and repeatedly frustrated – journeys through which to appeal to ever-higher offices for justice as she is not satisfied with the mediation, compromise and verdict offered by lower-level offices. The film's self-consciously documentary style marked a sharp turn in Fifth Generation cinematic language. It allows the film to descend from a compulsive aesthetic and philosophical height to address those important social issues such as rural justice and government, and Chinese legal and political reform in general. It continues the Fifth Generation tradition of observing Chinese rural life with an anthropological, sociological fervour and seriousness, but what sets *The Story of Qiu Ju* apart from a *Yellow Earth* is the fact that rural life, stylised by a modern cinematic language, no longer serves as the aesthetic basis for a fundamentally political and philosophical critique of tradition or the political culture of the communist state. Instead, rural or peasant life occupies the film screen as a *being in itself*, that is, as a form of life with its own historical and moral substance, even aesthetic self-sufficiency. The early Fifth Generation poetics of backwardness, so central to its cinematic distinction, is here replaced by a narrative form which can articulate the rhythms and material specificity of daily life. The embeddedness of the modernist sensibility in peasant life is evident in the strikingly suggestive image of the red chilli peppers hung to dry outside the house. These red chilli peppers exist in perfect harmony between use value (that is, value determined by quality and usefulness) and exchange value (prevailing market price), and between exchange value and aesthetic value. They are 'self-sufficient' symbols of a peasant form of life and when sold in the market they generate cash that funds Qiu Ju's repeated pursuit of justice as she understands it. A daily necessity and a reminder of material production, the red chilli peppers are an indication of the inherent aesthetic texture of manual labour and village life, even the latent moral dignity, unruliness and defiance of the Chinese peasantry.

In simple and misleading terms the film is a legal drama culminating in the court decision. The centrality of the legal, however, comes with its own ambiguity, even subversion. The sheer focus and intensity of the story gives rise to a kind of allegorical flight, as if everything in this film means something else. The central plot of the film, namely a lone peasant woman taking on the state apparatus in pursuit of justice, only triggers a different chain reaction leading to a different set of questions. If the film were about (in)justice and (il)legality in Chinese society, it would be nearly impossible for it to avoid the simplistic themes of state versus society, official versus non-official, modernity versus tradition, city versus country, and so forth, that is, binary opposites which still hold sway in much of the conventional media and academic writings about contemporary China. The fact that *The Story of Qiu Ju* does not seem to fall into the usual and uninteresting traps of those binaries has caused much uneasiness among its critics. In vague terms, some have suggested that the film (and Zhang Yimou as an increasingly successful filmmaker in China today) can be read as an endorsement of the Chinese government because it presents a somewhat humane, at least stable and tolerable, image of the everyday world in contemporary China. Such a transparent reading lacks resonance with and misses the complexity of a cultural text. It is imaginable, though, that the critics from both the far right and the far left, who, for radically different reasons, are unwilling to concede any legitimacy to the post-socialist state in name or in substance, will find their own ideological frameworks unfit for handling both the simplicity and the complexity of Zhang's cinematic narratives and, by extension, his latent cultural politics.

Before we move on to address the central questions regarding this film, let us take a look at the way it begins, which offers a telling clue to the significant change in both style and cultural politics of the filmmaker. The opening of *The Story of Qiu Ju* readily reminds us of the opening of Zhang Yimou's first film, *Red Sorghum* (1988). That is to say, the opening shots of the two films are diametrically opposed to one another. *Red Sorghum* notoriously starts with a sensuous, voyeuristic close-up of Gong Li trapped inside a wedding sedan, basking in amorous red colour. The striking image unmistakably announces the arrival of Zhang Yimou as a key figure in the Fifth Generation. It serves not only as a sign of objectified social desire, but also as a recognisable, indeed unforgettable, visual archetype and cinematic logo of many of Zhang Yimou's films to come. This naked, over-aestheticised human face can be read as a not-so-subtle *Mona Lisa* of a post-Mao Chinese secularisation. It reveals a social landscape, indeed a social libido, under the aesthetic veil called the 'modern cinematic language'. The aestheticised face of Gong Li, which evokes desire in the watching spectator, is also the first shot of a shot-reverse-shot between Gong Li and her object of desire, namely the half-naked sedan carrier. This is the standard Hollywood technique for suturing together a desiring subject and his/her 'object of desire' (the message: one is not a subject until you start desiring!). The shock effect was largely confined to the early years of the Chinese economic reform. For the jaded eyes of today's film critic, what is noteworthy about that image in a formalistic sense is its situational exclusiveness, namely the scene being inside the wedding sedan, a thoroughly enclosed space, and its relentless visual focus and homogeneity, namely the female face, the colour red, and the symbolic uniformity which gives the sequence both a visual pleasure almost as from an advertisement and a reassuring touch of high modernism. These are not to mention the implicit political rebelliousness in unleashing the mechanism of the daydream in the face of the still rigid, clumsy state discourse of the 'Four Adheres' (to Marxism and Leninism; to the socialist system; to the leadership of the Chinese Communist Party; and to proletarian dictatorship). In retrospect, the political ontology of early post-Mao culture requires such a sharply concentrated and ruthlessly exclusive optical situation to accomplish its aesthetic-philosophical build-up for the articulation of social desire.[3]

The opening scene of *Qiu Ju*, no less shocking, can be read as a social deconcealment of a different kind. It reveals, rather, exposes the concreteness and irreducibility of the everyday world by means of a patient and fascinated sociological-anthropological observation. One will recall the visual resemblance of the opening scene of *Qiu Ju* to a documentary on small-town life in rural China. Unlike the scene discussed above, in which the camera penetrates deeply into the physical texture of the everyday world and is literally 'inside' the wedding sedan, moving among objects of desire themselves (reminiscent of Walter Benjamin's famous observation that photography is a surgeon's scalpel cutting into the human body whereas traditional oil painting is a witch doctor's hand moving around it), the opening shot of *Qiu Ju* is made with a fixed hidden camera whose presence is predicated on its presumed absence or, better still, its secured, unnoticed being as part of the site. What faces the audience, what is presented by a supposedly passive camera that seeks to capture the world intact, is the continuous, endless flow of the crowd in a typical village bazaar. The shot lasts as long as two minutes (an eternity for a fixed shot in which 'nothing happens'), with Gong Li appearing, barely recognisable at first, in the last ten seconds. Revealed as a pregnant peasant woman, with her injured husband on a pushcart accompanied by her sister-in-law, played by an amateur actress, she thoroughly blends into the background. She comes to the fore not by means of a cinematic zoom-in, but rather through a patient, almost leisurely, long-take in which she approaches the hidden camera in the least 'self-conscious' manner. In the meantime, life swirls by, as indicated by the swarms of relaxed, slow-moving and semi-indifferent crowds in a small town market place. It takes a following series of horizontal-movement shots to set the main protagonists apart from the rest of the crowd, and at this point the narrative sequence of the story begins. If the initial shot is a declaration of the documentary impulse of the film, the following shot makes clear the melodramatic intent of it. The frontal encounter with the crowd is replaced by a scroll picture depicting a stream of quotidian life, a narrative reproduction deliberate in its shapelessness and contingency and yet structured in terms of a cinematic formation. In other words, the cinematographic device used to separate the central character is also meant to press her evenly and more firmly into the mosaic of the everyday world to which she belongs and from which she emerges almost indiscernibly as one among many.

One may be tempted to speculate that such a non-judgemental camera permits Zhang Yimou to cast a sympathetic light on the Chinese state, as it is itself considered a cluster of conflicting and coexisting moral and cultural codes from within and but one participant in the emerging and reconfiguring social sphere from without. It is in this light that such secondary characters in the film as the local policeman, the village chief, and the Director of the Public Security Bureau in the city must be viewed, that is, not as mere organs of an indifferent and abstract modern bureaucracy, but as mediators of an integral yet internally differentiated, even fragmented social totality, whose value system owes its very survival and legitimacy to the multiplicities and specificities of part-socialist Chinese everyday life.

To those utopian neo-liberal revolutionaries who are impatient with the existing Chinese socio-political reality, Zhang's film certainly would look like an apology for the status quo, which is too sluggish, messy and backward for a clean-cut free market complete with clear legal codes protecting private ownership and the political procedure of parliamentary democracy. Zhang may as well be considered guilty as charged, but his real or potential accusers easily forget the fact that his films are equally subversive to the unreformed loyalists for the old party-state, its fantastic central plans, and its unmediated, indifferent and often brutal reach into the social space. Indeed it is precisely the fantastic absolutism demonstrated in both the planners of socialist modernity and the visionaries of global capitalist homogeneity that is cast in doubt by Zhang Yimou's films about the commoners in the post-socialist Chinese everyday world. Against the ideological excess there emerges a new horizon and a new cultural politics that exist as the invisible social referent of his cinematic narrative.

LEGALITY VERSUS LEGITIMACY

In *The Story of Qiu Ju*, one must realise that the central polemic, the 'end' being pursued by the narrative, is not justice in a legalistic sense of the word, but something prior to it, which forms its historical and moral basis or 'pre-understanding' and constitutes its social, political and even cultural (one may dare to say) foundation. The conflict or antagonism cannot be described as a pristine, spontaneous civil society (one must not forget this concept's original Hegelian-Marxian connotation, namely bourgeois society) facing the grim superimposition of law by a modernising bureaucratic state. Nor can it conversely be viewed as a chaotic, backward peasant world indulged (at least for a few decades) by Chinese socialism and impossible to modernise, that is to say, to be brought into a commercial society complete with positive or procedural law as legal elaboration of the new socioeconomic contracts based on private property. What is deceptive – deception here constitutes the drama as well as providing the clue to putting together a narrative puzzle – in the film of *The Story of Qiu Ju* lies in its cinematic drama focusing on the legal mechanism or, rather, the comic ways by which a simple-minded peasant woman keeps missing it and missing its point in the same way as she keeps getting lost in the modern big city. Yet any careful and fruitful reading of the film will have to base itself on the plain observation that the film is about anything but formal, instrumental procedures and formulas (of law as well as of ideology). In *The Story of Qiu Ju*, the subject matter, which is legal, even legalistic, serves its truth content which is decidedly non-legalistic and indeed against abstract generality and exchangeability. The Law to be understood in Zhang Yimou's film is not a legal coding; it is not even culture – understood either naively in terms of 'natural psyche' or, with more intellectual sophistication, in terms of Jacques Lacan's 'symbolic order' (which turns the cultural back to the legal, albeit only 'metaphorically').[4] Rather, the Law here is something prior to the legal codes, something unwritten but rooted in and indicative of that which, even though not technical or formalistic, is constituted like a language – the nameless structure of a historically inherited ethical world.

I want to get into this analysis by noticing a slight yet crucial translation problem (isn't it true that, literally, one can say that all the problems of Chinese modernity, as a translated modernity, were caused by translation!) which comes with the film's international release, thus its transnational afterlife. The keyword in the film is 'justice' or 'apology', the two things which Qiu Ju is so determined to obtain and around which the film narrative unfolds. Whereas English subtitles render the keyword smoothly as either 'justice' or 'apology', often alternating the two as if they are interchangeable, the word consistently, stubbornly repeated by Qiu Ju throughout the film is, actually, 'shuofa'. The meanings and implications of 'shuofa' are not so much legal but moral, not putative but persuasive, not authoritative but communitarian and consensual, not judgemental but descriptive (or, better still, narrative). It is, indeed, close to something like 'explanation', as, literally as well as in everyday usage, 'shuo-fa' means the way things are discussed, talked about and, eventually, understood and accepted without coercion. The moral-cultural point of 'shuofa' is that the way things are must be accepted by those to whom it is explained; that the political-legal order must rest on a tacit agreement, a consent given by those to whom things are explained.

Notably and importantly, the English translation in the subtitles is a mistranslation because it ably and precisely 'translates' – anticipates and captures – the ways in which 'shuofa' is understood in the contemporary Chinese context and by the average Chinese audience as well, that is, as 'justice' and 'apology'. This observation may pre-empt any tendency to formulate the 'cultural' – here as a mere shorthand for the moral-political constitution of a people shaped by revolution and socialism – in terms of a false opposition or conflict between Chinese and Western societies or 'ethics'. In light of this close linguistic, pragmatic examination, what Qiu Ju demands, first and foremost, is not justice in the sense that an abstract general law must apply to all equally and indifferently, as a peasant versus mayor story seems to suggest, but for her values defined by her immediate surroundings to continue to make sense. It may not be an academic hyperbole to suggest that Qiu Ju's is not a legal battle but a hermeneutic struggle to ensure the coherence and integrity of the world of meaning and value, of understanding and, indeed, of being. She is not so much to litigate as to heal, above all her own peace of mind, for which an adequate notion of justice and individual dignity is indispensable but hardly sufficient.

The main thrust of the film goes against the grain of the notion of 'rule of law' introduced by the modernising state for its political legitimacy, but whose philosophical justification lies historically in the bourgeois pursuit of indifferent abstract generality based on exchange value and the universal individual as the social figure of property rights. Why does the husband get into a fight? It has to do with the fuzzy and overlapping property rights in rural China, a grey area between the government and the written law, on the one hand, and, on the other hand, peasant culture, everyday practice and plebeian sense of right and wrong as a sedimentation of Mao's China. The fact that the dramatic logic of the film is completely beyond the realm of the legal does not mean that the unfolding of the dramatic tension can develop without a legalistic logic. While the film covers Qiu Ju's fight at all levels of political administration below and at the provincial level (hence its everyday, if not comical, flavour), the real legal consequence that forces all the characters eventually to take Qiu Ju seriously is the possibility that she might, and she indeed threatens to, take her fight beyond the relative autonomy and normality of the local.

This possibility is indicated, comically and in passing, by a neighbour's cracking a joke on Qinglai, Qiu Ju's injured husband, by warning him to keep his legs tightly closed, in case he gets kicked again. For then Qiu Ju will sue all the way to Beijing. The sense of entitlement in, and the real probability of a peasant going to Beijing to appeal to the highest authority reveals a crucial and vital link of the individual to the absolute sovereign which exists above and beyond the rules, regulations, due process, and proper procedures.[5] In purely formalistic terms, this shows a resemblance to a peasant's belief in the good and benevolent emperor, and to the popular practice of 'appealing to the Emperor' (*gao yu zhuang*) in imperial China. Yet the history and socio-ideological density of the Chinese revolution and socialist modernity have given new substance to this belief and the PRC, at least in theory, still defines the sovereign that is above the law, a figure implicit in Mao's notion of mass democracy and proletarian dictatorship. Here lies the narrative device responsible for the film's comic touch as well as its intellectual-theoretical complexity: Qiu Ju perceives and fights against a lawlessness at the lower level of government where law, procedure and rules prevail as normality; but she seeks the rule of law at the highest level of government, that is, the realm of the sovereign, which is, by definition, outside and above the law but defines its moral-political constitution. In other words, she looks for justice in terms of moral substance where only justice defined by procedure and positivity can be given; and she searches for law where the law simply does not exist, that is, it exists only as something to be shaped, animated and simultaneously dissolved by the absolute concept of the sovereign. This is the legal-philosophical reason why Qiu Ju's repeated trips are doomed to fail.

There is no villain in this film; nor is there any indignant denouncement of lawlessness under totalitarianism. In that sense it is not a frontal assault on the communist regime. Yet the film puts the entire rational-legal foundation of the modern state system on trial at a deeper level and in an intellectually and politically more compelling way. Here the irony is threefold. First, the peasant fails the state by not understanding its effort at modernising its legal system, which alone protects their rights. Second, the state fails the peasantry by not understanding their inarticulate moral and political codes that constitute and underscore any real, substantial order. Third, Qiu Ju's quest for justice is bound to fail because a general, indifferent, legalistic justice is not what she wants and does not solve her problem, and yet is all that the modern rational social and state organisation has to offer. One may say that Qiu Ju makes explicit the unconscious fighting its own becoming-a-language, as becoming-a-language entails in itself and often manifests itself in reification and alienation. That is the reason why throughout the film we the audience feel both amused and frustrated, as Qiu Ju is either aiming too low or too high; she is either being too kind or too unrelenting, either too generous or too unforgiving; she is either asking too much or too little. Her stubbornness drives everyone crazy, both in and outside the film!

The dramatic and philosophic complexity of the film, in a way, is captured by the linguistic ambiguity of the word *shuofa*. The combination of the characters 'shuo' (to say, speak and talk about) and 'fa' (law; method; the way) produces the following three semantic possibilities: A: 'Speaking of law'; B: 'A way of explanation' (discussed above); and C: 'To talk about, or to comment on, the law'. One can see that the dramatic as well as philosophical unfolding of the film follows the ways in which the meaning of 'shuofa' evolves from A to C: it starts with a question regarding the law, in terms of a perceived injustice; it quickly moves on to becoming a persistent demand for an explanation; ultimately, the film becomes a commentary, a reflection on law and its limits. This is well beyond a problem of translation, but the difficulty of translation stands as a perfect metaphor for the multiplicity of forms of life and conflict of value which always pronounce themselves as a challenge to meaning and interpretation. It proves nearly impossible to render explicit and precise semantic meaning, let alone the pragmatic significance of this peasant usage, *shuofa* in this context. In a sense, the *The Story of Qiu Ju* is a sustained cinematic effort – a trial-by-error experiment of the 'uses of language' worthy of a late Wittgenstein – to determine the meaning of *shuofa* by examining its use in different everyday situations and contexts. To want an 'explanation' in these contexts, it gradually dawns on us, is to set in motion the quest for truth in a larger context as the articulation of something as yet undefinable. Thus, the difficulty the heroine encounters in this film is not so much the legal order understood as an abstract and general norm, but the value system of the everyday life in contemporary China struggling with its own fundamental moral, and political, self-understanding.

In the film narrative, the decisive conflict takes place in the city, in terms of an encounter between the urban and the rural, between formal-procedural law and the unwritten moral-ethical codes of the peasantry tinged with the political legacy of Chinese socialism, and between the modern rationality and what it sets out to overcome, which includes but is not limited to those conventional rubrics such as 'popular habit', 'social custom', 'natural right', or 'tradition'. This is the site in which the bureaucratic-legalistic machinery of the modernising state tries to show itself in abstract yet specific, impersonal yet socially 'responsible' terms. The reading of this effort by popular wisdom, the substitute for 'public opinion' where a free media is not in place, adds another layer of comic twist to the drama. The manager at the 'Workers' and Peasants' Guesthouse', an old man, confidently and, in fact, quite sensibly, predicts that Qiu Ju is going to win the lawsuit because, as he observes, the government, which is seldom known for its role in promoting the rule of law, needs to lose a few publicised trials to the ordinary folks to convince the public that this time it is being serious and playing fair. Yet the fact that Qiu Ju ends up losing the case only shows that the government is in fact more fair and more serious than conventional wisdom expected. The government, despite its sympathy for Qiu Ju – this sympathy embodied by the Director of the Public Security Bureau – cannot do anything about the legal procedure. This time the legal system seems all but determined to run its own course independent of meddling officialdom, personal sentimentalities and moral inclinations.

Yet the healing, the solution in real ethical and moral senses, is attainable only within the parameters of village life. If there is an emotional turning point in Qiu Ju's pursuit of 'justice', it is when the village chief saves her and her baby's life on New Year's Eve. For the village chief, that is merely the right thing to do as a fellow and elderly villager. It has nothing to do with the ongoing legal dispute between him and Qiu Ju. Yet this moment of harmony in the value system of daily life, so to speak, also provides a narrative solution outside the legal framework. The New Year, like the birth of the baby boy, is not a mere coincidence. For the festival and the delivery of Qiu Ju's baby emphasise community, mutual dependency and rebirth. Yet the ending of the film is nonetheless a harmony tinged with unsolved conflict – the conflict between a 'pre-modern' harmony within a rural community and the spread of modern positivistic rationality; the conflict between a culturally embedded notion of justice that remains prior to law and the modern realisation of law at a necessarily abstract, over-coded level. It is within this general ideological, or, rather, cultural-political framework, that a misplaced lawsuit sets in motion the fundamental discrepancies, conflict and coexistence of different systems of value, culture and social conduct – as a comedy but not a tragedy, in a documentary but not modernistic style.

This, to be sure, is but another way of looking at the historical conflict between the world of use value and that of exchange value. In light of this widening gap, the peasant concept of justice, as we realise in the film, is both less strict and rigid than the Law and, simultaneously, more demanding and inflexible than the Law in that it entails punishment from a higher, that is, more internalised, authority. So for people like Qiu Ju, the problem is not that the system is not modern or modern enough, but that it is too modern in an abstract, autonomous, impersonal or 'neutral' fashion and thus it threatens to separate itself from a concrete yet inarticulate value system which defines their daily life.

One should recall that the final verdict, which gives the village mayor a two-week jail term, is made belatedly and based on the new medical 'evidence' – an X-ray photo showing broken ribs, which elevates a civil dispute into 'aggravated assault'. The timing of the emergence of this new piece of legal evidence cannot be worse. Indeed it seems ridiculous, at least from the standpoint of a by-then reconciled village community. The X-ray photo proves to be an uncanny reminder – if not a metaphor in itself – of the philosophical differentiation between the legal and the legitimate as the distinction between two language systems. As a negative picture and a mirror-image of an isolated, 'deeper' and abstract fact, the X-ray photo speaks the positivistic language of technology and legal procedure, yet it is a language invisible and incomprehensible to the peasants as they still live in a pre-technological, pre-legalistic world. It registers a happening in a realm and a logic almost completely outside and independent of the *Lebenswelt* of the peasants. The only way by which the peasant world participates in the world of abstraction and positive law is linguistic mimicry and cultural pastiche, as performed by the old man in the market place who 'lends his pen' to the illiterate villagers seeking litigation. The hilariously hyperbolical but deadly precise legalistic-bureaucratic mimicries such as 'in gross violation of the national birth control policy', 'intent on homicide', and 'must be punished with the full force of the law' – all in reference to Qinglai's being kicked between the legs during his fight with the village chief – capture the comical but absurd discrepancy between the abstract legal codes and the everyday world lived by the villagers who cannot find their representation in the former.

REPETITION AND SINGULARITY: FURTHER THOUGHTS ON THE SELF-AFFIRMATION OF THE EVERYDAY WORLD AND PEOPLE'S SOVEREIGNTY

The law and justice a modern society promises to all, once so remote and unattainable, eventually reaches this peasant woman, but what it delivers is contrary to what she wants in the first place. Those who habitually and compulsively read anything from the People's Republic of China as either transparently pro-government or anti-government messages are understandably baffled and disappointed; and they are not alone in trying to decide whether this Zhang Yimou film is just an unabashed apology for the lingering communist state by bestowing it with a touch of normalcy under its tutelage, or, conversely, whether the unexpected twists and turns of the story of Qiu Ju in fact reveals a complicated and yet to be defined mix of forces at work in China today. Few, however, can dispute the fact that there is a discrepancy between the independent, impersonal legal(istic) procedure and what actually does and does not work for people like Qiu Ju in China today. What is clear, then, is that justice in the legalistic sense is not the point in this film.

In that light, the female protagonist's desire to 'find an explanation' must be seen as an allegory of the social-intellectual search for meaning, based on what is going on in contemporary China. The critical edge of the film is therefore not its exposing the rudimentary state of rule of law in China. In fact the film casts an overall positive or at least, understanding eye on the somewhat hasty implementation of a modern legal structure in a post-socialist society. Rather, what is critical and provocative is the way in which the film situates its dramatic intensity squarely in the structural gap between the legal and the political. The latter (the political) is no longer limited in its narrow confines to mean party politics, but ranges from value judgement based on a particular form of life to the moral courage and assertiveness by which to justify and defend it.

This invisible and inarticulate framework is prior to the legal and the legalistic order, yet it constitutes the very foundation of the latter. It persists in the rising money society in the form of Qiu Ju's pig-headed rejection of any abstract or formal equation between pre-legal and legal orders, between the unwritten law governing her universe and the elaborate and impersonal rules and codes which guarantee the smooth yet abstract functioning of a modern society. It is not about justice done in legalistic terms, but about 'right and wrong' in terms of 'natural right' rooted in the singularity (not generality) of a peasant community.

In one occasion early in the film, Qiu Ju's husband fumes that 'you ren guan ta' or 'there will be someone to set [the village chief] straight', which is translated, again quite mistakenly, as 'justice will be done' in the English subtitles. In light of these conflicting interpretations, the ultimate message or the central conflict of *The Story of Qiu Ju* is that the positivistic concept of a law is alien to the Chinese peasants, who uphold a notion of justice (and equality) which, as unwritten law, governs their world of everyday life and informs their moral and political behaviour. This unwritten law does not easily find its articulation in the symbolic order of the modern legal-social-political structure, but somehow can be converted to and achieve currency in the world of the modern as a relevant form of the utopian idealism of collectivity. Qiu Ju is still not happy at the end of the film. Once the social-moral chasm – which is merely alluded to by the distinction between the legal and the legitimate – becomes pronounced in social terms, she will never be happy again. But the last hint of this Zhang Yimou film seems to be that even the impossibility of happiness is not really a problem, as long as the subject here is not a bourgeois individual but someone embedded in and constituted by a collective. The being-in-the-world with a larger social being does not alter the life situation Qiu Ju faces, but the presence or survival of the concept of the people's sovereignty might change the ways it is approached, recognised and even transformed.

For Zhang Yimou, the sociological reality of contemporary China, like the mental world of Qiu Ju, simply exists. What is represented, then, is rather something unrepresentable, something which rejects mediation in the abstract 'symbolic' sense, but demands its own articulation through a different logic of narrative and expression. This, I would like to propose, is the logic of repetition and immediacy; of singularity and its irrepressible return. Zhang Yimou's approach to this narrative logic is that of comedy rather than tragedy. But in doing so he unambiguously indicates that the Chinese state form and peasant world must be viewed as actually existing forms of life whose justification (their 'shuofa') comes from their own internal differentiations, contradictions, unevenness, and their constant negotiations with one another. Such a perception of a mixed mode of production and its overlapping social, ideological and moral orders is made explicit by the random coexistence of political and commercial logos. One example is the 'cheapest inn in town' where Qiu Ju stays, which is called 'Workers' and Peasants' Guesthouse' (*gongnong lüshe*). The image not so much stands out in its own glaring and ironical anachronism, as it calmly and unself-consciously exists next door to a typical 'New Fashion Salon' (*xinchao fawu*). This 'flat' model of coexistence is coupled with a sort of 'depth' model that works only by means of its not working: while wandering on the street, utterly disoriented, Qiu Ju and her sister-in-law are told by well-meaning people to 'dress up like an urban dweller' so as to avoid being ripped off, which means to cover up their country-bumpkin clothes with fashionable urban attire. But when they re-emerge from the department store, new dresses on top of the old, they do not look a bit more urban, but just have more layers of what Ernst Bloch famously called 'non-synchronic contemporaneity'.[6]

The multiple trips Qiu Ju takes to search for an explanation may look repetitive. However, repetition can be said to be the most effective narrative device that helps the evolution of the idea, which is represented with astonishing immediacy as something uncoded and thus pre-linguistic. Each round of negotiation, mediation or conflict eliminates one possible solution and by exclusion sharpens the film's focus on the nameless 'way of things' as an explanation. Money, or financial compensation, is the first to go, as Qiu Ju does not accept the compensation the village chief pays off but in an insulting way. That is followed by the idea of a kind of culture-based rationalising effort made by the village policeman. The gift (two boxes of cakes) Officer Li brings to Qiu Ju, a reversed bribe, so to speak, is a comical but poignant way of highlighting the communal wisdom underlying the legalistic thinking required by the policeman's socio-political and bureaucratic functionality. It does not work, either. The last casualty in Qiu Ju's dogged pursuit of 'explanation' is, as we have discussed, the modern legal system itself.

Indeed, repetition as a narrative design seems to break its rigid, formal rhythm to suggest something philosophical, or what Roman Ingarden has identified as the ontological or metaphysical stratum of the work of art embracing 'represented entities' beyond the strata of word, syntax and semantics.[7] In light of the film's tendency against the abstract and the general in favour of the particular, repetition is a narrative device in service to the self-affirmation, if not self-assertion, of an as yet undefined and undefinable quality.

In *Difference and Repetition*, Gilles Deleuze provides a unique intuition into repetition as conducive to the evolving, self-differentiating, multiple, affirmative and productive dynamism of sameness. He writes:

> To repeat is to behave in a certain manner, but in relation to something unique or singular which has no equal or equivalent. And perhaps this repetition at the level of external conduct echoes, for its own part, a more secret vibration which animates it, a more profound, internal repetition within the singular.[8]

Deleuze, by re-establishing the conceptual and categorical links between his work and the questions of Bergson, Nietzsche and Spinoza, allows us to see the crucial historical, political, as well as philosophical mutual relevance between our own times and their prehistories, which together form the discontinuous continuity of the modern, capitalist society in its own 'eternal return'. Here, at a dizzying conceptual height but with sharp references to history, Deleuze shows how the residues of the past, the overcome, the redundant, and the repressed and the premature are always part and parcel of time and experience, which we try in vain to regulate, formalise and generalise, first in the name of mythology and metaphysics (Culture); then in the name of rationality and the modern (History). Yet in light of Qiu Ju, what Deleuze seeks to show is that all the identities and forms of life, like all the desires, fantasies and unfulfilled wishes, always come back in disguise for their own satisfaction and self-assertion instead of being happily 'negated', disappearing into the dustbin of universal history for good. It is in the unruliness of those identities and forms of life that their singular political nature manifests itself through repetition. And in light of Deleuze, the story of the Wan family's lawsuit is a fable of a historically, politically shaped form of life in search of its own affirmation, its own 'eternal return'. In *The Story of Qiu Ju*, each time the peasant woman in pursuit of justice comes home empty-handed, the audience is, in frustration and in awe, one step closer to capturing the meaning of that amorphous concept and to the understanding of the possibility of the impossible. Each repetition on Qiu Ju's part is an affirmation of something that is non-existent, missing or denied by the order of the world as a coding system for the general and the exchangeable; yet it is something concrete and singular which vibrates with a larger context beyond the formal institutions of modern rationality. In a literary sense, repetition in Zhang Yimou's film is a 'transgression [which] puts law into question, it denounces its nominal or general character in favor of a more profound and more artistic reality'.[9] Each repetition is to 'repeat the unrepeatable' which is the singularity of a concrete form of life. Thus, each trip made by Qiu Ju will not merely add one more time to the previous one, but, as Deleuze puts it, will 'carry [the first time] to the nth power'.[10]

The narrative-cinematic articulation of the dialectic of repetition and singularity in this Zhang Yimou film must not be taken as an articulation of a moral, let alone cultural, essence (of Chinese peasantry or of Chineseness as such). Rather, it is the historicity of the ongoing Chinese socioeconomic change – and its implicit or explicit friction and conflict with the prescriptive, normative 'universal' – that are brought to the fore before critical contemplation. As long as that prescriptive, normative universal is still defined in terms particular to Euro-American history of the bourgeois subject

– private property, contractual rationality, rule of law, universal rights, and the political ontology of exchange value, Qiu Ju's story ought to be read as a collective allegory of a form of life negotiating its cultural and political legitimacy between various traditions which constitute a natural history beyond the self-enclosed, moral-political self-understanding of the middle class.

A rigorous Marxist notion, natural history (*Naturgeschichte*) searches for a 'essential being' that is not 'essence' or 'genesis' in the metaphysical or mythological sense, but 'origin' (*Ursprung*), which contains and comprehends that which 'emerges from the [historical] process of becoming and disappearance'.[11] What is original, as Walter Benjamin tells us, 'is never revealed in the naked and manifest existence of the factual; its rhythm is apparent only to a dual insight':

> On the one hand it needs to be recognized as a process of restoration and reestablishment, but, on the other hand, and precisely because of this, as something imperfect and incomplete. There takes place in every original phenomenon a determination of the form in which an idea will constantly confront the historical world, until it is revealed fulfilled, in the totality of its history … The principles of philosophical contemplation are recorded in the dialectic which is inherent in origin. This dialectic shows singularity and repetition to be conditioned by one another in all essentials.[12]

In this light, we can conclude that what is unravelled and thrown into question by a simple peasant woman's pursuit for an 'explanation' is not so much the social-legal fabric of China under reforms, but indeed the sacrosanct codifications of universal rationality and law which lie at the bottom of the ideological assumptions of Chinese modernity. Conversely, the irrepressible feeling that Qiu Ju's strivings are not local but universal may serve as a reminder or confirmation that a solution that can completely satisfy her will have to call for a thoroughly transformed social system.

NOTES

1. For a critical study of Chinese cinematic modernism, see Xudong Zhang, *Chinese Modernism in the Era of Reforms, part III, Politics of a Visual Encounter* (Durham, NC: Duke University Press, 1997).
2. Chen Yuanbin, 'Wanjia susong', in *Zhongguo zuojia* (Chinese Writer), no. 1, 1991.

3. For a fuller analysis of *Red Sorghum*, see chapter 11, 'Ideology and Utopia in Zhang Yimou's *Red Sorghum*', in Xudong Zhang, *Chinese Modernism in the Era of Reforms*, pp. 306–29.

4. See Jacques Lacan, 'The Agency of the Letter in the Unconscious, or Reason Since Freud', in *Ecrits* (New York: W.W. Norton, 1977), pp. 146–78.

5. Here my discussion of the extra-legal nature of the sovereign, therefore the limits of the bourgeois positive law, is inspired by Carl Schmitt's intellectually brilliant but politically dubious works on the subject, organised around his proposition that 'the sovereign is that which decides on the exception'. Particularly relevant to the issues at stake are two of Schmitt's seminal texts: *The Concept of the Political* (translated and introduced by George Schwab, Chicago: University of Chicago Press, 1996) and *The Crisis of Parliamentary Democracy* (translated by Ellen Kennedy, Cambridge, MA: MIT Press, 1985).

6. See Ernst Bloch, *Heritage of Our Times*, trans. Neveille and Stephen Plaice (Berkeley, CA: University of California Press, 1990), Part II, and especially pp. 97–116.

7. See Roman Ingarden, *The Literary Work of Art*, trans. George G. Grabowicz (Evanston, IL: Northwestern University Press, 1973).

8. Gilles Deleuze, *Difference and Repetition*, trans. Paul Patton (New York: Columbia University Press, 1994), p. 1.

9. Deleuze, *Repetition and Difference*, p. 3.

10. Deleuze, *Repetition and Difference*, p. 9.

11. Walter Benjamin, *The Origin of German Tragic Drama*, trans. John Osborne (London: Verso, 1977), p. 47.

12. Benjamin, *The Origin of German Tragic Drama*, pp. 45–6.

11
Cinemas in Revolution: 1920s Russia, 1960s Cuba

Michael Chanan

STRUCTURAL CONDITIONS

The temptation to draw comparisons between Cuban cinema of the 1960s and Soviet cinema of the 1920s arises not only because these are the first decades of two communist revolutions which both placed great store by cinema, but also because the cinemas they produced were in both cases radical and experimental, in the vanguard of both politics and aesthetics, and precisely on that account, major movements in the history of world cinema. When the Cuban revolution took power in 1959, and quickly set up a film institute to promote their cause, cinema was in a very different situation from Russia after the Revolution of 1917, when it was a highly popular but still fledgling form of entertainment (which was also silent). Four decades later, cinema not only was the most universal form of mass culture both East and West, but was thoroughly dominated almost everywhere by Hollywood, which in 1917 was still nascent, and although gaining ground rapidly, not yet hegemonic. Indeed the 1920s would yet see the emergence in Europe of several national cinemas which represented alternatives to the Hollywood models, and of these one of the most powerful was in fact Russian cinema. Cuba in 1959 was in quite a different situation, a very small country that would not be supposed capable of sustaining a film industry of its own, which was merely an outpost of the Mexican film industry and occasional host to Hollywood films seeking exotic locations. The comparison between them therefore has important implications for our understanding of the relation between cinema and revolutionary socialism for, in both cases, cinema quickly found itself at the centre of cultural politics and became imbued with the euphoria of the revolutionary process, which allowed it to be treated as an experimental art form with the capacity, at least in theory, to overcome the class divisions of the old regime which had just been overthrown.

In both countries the new filmmakers belonged to a youthful intelligentsia for whom, with some exceptions, political loyalty to the new regime was axiomatic and Marxism a major influence on their thinking (although different Marxisms, as we shall see). In both situations, the claim was made that cinema had a critical role to play in the promotion of a revolutionary political culture; it was a prime ideological weapon which could not be left in the hands of industrialists. But it was also regarded as more and other than an industrial form of entertainment and means of mass propaganda: it aspired to the condition of the authentic artform of the twentieth century, a magnet for a new breed of contemporary artist. The result, because in both cases the filmmakers were initiates of dialectical thought, was a highly creative tension between individual and collective impulses which produced some of the most outstanding films of their period from any source. If the names of Eisenstein, Vertov, Pudovkin, Dovzhenko etc. are inseparable from the creation of a modernist political cinema in the 1920s, then those of Alea, Alvarez, Solás and others are inseparable from the new mode of radical political film which one of them, Julio García Espinosa, in a manifesto dating from 1969, called 'imperfect cinema'.[1] That tension, however, the friction between collective values and individual authorship – would play out differently in the two revolutions.

The sociologist George Huaco, in a book that seems to have been unduly forgotten, suggested that certain structural conditions are necessary for the emergence of major film movements like German Expressionism or Soviet Expressive Realism in the 1920s, or later, Italian Neo-Realism or the French New Wave.[2] With certain reservations we shall come to later, the same considerations apply to Cuba's 'imperfect cinema'. Each of these film movements depended on a coming together of certain social resources and modes of organisation, a favourable political and ideological climate, and the particular artistic traditions that informed them. If these factors, in the scheme of classical Marxism, belong to either the base or the superstructure, there are four basic conditions, says Huaco, that need to be met. First, there needs to be the necessary technical and industrial infrastructure and, second, a cadre of trained personnel, including directors, cinematographers, editors and actors. Third, there needs to be a mode of organisation that is conducive to the movement's ideology, and fourth, the political regime must be tolerant of or favourable towards both the ideology and style of the films. In Cuba, the last two factors were initially satisfied even more rapidly than in Russia.

In both countries, the first imperative was to rescue the cinema from actual or imminent collapse. In Russia the industry reacted to the Bolsheviks with open hostility and many producers simply left the country taking their equipment with them, prompting the nationalisation decree of 1919 (which to begin with only made matters worse). Similar conditions occurred in Cuba. When the dictator Batista fled the country, leading figures in the film business were hard on his heels, and the new Cuban film institute, ICAIC – *Instituto Cubano de Arte y Industria Cinematográficos*, Cuban Institute of Film Art and Industry – was originally set up to take over their property. But if this was the new regime's first decree in the cultural field, a close reading of the text reveals a good deal about the politics, intelligence and intentions of its authors, members of the revolutionary vanguard that stood behind the Provisional Government, which was not yet publicly known as socialistic in its leanings. However, this is not the kind of law that would be passed by a government which happened to acquire a film studio without knowing what to do with it; it exhibits a clear understanding of the character of the forces that had prevented the growth of an independent film industry in Cuba until then, and an analysis of the structure needed to set up an industry which might be able in the future to escape those forces. This indicates a certain difference between the two revolutionary moments, in which the latter had the ironic benefit of coming much later, when the further development of the cinema had made very clear the transnational forms of dominance and control through which Hollywood exercised its hegemony.

Another difference is seen in contrasting approaches to the evident need for new technical cadres. While the Bolsheviks immediately set up a film school, the first in the world, the Cubans considered a film school beyond their means, and opted instead for a system of in-house apprenticeship (the famous film school at San Antonio de Los Baños came 25 years later). But this approach provided for more than a technical education. In both countries, for both ideological and material reasons, the early years of revolution favoured newsreel and documentary – in the first years of the Soviet Revolution, the conditions of civil war and armed foreign intervention made any other kind of filmmaking practically impossible. In Cuba, ICAIC developed a system in which all new recruits passed through the newsreel and documentary department before they could go on to make fiction, a crucial schooling in direct encounter with a rapidly changing reality which fed into their subsequent films.

In Russia, the founding principles of film policy were derived from Lenin by way of the Cultural Commissar Lunacharsky. If Lenin told Lunacharsky that 'of all the arts for us the most important is cinema', one of the primary reasons was its ability to reach a widespread and largely illiterate population with a vivid portrayal of great propaganda value. The country was vast and heterogeneous, people spoke dozens of different languages and dialects; cinema was a terrific instrument for the enormous job of educating them in the basic tenets of the communist state. It was also and necessarily more than that. Cinema participates here in a transformation of the public space in which it is seen, the domain of common knowledge of the historically existing world which underpins political life; a transformation which, like everywhere else, it both promotes and reflects, as agent and instrument, source and effect, vehicle and catalyst. This indeed was one of the factors which encouraged Vertov to push beyond the fragmentary imagery of the early newsreel. To begin with, working with barely adequate technical resources and meagre supplies of raw film, Vertov was engaged in assembling bits of footage of the civil war from different sources – 'fragments of struggle, crisis, disaster, victory', in one description[3] – organising them and adding simple captions to make *agitki* – short agitational illustrations of communist ideas and slogans, one of the classic forms of agitprop (agitational propaganda). The second newsreel series, *Kino-Pravda* ('Cine Truth'), launched in 1922, became a sustained attempt to create a more fluid and dynamic screen language. In the urgency to keep up with social reality, each newsreel was different from the previous one. 'The system of editing changed', wrote Vertov later,

> The approach to the process of filming changed. The character of the captions and the way in which they were used changed ... Every day one had to invent something new. There was no-one to learn from. We were exploring unknown ground. Inventing and experimenting.[4]

In this unusual laboratory, 'slowly but surely the alphabet of film-language was built up', and thus emerged the principles of montage which were systematically explored by Kuleshov and developed in different directions by Eisenstein, Pudovkin and others.

In short, if Lenin set the agenda for cinema, the forcing ground was the Revolution itself, which was nothing less than a new kind of totalisation of society that involved rethinking everything from the ground up. The overthrow of the old order gave licence to iconoclasm, experimentation and re-evaluation in all the arts, and artists in every field argued the need to repudiate bourgeois ideas and forge a new proletarian culture. Great hopes were pinned on cinema precisely because of its originality, its dynamic potential, and its unencumbrance with the norms of bourgeois aesthetics. Here, for the first time in its short life, cinema was taken seriously by intellectuals, politicians and artists alike. The social and economic pragmatism of the day was accompanied by significant artistic tolerance which allowed artistic experiment and debate to flourish, and Vertov developed his methods and ideas in close dialogue with critical currents in the avant garde to which he belonged: he was close to the Lef group, the revolutionary wing of the Russian Futurism led by the poet Mayakovsky, who declared that 'art is not a mirror which reflects the historical struggle, but a weapon in that struggle',[5] and the Constructivists, who compared the fabrication of the work of art to the tasks and methods of building and engineering.

If the Cuban revolution produced a similar engagement in cultural renewal, it was strongly supported by the social cohesion generated by the literacy campaign of 1961. Teenagers from the cities taught peasants in the countryside to read and write using texts and ideas which were new to both, so that the words which expressed a new political discourse created a new set of shared values. With this extraordinary piece of social and political engineering, which virtually eliminated illiteracy within a couple of years, written language and everything that comes with it translated into access to a new sense of national culture on a mass scale from which the filmmakers greatly benefited but to which they also greatly contributed. According to the political scientist Rafael Hernández, it was as if language itself was liberated from the structures of control which previously divided the social classes into different linguistic communities; the traditional socio-linguistic stratification was ruptured; the most humble people took possession of linguistic territories previously veiled from them; knowledge and culture became central elements of prestige in the new social order.[6] Cuban cinema was infused with this expansive popular culture, which allowed Cuban filmmakers considerable leeway to experiment. The boldest innovator in Cuba, Santiago Alvarez, reinvented the newsreel, the compilation film, the travelogue and every other documentary genre he laid hands upon, in an irrepressible frenzy of filmic bricolage licensed by that supreme act of bricolage, the Cuban revolution. And the literacy campaign is at the root of the playful way in which he replaced the conventional spoken commentary of the newsreel and documentary with animated words moving backwards and forwards across the screen.

When Alvarez's films began to circulate abroad, film critics began to compare them to the work of Vertov in 1920s Soviet Russia. Then it turned out that Alvarez had never seen any Vertov. When he finally did so, and of course recognised the similarities, he could only explain them as a consequence of an historical parallel: the discovery of cinema in both countries in and through the revolutionary process.[7]

WORDS TO THE INTELLECTUALS

In Russia, the watchword was 'the Leninist proportion' – the imperative to sustain a good level of politically correct newsreel and didactic films. Lenin told Lunacharsky he thought the production of films 'imbued with Communist ideas and reflecting Soviet reality should begin with the newsreel'.[8] Since the word 'documentary' was not yet in use, the term 'newsreel' should not be interpreted narrowly. In his 1922 directive on cinema, he wants every programme to contain a proper proportion of the two types of film, entertainment and propaganda. He imagines a series called *From the Life of the Peoples of the World* on subjects like 'the colonial policy of the British in India, the work of the League of Nations, the starving in Berlin, etc., etc.' Entertainment films had to be monitored and censored for obscenity and counter-revolutionary content, but within these limits, producers should be allowed broad initiative. Lenin was clearly being pragmatic. The dire state of an economy under attack through civil war and foreign invasion, which meant that Vertov's first newsreel series came to a halt and the film school had to open without any film, had prompted a retreat from pure socialist theory and the introduction of the NEP, or New Economic Policy, a temporary return to forms of private enterprise; the results restored the shattered country to the point where, among other things, regular film production was once again a possibility, and fiction film production began again.

While the Cubans shared a certain leaning towards propaganda – several of the early documentaries supported and explained the new urban and agrarian reform laws, for example – they also faced different problems. To begin with the economy was not in crisis. On the contrary, it was pretty healthy, and ICAIC was able to obtain credit to purchase equipment abroad and embark immediately on production of their first features. There was no civil war, only a seriously botched attempt at invasion, the US-sponsored incursion at the Bay of Pigs, which the Cubans rapidly defeated in a crucial moment of revolutionary self-definition (although they had to fight counter-revolutionary bandits for several years). There was, however, a serious struggle for power with the liberal bourgeoisie, in which cinema played a deeply symptomatic role, and which came to a head in 1961 when ICAIC declined to exhibit a short independent documentary called *P.M.* because it seemed to them ideologically ambiguous. The resulting commotion led to a meeting where Fidel, after listening to the arguments on both sides, gave the speech known as the 'Words to the Intellectuals', where he pronounced the formula which henceforth defined the revolution's cultural policy: *dentro de la Revolución, todo; contra la Revolución, nada* – 'within the Revolution, everything; against it, nothing'.[9] The formula is remarkable not only for its openness, which would mean that the extent of freedom of artistic creation would be periodically put to the test, but also for what lay behind it. The cultural politics which it implied had a precedent in the ideas of the *Manifesto: Towards a Free Revolutionary Art*, published in 1938 over the signatures of Diego Rivera and André Breton, which Trotsky is said to have had a hand in drafting: 'True art is unable *not* to be revolutionary, *not* to aspire to a complete and radical reconstruction of society.'[10] If this was an advance on the position Trotsky maintained in 1920s Russia, which, while looking forward to a new proletarian culture, also defended the universal values of bourgeois culture, then to reassert such a position in Cuba four decades later was not only to outmanoeuvre the liberals but also to stymie the sectarians of the left, whom Ambrosio Fornet once described as 'a quartet of night-prowling tomcats who still confused jazz with imperialism and abstract art with the devil'.[11]

This is not to claim some unexpected Trotskyist influence on Cuban Marxism, which in fact has been generally closer to Gramsci.[12] In any case it is better to look at this through a Latin American prism. Here it is relevant to know that ICAIC's president, Alfredo Guevara, was a close friend of Fidel's from student days who had worked for a time in Mexico as an associate producer with Buñuel. The anticlericalism that was an essential characteristic of this milieu was shared by Fidel. In European terms, this position is more like the critique that Sartre directed against what he called 'lazy Marxism' (and no wonder, therefore, that Sartre was among the staunchest of Fidel's early supporters). Fidel himself directly addressed the problem of sectarianism in the strongest terms in the spring of 1962, during the so-called Escalante affair, when he declared in a television broadcast that 'the suppression of ideas was a myopic, sectarian, stupid and warped conception of Marxism that could change the Revolution into a tyranny. And that is not revolution!'[13]

There has often been speculation about the benefits to ICAIC of the special relationship with the centre of power which came from Alfredo Guevara's close connection with Fidel, but the crucial factor was Guevara's political capacity in founding ICAIC to persuade his personal friend and political chief to let him place art rather than propaganda at the centre of the Institute's vision. In other words, to allow him the rule of artistic freedom which Fidel then supported in the 'Words to the Intellectuals'. This support would also play a role when it came to confronting the communist old guard over exhibition policies. Here the problems of Cuba in the 1960s and Russia in the 1920s were fundamentally similar. Both countries were dependent for the vast bulk of their supply of new films on imports which were often ideologically inimical. As Guevara wrote in the Institute's journal, out of 484 films exhibited in Cuba in 1959, 266 were North American. More serious, however, was

> the character of the films being shown. Out of the 484 films, 140 represented sentimental dramas and conflicts, generally of the quality of syrup and magazine serials, sometimes psychological in a visually spectacular way; 34 were war movies and 27 police, 43 westerns and 92 action and adventure … Average taste has been maltreated and certain overriding influences have created 'habits' of cinema difficult to eradicate … [T]he genres together with the star system predominate and their formulae amount to anti-cinema.[14]

He was therefore incensed when a senior Party figure, Blas Roca, attacked ICAIC for exhibiting Fellini's *La Dolce Vita* on the grounds that it was hardly wholesome entertainment for the Cuban working class. Guevara replied in withering tones. 'To men like you,' he wrote, 'the public is made up of babies in need of a wet-nurse who will feed them with ideological pap, highly sterilised, and cooked in accordance with the recipes of socialist realism.'[15]

Here, however, we reach the limits of any possible comparison between the two moments. Russia in the 1920s was a site of debate between a number of aesthetic responses to the political currents of the Revolution, mostly representing different varieties of the modernist sensibility, and it would be quite wrong to suppose that the eventual supremacy of Socialist Realism was predictable (even if in the end it was politically overdetermined). For the Cubans, on the other hand, Socialist Realism was an historical given which seemed to them a dubious doctrine on at least two counts. First, because it represented a purely populist position. A filmmakers' manifesto dating from 1963, in the middle of this debate, and boasting 29 signatories, was quite lucid about this.[16] It was a forthright document which declared that while it was both the right and duty of the state to promote cultural development, aesthetic tendencies and ideas are always in a state of conflict with each other and it is mistaken to try to impose solutions. Moreover, the relationship between bourgeois and proletarian culture is not exclusively antagonistic (as Lenin too had pointed out) and 'the obvious fact that a liberal bourgeois like Thomas Mann is a better writer than Marxist-Leninist Dmitir Furmanov shows that a specifically aesthetic criterion exists which cannot be reduced to the ideological position of the writers'. Art cannot be reduced to its external determinants and formal categories have no class character. The conclusion is therefore that in the battle between aesthetic ideas, suppression on the grounds that certain forms have an undesirable class character impedes the evolution of art by restricting the struggle between the ideas themselves.

Second, it didn't suit them. This is to speak of what Huaco called the particular artistic traditions by which each film movement is informed. Cuban artists and intellectuals were schooled in a highly syncretistic culture which celebrated rumba and surrealism, Yoruba gods and Catholic transcendentalism in equal measure – the heritage of a colonial history very different from the history of Russia and Europe. As they entered the period that the Uruguayan poet Mario Benedetti has described as 'the splendour of those first seven, eight, nine years which produced the coincidence between ideological avant-gardism and artistic avant-gardism',[17] the cineastes paid homage equally to Eisenstein and Chaplin, Hollywood and Italian Neo-Realism, the French New Wave and Brazilian Cinema Novo. Benedetti's description applies equally well to Soviet Russia in the 1920s, but the difference in geo-cultural perspective is crucial; a difference the Cubans began to detect with the first Soviet-Cuban co-production, *Soy Cuba* (I am Cuba, 1964), directed by Mikhail Kalatozov from a script by Yevgeni Yevtushenko and Enrique Pineda Barnet, which principally impressed for the delirium of Sergei Urusevsky's cinematography. While this and other co-productions with East European countries in those years made good political and economic sense, even Yevtushenko was unable to go beyond the traveller's image of an exotic island which Russian poetry inherited from Mayakovsky's visit in the 1920s.

AESTHETIC LABOUR

ICAIC played a leading role in the ideological confrontations through which Cuba's new cultural politics were defined. The film institute developed and defended positions more lucidly than any comparable organisation against both the sometimes near-hysterical attacks of liberals who feared the encroachment of the state, and the mechanical application of schemes for socialist realism on the part of more orthodox and traditional Marxists associated with the old guard of the Communist Party. Nor, they said, should the audience be refused the right to see the work of aesthetically progressive European filmmakers because they supposedly dealt in the portrayal of bourgeois decadence. Instead of such communist orthodoxies, ICAIC's filmmakers wanted to undermine the adverse powers of the dream screen of commercial entertainment cinema by building on what started as the audience's spontaneous change of perspective in order to create both a more critical disposition in the viewer and a radical film language. The result was a series of exhilarating, experimental films by Tomás Gutiérrez Alea, Julio García Espinosa, Humberto Solás, Manuel Octavio Gómez, Santiago Alvarez and others in the late 1960s which were recognised on every continent of the globe as a major new presence in world cinema – a moment it would prove hard to maintain.

Defending the right of its members to experiment in the most varied styles and techniques, at the same time ICAIC argued that artistic creation could neither be reduced to propaganda or merely didactic functions, nor could it be subjected to economic criteria of productivity, because the value of a work of art is determined by qualitative, not quantitative characteristics. The Russian filmmakers of the 1920s, recognising the cooperative nature of the filmmaking process, and in a spirit of antagonism towards bourgeois individualism, had begun by embracing the idea of collective authorship. The Cuban position, which was less voluntaristic, went far beyond this, calling on arguments in Marxist aesthetics which had not yet been developed in the 1920s. These arguments were not widely disseminated, even in Marxist circles, but the Cubans found them in books they translated and published by writers like John Howard Lawson, the blacklisted

American screenwriter, and the Italian writer and theorist Umberto Barbaro, the person who gave Italian Neo-Realism its name. Both were Marxists who saw the cinema as an exemplification of the hostility of the capitalist mode of production towards artistic creation. According to this position, and to put it in formal terms, the quantification of aesthetic labour by means of its reduction to the same criteria as regular labour under normal conditions of production is of no use in evaluating the work of the artist. To apply a common quantitative denominator to artistic production can only lead in practice to a standardisation of aesthetic creation, the mechanical reproduction of repetitive formulae which are totally incompatible with the creative character of the imagination – precisely what Alfredo Guevara spoke out against at the National Cultural Congress in 1962, which followed Fidel's speech to the intellectuals. ICAIC was not to be in the business of making genre movies.

Here, then, we find the third and fourth of the structural factors mentioned by Huaco, the need for a conducive mode of organisation, and a political regime favourable to the filmmakers' ideology and style. It is perhaps ironic, given ICAIC's opposition to orthodox communist aesthetics, that with the transition to communist rule which followed Russia's embrace of Cuba, the Institute came to be financed according to the system of central planning practised by communism in power. But then here profitability plays no direct role in the evaluation of the enterprise, which instead receives a pre-arranged sum from the state budget (any net income goes back to the treasury from which centrally budgeted funds are allocated). In short, it is a system which allows social and political considerations to take precedence over market mechanisms, although it can (and later did) also lead to unrealistic economic judgements.

This is not the place to debate the contradictions of communist economics. The fact is that this economic regime was of great benefit to ICAIC and Cuban cinema, because it also produced two other effects which helped to keep production costs down. One is that the economics of the star system no longer exerted any influence. Since the regime established control over inflation and rationalised salaries and wages, there was no longer any pressure to keep increasing the pay of actors and specialised technical personnel – which is a major factor in the constantly increasing production budgets of the capitalist film industries. (This is because film production is labour intensive, and in Marxist language, this makes it almost impossible to improve the organic composition of capital.) At the same time,

ICAIC's vertical integration also accomplished the elimination of the numerous small individual companies which buy and sell each other their services and facilities in every capitalist film industry after the demise of the studio system, each one raking off its own profit. Again under such a system the costs tend upwards, production is risky, employment uncertain. At ICAIC, which came to employ about a thousand people in the 1980s, such uncertainty became a thing of the past (until the 1990s and the collapse of the European communist bloc created uncertainties of a different order, and ICAIC would enter into crisis and lose many of its personnel).

In Russia, the early 1920s saw the emergence of groups who argued aggressively in support of a new proletarian culture, an aspiration that readily embraced the evolving art of film; which at the same time, however, remained an open field of experiment precisely because of its evolving character. In this minefield, Lenin's view, says Huaco, seems to have been a cautious tolerance towards experiment, and an unwillingness to impose his own prejudices, a trait which would be shared by Fidel. Trotsky entered the debate with his book *Literature and Revolution* of 1923, where he held that, while it was impossible to allow the political use of art by the Revolution's enemies, aesthetic questions were not the concern of the Party. But this was a position upheld by other Bolshevik leaders like Bukharin, the editor of *Pravda*, so that while Trotsky quickly became marginalised following Lenin's death, a policy of tolerance towards the gamut of artistic currents was still being affirmed by the Politburo in the middle of 1925. The emergence of a more intolerant line towards literary and artistic questions surfaced in the summer of 1928, followed by the first signs of rift between the Stalin and Bukharin factions, which came into the open in April 1929, after Trotsky had been expelled from the country; by the end of that year, Bukharin and Lunacharsky had both been removed from their posts. In Huaco's reading, the ascendancy of the Stalinist faction represented the capture of the Revolution from within by a xenophobic nationalism which would wipe out the cultural fruits of the previous decade. The impact of these changes on the cinema began almost immediately with the replacement of Sovkino by a new All-Union film industry combine, Soyuzkino, by which it was removed from the domain of the Commissariat of Education to the Supreme Council of the National Economy, the body responsible for overseeing the first Five Year Plan. There were still experimental films being made in the early 1930s, but by the middle of the decade Soviet cinema had succumbed to a stylistic conformity under the banner of Socialist Realism which is like a mirror image of Hollywood: stereotyped characters, formulaic plots with happy endings, naturalistic photography and continuity editing, avoidance of controversial subject matter, a Victorian code of sexual morals, in short, a mass-culture product addressed to the lowest common denominator of popular taste.

The impression that the same thing happened in Cuba is only superficial. Che Guevara once described the Cuban revolution, evoking a popular Cuban dance of the time, as 'socialism with pachanga' – a kind of libertarian socialism with a Caribbean flavour. Later, they would have to rein themselves in somewhat, but the repression of so-called dissidents which spilled out with the Padilla affair in 1971, when Western leftist intellectuals (including Sartre) criticised Cuba over the treatment of the poet Heberto Padilla, must not be confused with real Stalinism. The comparison with the Soviet experience breaks down as soon as you go beyond the first period of effervescent euphoria. Yes, Cuba has had its political prisoners, but no gulags. The episode of the work camps (known as UMAPs, or Military Units to Augment Production) in the late 1960s was short, and the camps were quickly reformed. Many of those who suffered from sectarian repression in the early 1970s were later reinstated. There is a difference here from more recent episodes of moves against so-called dissidents, who are incriminated by association with anti-Cuban elements in Miami or Washington. From my own researches, including an investigation carried out for a television documentary on human rights in Cuba in 1988, I have concluded that while anti-government activities have generally led to harsh treatment, and the legal system is both inefficient and politically controlled, the prison regime is pretty humane – one can see this in the footage we shot. In short, Cuban Stalinism is an invention of the disinformers, based, as disinformation always is, on half-truths.[18]

Throughout the ups and downs of sectarianism over the ensuing decades, ICAIC constituted a space of relative safety, because instead of coming under the heavy hand of the Ideological Office of the Central Committee like the rest of the mass media, it was assigned to the Ministry of Culture and thus retained a good degree of autonomy. As a result, even with only a handful of films each year, ICAIC managed to sustain a diversity in its output which prevented the predominance of any particular style or form, even when directors played safe and turned to the kind of genre film that García Espinosa warned against. On the other hand, according to Fornet, referring to Fidel's formula of 1961, 'The fact is that, in the context of a state of siege, aesthetic discourse, perhaps because of its own polysemic nature, delights in the license of this "inside" where everything – or almost everything – is permitted.' Nor are the limits ever fixed, because 'the "everything" permitted is not a permanent right but an arena of conflict that must be renegotiated every day, with no quarter granted to the bureaucracy and with the temptation of irresponsible whimsy firmly resisted'.[19]

NOTES

1. For a discussion of imperfect cinema, see Michael Chanan, *Cuban Cinema* (Minneapolis and London: University of Minnesota Press, 2004), ch.13. These ideas were not limited to Cuba. Imperfect cinema is the cousin of 'Third Cinema': neither the genre movie of Hollywood and its imitators (First Cinema), nor the European tradition of auteur cinema (Second Cinema), but the oppositional and militant form advocated by Solanas and Getino in Argentina. See Michael Chanan, 'The Changing Geography of Third Cinema', *Screen*, vol. 38, no. 4 (1997), pp. 372–88; and at <www.mchanan.dial.pipex.com>.

2. George A. Huaco, *The Sociology of Film Art* (New York & London: Basic Books, 1965).

3. Eric Barnouw, *Documentary: A History of the Non-Fiction Film* (Oxford: Oxford University Press, 1974), p. 52.

4. Dziga Vertov quoted in Masha Enzensberger, 'Dziga Vertov' in *Screen Reader 1, Cinema/Ideology/Politics* (SEFT, 1977), p. 395.

5. Enzensberger, 'Dziga Vertov', p. 395.

6. See Rafael Hernández, *Mirar a Cuba, Ensayos sobre cultura y sociedad civil* (Looking at Cuba, Essays on Culture and Civil Society) (Havana: Editorial Letras Cubanas, 1999), pp. 128–9.

7. Personal communication in conversations with Alvarez, Havana, 1979/80.

8. Anatoli Lunacharsky, 'Conversation with Lenin', in Richard Taylor and Ian Christie (eds), *The Film Factory* (London: Routledge, 1988), p. 57.

9. Fidel Castro, 'Words to the Intellectuals', in Lee Baxandall (ed.), *Radical Perspectives in the Arts* (London: Penguin, 1972). For a full account of the whole episode, see Chanan, *Cuban Cinema*, pp. 133ff.

10. 'Manifesto: Towards a Free Revolutionary Art', in Paul Siegal (ed.), *Leon Trotsky on Literature and Art* (New York: Pathfinder Press, 1970), pp. 115–21.

11. Ambrosio Fornet, in *El intelectual y la sociedad* (The Intellectual and Society) Colección Minima No. 28 (Mexico: Siglo Veintiuno Editores, 1969), p. 48.

12. See Michael Chanan, 'Cuba and Civil Society, or Why Cuban Intellectuals are Talking About Gramsci', *Nepantla*, vol. 1, no. 2 (2001), pp. 387–406.

13. See Chanan, *Cuban Cinema*, p. 167.

14. Alfredo Guevara, 'Una nueva etapa del cine en Cuba' (A New Hope in Cuban Cinema), *Cine Cubano*, no. 3 (n.d.).

15. Alfredo Guevara in *Hoy*, 17 December 1963.
16. *La Gaceta de Cuba*, August 1963.
17. Manuel Vásquez Montalbán, *Y Dios entró en La Habana* (And God Entered Havana) (El Pais/Aguilar, 1998), p. 353.
18. I have presented evidence on this subject in three places, my book on Cuban cinema, a television report on human rights in Cuba in 1988 ('Cuba from Inside', for *Despatches*, Channel Four), and the essay, 'Cuba and Civil Society'.
19. Ambrosio Fornet, Introduction to A. Fornet (ed.), *Bridging Enigma: Cubans on Cuba*, Special Issue of *South Atlantic Quarterly*, vol. 96, no. 1 (Winter 1997), pp. 11–12.

Notes on Contributors

Michael Chanan is Professor of Cultural Studies at the University of the West of England, Bristol. As well as being a documentary filmmaker, he has written about early cinema, Latin American cinema, the social history of music and the history of recording. His latest publication is *Cuban Cinema* (University of Minnesota Press, 2004), being a revised and updated edition of his earlier book on film in Cuba, *The Cuban Image*.

Douglas Gomery teaches media history and economics at the University of Maryland and is Resident Scholar at the Library of American Broadcasting. His latest book, co-authored with Benjamin Compaine, *Who Owns the Media?* (Lawrence Earlbaum Associates) earned the Picard Prize for the best media economics book of 2000. He is author of a dozen other books and more than 1,000 articles.

Anna Kornbluh is pursuing her Ph.D in English at the University of California, Irvine. Her research focuses on forms of bourgeois libidinal economy in both Victorian and Hollywood melodrama.

Marcia Landy is Distinguished Service Professor of English and Film Studies at the University of Pittsburgh with a secondary appointment in the Department of French and Italian. In addition to numerous essays in journals and anthologies, her publications include *Fascism in Film: The Italian Commercial Cinema, 1930–1943* (Princeton, 1986); *British Genres, 1930–1960* (Princeton, 1991); *Imitations of Life: A Reader on Film and Television Melodrama* (Wayne State University Press); *Film, Politics, and Gramsci* (Minnesota University Press, 1994); *The Folklore of Consensus: Theatricality in Italian Cinema, 1930–1943* (SUNY Press, 1998); *Italian Film* (Cambridge, 2000); and *The Historical Film: History and Memory in Media* (Rutgers, 2000).

Hyangjin Lee is a lecturer in the School of East Asian Studies at the University of Sheffield, UK. She is the author of *Contemporary Korean Cinema: Identity, Culture and Politics* (Manchester University Press, 2000), and various articles on North and South Korean cinema and culture.

Esther Leslie teaches in the School of English and Humanities, Birkbeck, University of London. Her writings include *Walter Benjamin: Overpowering Conformism* (Pluto, 2000), and *Hollywood Flatlands, Animation, Critical Theory and the Avant Garde* (Verso, 2002). Her next book is a study of the German chemical industry in relation to the Romantic philosophy of nature, and the politics and poetics of modernity. She is actively involved in editing three journals – *Historical Materialism: Research in Critical Marxist Theory*, *Radical Philosophy* and *Revolutionary History*, and has also edited and contributed to a collection called *Mad Pride: A Celebration of Mad Culture*. She translated Georg Lukács' *A Defence of History and Class Consciousness: Tailism and the Dialectic* (Verso, 2000).

Colin McArthur was formerly Head of the Distribution Division of the British Film Institute and is now a freelance teacher, writer and graphic artist. He has written extensively on diverse national cinemas, particularly Hollywood, British television and Scottish culture. His most recent books are *Whisky Galore! and The Maggie* (2002), in I.B. Tauris's 'Guides to British Films' series, and *Brigadoon, Braveheart and the Scots* (I.B. Tauris, 2003).

Toby Miller is Professor of English, Sociology, and Women's Studies at the University of California, Riverside where he directs the Program in Film and Visual Culture. He is the author and editor of 21 books including: *The Well-Tempered Self: Citizenship, Culture, and the Postmodern Subject* (The Johns Hopkins University Press, 1993); *Contemporary Australian Television* (University of New South Wales Press, 1994 – with Stuart Cunningham); *The Avengers* (British Film Institute, 1997/Indiana University Press, 1998); *Technologies of Truth: Cultural Citizenship and the Popular Media* (University of Minnesota Press, 1998); *Popular Culture and Everyday Life* (Sage Publications, 1998 – with Alec McHoul); *A Companion to Film Theory* (Basil Blackwell, 1999 – edited with Robert Stam); *Film and Theory: An Anthology* (Basil Blackwell, 2000 – edited with Robert Stam); and *Global Hollywood* (British Film Institute/Indiana University Press, 2001 – with Nitin Govil, John McMurria and Richard Maxwell).

Deborah Philips teaches at Brunel University, and has written on feminism and popular culture. She was one of the founding members of *Women's Review*, and her publications include *Brave New Causes*

(Cassell, 1998) with Ian Haywood, and *Writing Well* (Jessica Kingsley, 1999) with Debra Penman and Liz Linington.

Mike Wayne teaches film, television and video practice at Brunel University. He is the author of *Marxism and Media Studies: Key Concepts and Contemporary Trends* (Pluto, 2003), *The Politics of Contemporary European Cinema, Histories, Borders, Diasporas* (Intellect Books, 2002), *Political Film: The Dialectics of Third Cinema* (Pluto, 2001), *Theorising Video Practice* (Lawrence and Wishart, 1997) and is the editor of *Dissident Voices: The Politics of Television and Cultural Change* (Pluto, 1998). He is the co-editor with Esther Leslie of the Marxism and Culture series (Pluto).

Xudong Zhang teaches Chinese and Comparative Literature at New York University. He is the author of *Chinese Modernism in the Era of Reforms: Cultural Fever, Avant-Garde Fiction, and the New Chinese Cinema* (Duke University Press, 1997) and *Post-Socialism and Cultural Politics: China, 1989–2002* (Duke University Press, 2005); and editor of *Postmodernism and China* (with Arif Dirlik, Duke University Press, 2000) and *Whither China: Intellectual Politics of Contemporary China* (Duke University Press, 2001). In Chinese he is the author of *The Order of the Imaginary: Critical Theory and Modern Chinese Literature Discourse* (Oxford University Press, Hong Kong, 1996); *Traces of Criticism: Essays in Cultural Criticism and Cultural Theory* (Sanlian shudian, 2003), and *Cultural Identity in the Age of Globalization: A Historical Critique of Discourses of Universalism* (Peking University Press, 2005). He is also the Chinese translator of Walter Benjamin's *Charles Baudelaire* (Sanlian shudian, 1989) and *Illuminations* (Oxford University Press, Hong Kong, 1998).

Index